SECURWARE 2022

The Sixteenth International Conference on Emerging Security Information, Systems and Technologies

October 16 - 20, 2022

Lisbon, Portugal

SECURWARE 2022 Editors

George O. M. Yee, Aptusinnova Inc. / Carleton University, Ottawa, Canada

Printed from e-media with permission by:

Curran Associates, Inc.
57 Morehouse Lane
Red Hook, NY 12571

Some format issues inherent in the e-media version may also appear in this print version.

Printed with permission by Curran Associates, Inc. (2023)

International Academy, Research, and Industry Association (IARIA)
412 Derby Way
Wilmington, DE 19810

Phone: (408) 893-6407
Fax: (408) 527-6351

petre@iaria.org

Additional copies of this publication are available from:

Curran Associates, Inc.
57 Morehouse Lane
Red Hook, NY 12571 USA
Phone: 845-758-0400
Fax: 845-758-2633
Email: curran@proceedings.com
Web: www.proceedings.com

Table of Contents

Joanna Taneva

SECURWARE 2022

Forward

The Sixteenth International Conference on Emerging Security Information, Systems and Technologies (SECURWARE 2022), held on October 16-20, 2022, continued a series of events covering related topics on theory and practice on security, cryptography, secure protocols, trust, privacy, confidentiality, vulnerability, intrusion detection and other areas related to low enforcement, security data mining, malware models, etc.

Security, defined for ensuring protected communication among terminals and user applications across public and private networks, is the core for guaranteeing confidentiality, privacy, and data protection. Security affects business and individuals, raises the business risk, and requires a corporate and individual culture. In the open business space offered by Internet, it is a need to improve defenses against hackers, disgruntled employees, and commercial rivals. There is a required balance between the effort and resources spent on security versus security achievements. Some vulnerability can be addressed using the rule of 80:20, meaning 80% of the vulnerabilities can be addressed for 20% of the costs. Other technical aspects are related to the communication speed versus complex and time consuming cryptography/security mechanisms and protocols.

Digital Ecosystem is defined as an open decentralized information infrastructure where different networked agents, such as enterprises (especially SMEs), intermediate actors, public bodies and end users, cooperate and compete enabling the creation of new complex structures. In digital ecosystems, the actors, their products and services can be seen as different organisms and species that are able to evolve and adapt dynamically to changing market conditions.

Digital Ecosystems lie at the intersection between different disciplines and fields: industry, business, social sciences, biology, and cutting edge ICT and its application driven research. They are supported by several underlying technologies such as semantic web and ontology-based knowledge sharing, self-organizing intelligent agents, peer-to-peer overlay networks, web services-based information platforms, and recommender systems.

To enable safe digital ecosystem functioning, security and trust mechanisms become essential components across all the technological layers. The aim is to bring together multidisciplinary research that ranges from technical aspects to socio-economic models.

We take here the opportunity to warmly thank all the members of the SECURWARE 2022 technical program committee, as well as all the reviewers. The creation of such a high quality conference program would not have been possible without their involvement. We also kindly thank all the authors who dedicated much of their time and effort to contribute to SECURWARE 2022. We truly believe that, thanks to all these efforts, the final conference program consisted of top quality contributions.

We also thank the members of the SECURWARE 2022 organizing committee for their help in handling the logistics and for their work that made this professional meeting a success.

We hope that SECURWARE 2022 was a successful international forum for the exchange of ideas and results between academia and industry and to promote further progress in the area of security information, systems and technologies. We also hope that Lisbon provided a pleasant environment during the conference and everyone saved some time to enjoy the historic charm of the city.

SECURWARE 2022 Chairs

SECURWARE 2022 Steering Committee
Steffen Fries, Siemens, Germany
George O. M. Yee, Aptusinnova Inc. / Carleton University, Ottawa, Canada
Ki-Woong Park, Sejong University, South Korea
Rainer Falk, Siemens AG, Corporate Technology, Germany
Hans-Joachim Hof, INSicherheit - Ingolstadt Research Group Applied IT Security, CARISSMA – Center of Automotive Research on Integrated Safety Syst, Germany

SECURWARE 2022 Publicity Chair
Sandra Viciano Tudela, Universitat Politecnica de Valencia, Spain
Jose Luis García, Universitat Politecnica de Valencia, Spain

SECURWARE 2022

Committee

SECURWARE 2022 Steering Committee
Steffen Fries, Siemens, Germany
George O. M. Yee, Aptusinnova Inc. / Carleton University, Ottawa, Canada
Ki-Woong Park, Sejong University, South Korea
Rainer Falk, Siemens AG, Corporate Technology, Germany
Hans-Joachim Hof, INSicherheit - Ingolstadt Research Group Applied IT Security, CARISSMA – Center of Automotive Research on Integrated Safety Syst, Germany

SECURWARE 2022 Publicity Chair
Sandra Viciano Tudela, Universitat Politecnica de Valencia, Spain
Jose Luis García, Universitat Politecnica de Valencia, Spain

SECURWARE 2022 Technical Program Committee

Aysajan Abidin, imec-COSIC KU Leuven, Belgium
Abbas Acar, Florida International University, Miami, USA
Rabin Acharya, University of Florida, USA
Afrand Agah, West Chester University of Pennsylvania, USA
Chuadhry Mujeeb Ahmed, University of Strathclyde, UK
Sedat Akleylek, Ondokuz Mayis University, Samsun, Turkey
Oum-El-Kheir Aktouf, Greboble INP | LCIS Lab, France
Mamoun Alazab, Charles Darwin University, Australia
Ashwag Albakri, University of Missouri-Kansas City, USA / Jazan University, Saudi Arabia
Asif Ali laghari, SMIU, Karachi, Pakistan
Aisha Ali-Gombe, Towson University, USA
Luca Allodi, Eindhoven University of Technology, Netherlands
Mohammed Alshehri, University of Arkansas, USA
Eric Amankwa, Presbyterian University College, Ghana
Prashant Anantharaman, Dartmouth College, USA
Mohammadreza Ashouri, Virginia Tech, USA
Alexandre Augusto Giron, Federal University of Santa Catarina (UFSC) / Federal University of Technology (UTFPR), Brazil
Antonio Barili, Università degli Studi di Pavia, Italy
Ilija Basicevic, University of Novi Sad, Serbia
Luke A. Bauer, University of Florida, USA
Malek Ben Salem, Accenture, USA
Smriti Bhatt, Purdue University, USA
Catalin Bîrjoveanu, "Al. I. Cuza" University of Iasi, Romania
Robert Brotzman, Pennsylvania State University, USA
Francesco Buccafurri, University Mediterranea of Reggio Calabria, Italy
Erik Buchmann, DEUTSCHE TELEKOM AG / Hochschule für Telekommunikation Leipzig, Germany
Arun Balaji Buduru, IIIT-Delhi, India

Enrico Cambiaso, Consiglio Nazionale delle Ricerche (CNR) - IEIIT Institute, Italy
Paolo Campegiani, Bit4id, Italy
Juan-Vicente Capella-Hernández, Universitat Politècnica de València, Spain
Roberto Carbone, Fondazione Bruno Kessler, Trento, Italy
Juan Carlos Ruiz, Universidad Politécnica de Valencia, Spain
Christophe Charrier, Nomandie Univ. | UNICAEN | ENSICAEN | CNRS GREYC UMR 6072, France
Bo Chen, Michigan Technological University, Houghton, USA
Liquan Chen, Southeast University, China
Zelei Cheng, Purdue University, USA
Tan Saw Chin, Multimedia University, Malaysia
Jin-Hee Cho, Virginia Tech, USA
Stelvio Cimato, University of Milan, Italy
Marijke Coetzee, Academy of Computer Science and Software Engineering | University of Johannesburg, South Africa
Jun Dai, California State University at Sacramento, USA
Dipanjan Das, University of California, Santa Barbara, USA
Alexandre Debant , Université de Lorraine | CNRS | Inria | LORIA, Nancy, France
Raffaele Della Corte, "Federico II" University of Naples, Italy
Jean-Christophe Deneuville, ENAC | University of Toulouse, France
Jintai Ding, Tsinghua University, Beijing
George Drosatos, Athena Research Center, Greece
Jean-Guillaume Dumas, Univ. Grenoble Alpes | Laboratoire Jean Kuntzmann, France
Navid Emamdoost, University of Minnesota, USA
Alessandro Erba, CISPA Helmholtz Center for Information Security, Germany
Rainer Falk, Siemens AG, Corporate Technology, Germany
Yebo Feng, University of Oregon, USA
Eduardo B. Fernandez, Florida Atlantic University, USA
Anders Fongen, Norwegian Defence University College, Norway
Steffen Fries, Siemens Corporate Technologies, Germany
Amparo Fúster-Sabater, Institute of Physical and Information Technologies (CSIC), Spain
Olga Gadyatskaya, LIACS - Leiden University, The Netherlands
Clemente Galdi, University of Salerno, Italy
Rafa Gálvez, KU Leuven, Belgium
Kevin Gomez Buquerin, Technical University Ingolstadt, Germany
Nils Gruschka, University of Oslo, Norway
Jiaping Gui, NEC Laboratories America, USA
Chun Guo, Shandong University, China
Bidyut Gupta, Southern Illinois University, Carbondale, USA
Saurabh Gupta, IIIT-Delhi, India
Emre Gursoy, Koc University, Istanbul, Turkey
Muhammad Shadi Hajar, Robert Gordon University, UK
Amir Mohammad Hajisadeghi, Amirkabir University of Technology (Tehran Polytechnic), Iran
Mohammad Hamad, Technical University of Munich, Germany
Jinguang Han, Southeast University, China
Petr Hanáček, Brno University of Technology, Czech Republic
Dan Harkins, Hewlett-Packard Enterprise, USA
Mohamed Hawedi, École de Technologie Supérieure Montreal, Canada
Zecheng He, Princeton University, USA

Hans-Joachim Hof, INSicherheit - Ingolstadt Research Group Applied IT Security, CARISSMA – Center of Automotive Research on Integrated Safety Syst, Germany
Jiaqi Hong, Singapore Management University, Singapore
Gahangir Hossain, West Texas A&M University, Canyon, USA
Fu-Hau Hsu, National Central University, Taiwan
Fatima Hussain, Royal Bank of Canada, Toronto, Canada
Ibifubara Iganibo, George Mason University, USA
Sergio Ilarri, University of Zaragoza, Spain
Mariusz Jakubowski, Microsoft Research, USA
Prasad M. Jayaweera, University of Sri Jayewardenepura, Sri Lanka
Kun Jin, Ohio State University, USA
Hugo Jonker, Open Universiteit, Netherlands
Taeho Jung, University of Notre Dame, USA
Kaushal Kafle, William & Mary, USA
Sarang Kahvazadeh, Centre Tecnològic de Telecomunicacions de Catalunya (CTTC), Spain
Harsha K. Kalutarage, Robert Gordon University, UK
Georgios Kambourakis, University of the Aegean, Greece
Mehdi Karimi, The University of British Columbia, Vancouver, Canada
Georgios Karopoulos, European Commission JRC, Italy
Sokratis K. Katsikas, Norwegian University of Science and Technology, Norway
Basel Katt, Norwegian University of Science and Technology, Norway
Joakim Kävrestad, University of Skövde, Sweden
Ferdous Wahid Khan, Airbus Digital Trust Solutions, Munich, Germany
Hyunsung Kim, Kyungil University, Korea
Paris Kitsos, University of the Peloponnese, Greece
Andreas Kogler, Graz University of Technology (TU-Graz) | Institute of Applied Information Processing and Communications (IAIK), Austria
Harsha Kumara, Robert Gordon University, UK
Hiroki Kuzuno, SECOM Co. Ltd., Japan
Hyun Kwon, Korea Military Academy, Korea
Romain Laborde, University Paul Sabatier Toulouse III, France
Cecilia Labrini, University of Reggio Calabria, Italy
Vianney Lapôtre, Université Bretagne Sud, France
Martin Latzenhofer, AIT Austrian Institute of Technology | Center for Digital Safety and Security, Vienna, Austria
Wen-Chuan Lee, Apple Inc., USA
Ferenc Leitold, University of Dunaújváros, Hungary
Albert Levi, Sabanci University, Istanbul, Turkey
Shimin Li, Winona State University, USA
Wenjuan Li, The Hong Kong Polytechnic University, China
Zhihao Li, Meta Platform Inc., USA
Stefan Lindskog, SINTEF Digital, Norway / Karlstad University, Sweden
Guojun Liu, University of South Florida, Tampa, USA
Shaohui Liu, School of Computer Science and Technology | Harbin Institute of Technology, China
Shen Liu, NVIDIA, USA
Giovanni Livraga, Universita' degli Studi di Milano, Italy
Jakob Löw, Technische Hochschule Ingolstadt, Germany
Flaminia Luccio, University Ca' Foscari of Venice, Italy

Duohe Ma, Institute of Information Engineering | Chinese Academy of Sciences, China
Bernardo Magri, Aarhus University, Denmark
Rabi N. Mahapatra, Texas A&M University, USA
Mahdi Manavi, Mirdamad Institute of Higher Education, Iran
Antonio Matencio Escolar, University of the West of Scotland, UK
Wojciech Mazurczyk, Warsaw University of Technology, Poland
Weizhi Meng, Technical University of Denmark, Denmark
Aleksandra Mileva, University "Goce Delcev" in Stip, Republic of N. Macedonia
Paolo Modesti, Teesside University, UK
Adwait Nadkarni, William & Mary, USA
Vasudevan Nagendra, Plume Design Inc., USA
Priyadarsi Nanda, University of Technology Sydney, Australia
Chan Nam Ngo, University of Trento, Italy
Duc Cuong Nguyen, HCL Technologies, Vietnam
Liang Niu, New York University (NYU) Abu Dhabi, UAE
Nicola Nostro, Resiltech, Italy
Jason R. C. Nurse, University of Kent, UK
Rajvardhan Oak, Microsoft, India
Livinus Obiora Nweke, Norwegian University of Science and Technology, Norway
Catuscia Palamidessi, INRIA, France
Carlos Enrique Palau Salvador, Universitat Politècnica de València, Spain
Lanlan Pan, Guangdong OPPO Mobile Telecommunications Corp. Ltd., China
Brajendra Panda, University of Arkansas, USA
Ki-Woong Park, Sejong University, Republic of Korea
Balázs Pejó, CrySyS Lab - BME, Budapest, Hungary
Wei Peng, University of Oulu, Finland
Travis Peters, Montana State University, USA
Josef Pieprzyk, Data61 | CSIRO, Sydney, Australia / Institute of Computer Science | Polish Academy of Sciences, Warsaw, Poland
Nikolaos Pitropakis, Edinburgh Napier University, UK
Thomas Plantard, University of Wollongong, Australia
Tassilo Pellegrini, St. Pölten University of Applied Sciences, Austria
Tran Viet Xuan Phuong, University of Wollongong, Australia / Old Dominion University, USA
Bernardo Portela, University of Porto, Portugal
Mila Dalla Preda, University of Verona, Italy
Maxime Puys, Univ. Grenoble Alpes | CEA | LETI | DSYS, Grenoble, France
Yiyue Qian, University of Notre Dame, USA
Alvise Rabitti, Università Ca'Foscari - Venezia, Italy
Khandaker "Abir" Rahman, Saginaw Valley State University, USA
Mohammad Saidur Rahman, Rochester Institute of Technology, USA
Keyvan Ramezanpour, ANDRO Computational Solutions LLC, USA
Mohammad A. Rashid, Massey University, New Zealand
Alexander Rasin, DePaul University, USA
Danda B. Rawat, Howard University, USA
Leon Reznik, Rochester Institute of Technology, USA
Ruben Ricart-Sanchez, University of the West of Scotland, UK
Martin Ring, Bosch Engineering GmbH, Germany
Heiko Roßnagel, Fraunhofer IAO, Germany

Salah Sadou, IRISA - Universite de Bretagne Sud, France
Nick Scope, DePaul University, USA
Rodrigo Sanches Miani, Universidade Federal de Uberlândia, Brazil
Stefan Schauer, AIT Austrian Institute of Technology | Center for Digital Safety and Security, Vienna, Austria
Stefan Schiffner, University of Münster, Germany
Savio Sciancalepore, Hamad Bin Khalifa University (HBKU), Doha, Qatar
Giada Sciarretta, Fondazione Bruno Kessler (FBK), Trento, Italy
Haoqi Shan, University of Florida, USA
Amit Kumar Sikder, Georgia Institute of Technology, USA
Christian Skalka, University of Vermont, USA
Rocky Slavin, University of Texas at San Antonio, USA
Liwei Song, Princeton University, USA
Christoph Stach, University of Stuttgart, Germany
Dean Sullivan, University of New Hampshire, USA
Zhibo Sun, Drexel University, USA
Sheng Tan, Trinity University, USA
Michael Tempelmeier, Giesecke+Devrient, Germany
Nils Ole Tippenhauer, CISPA Helmholtz Center for Cybersecurity, Germany
Scott Trent, IBM Research - Tokyo, Japan
Yazhou Tu, University of Louisiana at Lafayette, USA
Vincent Urias, Sandia National Labs, USA
Emmanouil Vasilomanolakis, Aalborg University, Denmark
Andrea Visconti, Università degli Studi di Milano, Italy
Qi Wang, University of Illinois Urbana-Champaign / Stellar Cyber Inc., USA
Shu Wang, George Mason University, USA
Wenhao Wang, Institute of Information Engineering | Chinese Academy of Sciences, China
Wenqi Wei, Georgia Institute of Technology, USA
Ian Welch, Victoria University of Wellington, New Zealand
Zhonghao Wu, Shanghai Jiao Tong University, China
Lei Xue, The Hong Kong Polytechnic University, China
Nian Xue, New York University (NYU), USA
Ehsan Yaghoubi, University of Beira Interior, Portugal
Ping Yang, Binghamton University, USA
Wun-She Yap, Universiti Tunku Abdul Rahman, Malaysia
Qussai M. Yaseen, Jordan University of Science and Technology, Irbid, Jordan
George O. M. Yee, Aptusinnova Inc. / Carleton University, Ottawa, Canada
Kailiang Ying, Google, USA
Amr Youssef, Concordia University, Montreal, Canada
Chia-Mu Yu, National Yang Ming Chiao Tung University, Taiwan
Wei Yu, Institute of Information Engineering | Chinese Academy of Sciences, China
Apostolis Zarras, Delft University of Technology, The Netherlands
Thomas Zefferer, Secure Information Technology Center Austria (A-SIT), Austria
Dongrui Zeng, Palo Alto Networks, Santa Clara, USA
Linghan Zhang, Florida State University, USA
Penghui Zhang, Meta Platforms Inc., USA
Tianwei Zhang, Nanyang Technological University, Singapore
Yubao Zhang, Palo Alto Networks, USA

Yue Zheng, Nanyang Technological University, Singapore
Tommaso Zoppi, University of Florence, Italy

Copyright Information

Importance of Human Factors on Cybersecurity within Organizations

A Study of Attitudes and Behaviors

Elham Rajabian Noghondar
Data Center
Tamin ICT& Management Consultancy
Tehran, Iran
Elham.rajabian@hotmail.com

Abstract—**The rise of cybersecurity incidents is a threat to most organizations, while the impact of the incidents is unique for each of the organizations. There is a requirement to create the right conditions which provide rhythm to cybersecurity growth and a fully developed cybersecurity resilience. Having a mindset of cybersecurity resilience works actively to adapt people, processes and technology. Meanwhile, the adequate cultural cybersecurity conditions need to be achieved. It seems necessary to employ behavioral sciences to concentrate on employees' behavior in order to achieve concrete security mitigation preparedness regarding cybersecurity incidents. There are noticeable differences among users of a computer system in terms of complying with security behavior. The people differences can be studied under several headings, such as delaying tactics on something that must be done, the tendency to act without thinking, future thinking about unexpected implications of present-day issues, and risk-taking behaviors in security policy compliance. In this article, we introduce high profile cyber-attacks and their impacts on weakening cyber resilience in organizations. We also give attention to human errors and behaviors that weaken general security readiness in organizations. The human errors are discussed as a part of psychological matters to enhance compliance with security policy.**

Keywords-cyber resilience, human factors, cybersecurity behavior, attitude, usability, security culture

I. INTRODUCTION

In a world of continuous change, addressing cyber risks within organizations is already a huge leadership challenge. Regardless of organization size, it is critically important that each organization develops its own cyber crisis preparation response plan. Moreover, having a cyber-resilience approach in place prohibits a serious financial and reputational harm to organizations and their leaders.

Digital, dynamic and complex workplaces are great targets for cyber-criminals [1]. Cyber-criminal actors are people who search for any chance to steal data, blocking access with ransomware, or install evasive malware to remain undetected for long-term malicious effect. They utilize security breaches that emerge from weak links in, for instance, embedded software and applications in organization environment. Hence, technology and tools alone are not the answer for the cyber risks; after all, we have not seen the high- profile breaches in the headlines. In addition, the nature of attacks has altered from theft to become more harmful than ever since the threats become more complicated and harder to recognize. For instance, current attack scenarios target backup data repositories and administrator functions, which are the last lines of defense in organizations [5].

The two main high-profile cyber-attacks in 2021 involved confidential data lost and various forms of ransomware attacks. Confidential data was stolen from large organizations like Singtel, the University of Colorado, Aerospace Company Bombardier and the Australian Securities and Investments Commission. Moreover, various types of ransomware attacks have occurred in organizations such as Acer Company, United States CAN Insurance, Scotland's University of the Highlands, United States Colonial Pipeline, California Water and Wastewater System, etc. Furthermore, based on the GDATA news in 2021, the most recognized type of security attacks include phishing, clever ransomware, polyglot files, IoT attacks, social engineering, malvertising on Facebook feeds, identity theft, password and data breach, zero-day exploits, insider threats and deep fake attacks.

Organizations with integrated information technology systems and operational technology systems propose clear and unclear points of convergence that directly threaten functionality of the technical systems [2] [3], like the attack against the Water and Wastewater System in California. The attacks usually work against the four main functions of information communications technology systems: quality and efficiency of services, data confidentiality, improved usability and people privacy and safety.

Organizations need awareness about immaturity in their risk mitigation measures. They also should recognize depth of threats that result from insiders at the same time [4]. We believe that insiders' threats are becoming more frequent, as they are difficult to detect and insiders already have legitimate access to the network infrastructure [4]. In addition, variety in embedded applications is a source of data leakage [5]. The growth in the amount of stored data widens the cyber-attack surface. Transition to cloud computing technologies poses major difficulties in identifying insider attacks as well [6]. Because of all the mentioned complexities, such as immature risk mitigation measures, the role of insiders, difficulty in recognizing threats from insiders to a wide range of embedded software and business applications, stored data growth and cloud data repositories, more research is needed in order to enhance organizational resilience. In this article, we aim to discuss how a people-centric approach in parallel with a technology-centric approach can largely mitigate cybersecurity risks in organizations. We also investigate how cyber resilience limits the scope of cybercrime within organizations. The research methodology is a qualitative method based on systematic literature study along with case studies that prove the importance of human factors in cybersecurity. The case studies are used to shape discussions, to locate gaps and draw conclusions. The organizational challenges are studied to shape a sustainable cyber risk management approach in the related work section. Insider behaviors are viewed as a cybersecurity gap to draw proper cyber resilience in Section 3. The challenges to perform the best cybersecurity practices are mentioned in Section 4. Some guidelines and metrics are provided to measure cyber resilience in organizations in Section 5. At the end, we indicate some points to build a cybersecurity culture based on individual behavior.

II. Related Work

Sometimes organizations encounter problems to manage cyber risks and develop a sustainable security framework. They don't pay enough attention to knowledge, guidance and research for the technologies' innovations. In addition, there are no incentives like market forces and no regulation for utilizing the emerging technologies in a secure manner [7]. A sustainable security framework should mitigate the issues such as skills gaps, fragmented security approaches, obscure liabilities in cyber resilience, lack of operational security capabilities and lack of technical solutions in responding to incidents.

Organizations face a competitive market and they are concerned about the sustainability of their operations from economic, environmental and social viewpoints. This is called the sustainability of business. It means that business strategy and competitiveness don't necessarily interfere with sustainability of environment and society [8]. On the other hand, digitalization also brings complexity in cyber space and organizations are exposed to cyber threats as a result [9]. Therefore, organizations need to understand cyber resilience as an ability to plan ahead, to respond, to recover from and adapt to the cyber threats.

Cyber resilience can be achieved through a secure information infrastructure and a proactive workforce that takes both the human factor and the organizational factor serious simultaneously. Based on our organizational experience, there are many opportunities for purchasing technical devices to get ready against cybersecurity attacks. Many organizations have cybersecurity risks at their core due to untuned embedded devices and other negligent factors. Moreover, during the last few years, there is noticeable attention to the human side of the cyber risk but there is still growth in data breach and other human-related threats [5]. One reason to consider just objective activities and pay too little attention to people and their behavioral aspect. In addition to this, there is a lack of proper policies and of procedures to encourage the desired human behavior. These are the main reasons why current cybersecurity solutions are not effective.

To specify security problems, besides the above issues, organizations should also keep an eye on the numerous technological transformations intended to enhance profitability, and consider them in their security checklists. Most such transformations have potential to generate new systemic risks [11]. Examples are artificial intelligence and advanced machine learning [6], ubiquitous connectivity, quantum computing solutions and next-generation digital identity systems [11]. Append to these the current cybersecurity problems such as distributed cloud-based infrastructure, integrating software, web applications that reside on premises behind firewalls, etc. [7]. Some organizations set policies, standards, apply the best security practices and make partnership to avert such cybersecurity threats. In addition, organizations need to share and develop research, insights and solutions to manage the future-risks as a community. At the same time, there is a need for adopting a defense-in-depth security strategy with the aim of receiving perfect cooperation from the main fundamental cybersecurity components including people, processes and technology [13]. We contribute with an analysis of different incidents and threats reports to show that current cybersecurity breaches are the result of too little attention to human factors and too much focus on tech-centric solutions. We collect the latest cybersecurity reports and study the cause and effect for each incident. In addition, the components of cyber resilience strategy and corresponding metrics are discussed as a limitation for cybercrime impacts. We also introduce a cybersecurity training scheme for employees' preparation to recognize the signs of malicious activity in advance. We carry out pillars for cybersecurity culture and the desired behavioral pattern toward a well-structured cybersecurity culture as well.

III. The Cybersecurity and Human Factor

As we mentioned earlier, organizations usually display great progress to employ different technical security solutions such as firewalls, virus scanners, web application firewalls and intrusion detection systems to control the potential cybersecurity threats [14]. This happens because CIS normally recommend a technology-centric approach with little emphasis on human factors, needs and motivations [15]. But there is a demand for a holistic security approach, as technical solutions merely cannot handle cybersecurity attacks. This is the way to acquire cyber resilience. Thus, we have to discuss insiders' threats besides the threats related to the information infrastructure and the processes. Insiders are the individuals who have access to resources, detailed knowledge about the computer network infrastructure, and data storage technical infrastructure. They include staff, contractors, partners, vendors and other stakeholders [16]. Insiders usually are aware of the location of sensitive data, what protective measures are in place, such as firewalls and the designed security policies. They often know of cybersecurity concerns and bottlenecks. They also have capabilities and skills to conceal the crime footprint for a long time or sometime forever [17]. Therefore, insiders present much more danger with potentially higher damage than external cyberattacks.

According to Data Breach Investigations Report in 2021, insiders are in charge of 22% of security incidents. Furthermore, based on Stanford University, around 88% of data breaches are caused by staff mistakes. Bitglass [49] report in 2022 revealed that top insider actors of security incidents are privileged users and administrators (63%), privileged business users and C-level executives with access to sensitive data (60%), third parties and temporary workers such as contractors and consultants (57%) and regular employees (51%) as shown in Fig. 1.

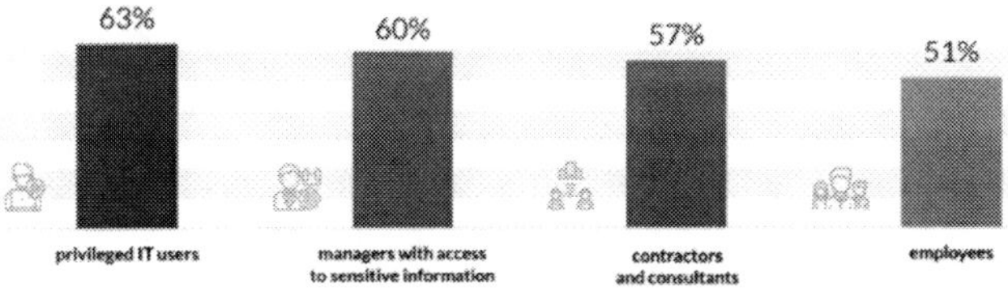

Figure 1. Top Insider Threat Actors in 2022.

Moreover, 62% of the security incidents result from negligent employees or contractors while 14% of the incidents were caused by malicious insiders, according to Panda security report in 2020 [18].

Fortinet [47] described that the most prevalent type of insider threats is phishing, about 38% in 2019. For instance, exploitation of insecure RDP, and unsupported or outdated operating systems and software result in the phishing attack. Moreover, according to US Securonix [48] report in 2020, the most frequent cyber incidents include data extrusion accounting for 62%, privilege misuse about 19%, data snooping for 9.5%, infrastructure sabotage around 5% and circumvention of IT controls for 3.8%. Fortinet also defines fraud as the primary motivation behind insider threats around 55%, monetary gain for 49% and IP theft for 44% in 2019. The most frequent types of attacks related to human factor involve online fraud like phishing, DDOS, ransomware and social engineering [20]-[23]. Fig.2, displays stop motivations for insider attacks.

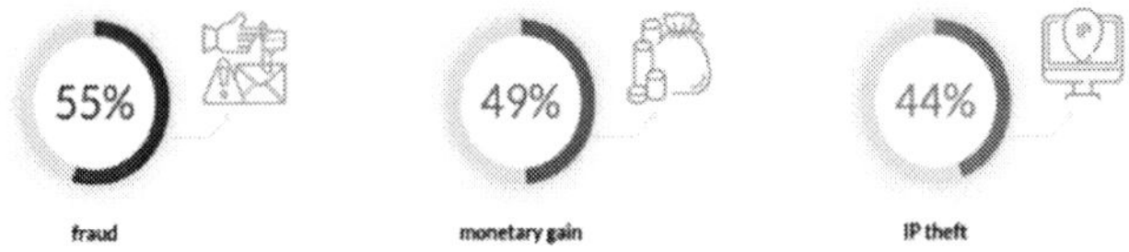

Figure 2. Top Motivations for Insider Attacks.

For several reasons, finding solutions for the insider threats is even more difficult than implementing measures to protect against foreign and external threats. Most companies and organizations rely on security awareness training, followed by company policies, procedures and intelligent automation to protect themselves against the insider threats. Ironically most employees say they understand the company policies and the procedures. Comprehension does not help to prevent incidents due to malicious behavior or negligence. The early indicators of such actions distribute themselves across vast data silo repositories that historically defied our ability to wrap our cognitively limited minds around [17]. To reduce the cyber risk gaps organizations' top managers need to learn about threats by implementing a mature cybersecurity risk management. They need to consider one key lesson: while technical upgrades are important, minimizing human errors by studying employees' attitudes is even more vital. Mistakes by network administrators and users' failures to patch vulnerabilities in legacy systems, misconfigured settings, violations of standard procedures-open the door to the overwhelming majority of successful attacks [23]. To flourish, they should move beyond protection to resilience.

IV. THE CHALLENGES TO CYBERSECURITY PRACTICES

Hidden interconnections among organizational factors affect the quality of services provided by organizations. They may influence in individual's total performance and their actions. For example, poorly written rules, faulty equipment, web application misconfiguration, poor management practices and vague procedures [24] [25]. These refer to more breaches and create consequences that are more adverse. There are four discussable CIS challenges in path of implementing cybersecurity best practices and attack mitigation in organizations. They include individual factors, organizational factors, technological factors and ethical matters [26].

When we talk about the individual factor, it is about inadequate security actions causing both errors and/or violations. Incorrect configurations of work elements will cause unintentional errors and conscious actions of non-malicious attempts [27]. The theory of Reasoned Action [19] and the theory of Planned Behavior discuss two solid models that link behaviors and attitudes. It is about an indirect psychological connection that is called "behavioral intention" [27]. It makes clear that there is a feasibility to define human failures and violations via studying staffs' attitudes versus cybersecurity critical behaviors. Reasonably, cybersecurity behaviors can directly predict attitudes and the exact behavioral purpose of high-risk behaviors. Thus, it is important to understand the relation between attitudes and deliberate actions in order to avoid the CIS breaches [17]. Furthermore, to enhance the cybersecurity situation, there is a need to set bases to form attitudes like subjective norms and beliefs to perceive consequences of an action, acquire actual knowledge about the cybersecurity matter, the cognitive strategies utilized in decision-making process, etc. Staff attitudes can also encourage the impact of social and organizational factors. For instance, social norms, ethical dilemmas, and different levels of behavioral control understood by staff members such as the degree of freedom taken in to display a given behavior and contextual enablers in place, are connected to such given behavior [27]. There are psychological frameworks that can be applied with the aim of reducing the security violations and giving emphasis to the role of norms and the ethical values informing staff attitudes. The Norm Activation Theory [37], makes clear that attitudes are certainly impressed by the moral obligation levels, self-responsibility and clear awareness about emerging consequences of a given behavior [27]. Employees' awareness and training downgrade the probability of sudden and unintentional behaviors which cause a violation from cybersecurity rules. In consequence, it largely minimizes the information security risks and preserves the important organizational assets and the intellectual property [28]. Therefore, perceiving the tiny differences between human errors and violations specifies organizational bottleneck points. In addition, building an information security culture based on behavioral issues, and incorporate the created culture framework into organizational levels contribute towards reducing the risk from employees' behavioral fault and related human errors.

The second discussable cybersecurity challenge is the organizational factor. Many organizations proceed towards mitigating the cyber security vulnerabilities by forming policies, processes and procedures. Although the organizations require their employees' compliance with the regulations and the procedures, the formal regulations merely do not construct the desired human behavior [29] [33]. For instance, the complex architecture of computer networks, resources and data storage infrastructure provide possibility for individuals to use the system in unprotected modes, pretending as a usual and useful activity [18]. Deviating from security practices can occur because informal procedures and intuitional cost-benefit estimations override potential negative results of one's activity. For example, passwords are written down or shared with colleagues. Therefore, employees will not follow the organizational policies and rules if they are too costly or it is unclear how to implement them [27] [30].

The third imaginative challenge is the technological factor. In this regard, CIS supplies an effective and useable security design. Users certainly refuse security mechanisms that are hard to utilize or cause faults that weaken security [32]. Usability is a degree of effectiveness, efficiency, and satisfaction with which users of a system can recognize predesignate tasks. Low usability may directly threaten safety, quality and efficiency, especially when it leads to human errors and slows down organizational processes. Inadequate usability might cause indirect cybersecurity risks. For example, when aggressive warning notifications encourage users to deactivate the security notifications [34]. In addition, it is difficult to integrate employees' differences and socio-cultural variables without a usable security design [35]. To improve usability, the security principles should be user-experience based. This is still a real issue with the CIS implementation in organizations. Weak usability in the security design leads to improper operation of cybersecurity tools and poor functionality. It ultimately creates in-effectiveness [31]. A unified user interface for various user domains may solve some usability and acceptability related issues [36]. Therefore, giving priority to the user interface design and good user experience leads to positive attitudes and facilitates the usage of procedures, software and applications [27].

The fourth challenge, ethical matter is discussable under role of the norms in shaping employee's attitude based on the Norm Activation Theory. In other words, employees' attitude is directly impressed by moral obligation, the ethical norms, and their clear knowledge about the consequences of a particular behavior [37]. In collective actions, individual efforts are negligible when others do not perform their role as desired. Thus, having information about others behavior supplies clear overview about behavioral norms, which have an independent influence on behavior [38].

V. CYBER RESILIENCE OVER CYBERSECURITY

Cyber resilience should restrict the impact of cybercrime in organizations, business brand reputation, financial commitment, legal, and customer trust obligations. These areas demand resources and executive support, as they are important subjects in case of an actual threat [39]. In other words, cyber resilience should bring a certain level of confidence for business continuity and ability to respond to security attacks with purpose of preserving the obligations [40]. Fig. 3 illustrates the relationship between cyber resilience, crisis management and reconstruction.

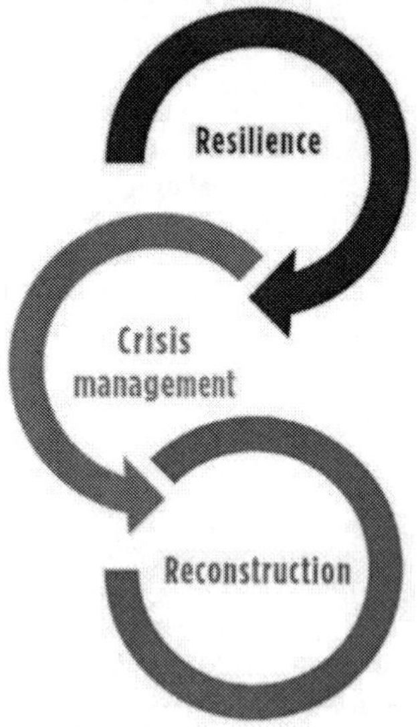

Figure 3. Cyber Resilience Crisis Management and Reconstruction.

Cyber resilience should present some cybersecurity basis such as patching vulnerabilities, detecting and lessening threats, and training programs for employees on how to defend their organization's security [41]. It is about a continuous functionality not a yearly action as well. In addition, the cyber resilience idea must build into each part of the organizational departments, from business process mapping to service availability engineering to critical stakeholder and vendor dependency [42]. Fig. 4 presents components of a cyber-resilience strategy:

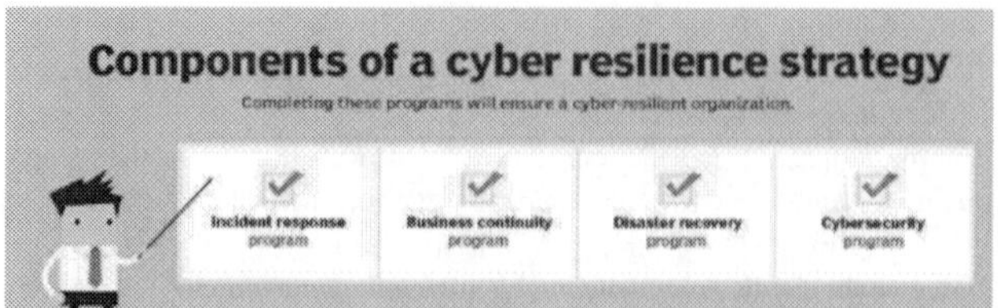

Figure 4. Components of Cyber Resilience Strategy.

Currently, there is a demand for a mature cyber resilience framework and specific metrics to measure cyber resilience. The mature cyber resilience framework must propose a set of features including quick response and recovery procedures in minimal time in case of an incident while supporting organizational priorities [43]. The cyber resilience framework helps leaders to understand what cyber resilience is and what attitudes can support the intended cyber resilience [16]. Organizations need to prioritize human-related solutions into their cyber resilience strategy for workforces. Cyber resilience is not about comparison, and there is no final destination. It is about a measurement framework that scales businesses by focusing on people, processes and technology to make sure that entire value chains are resilient while adopting the desired security culture [39].

The training program should empower staff to actively consider cyber risk. Employees require to be trained about different possible security layers. As nowadays the most common attacks are again web applications they ought to know about the most popular web vulnerabilities and the impacts. For instance, phishing, social engineering, password-based attacks, injection attacks, information leakage, email attacks, malware attacks, ransomware, DDOS, etc. In addition, the role of insiders should be part of the cybersecurity training scheme. To follow up the effectiveness of the training package, random testing of employees should be performed. For example, a test email including malware can be sent to employees and their responses are evaluated. Therefore, it is an appropriate measure to undertake further education. CEO should have an active role in forming an impressive cyber training program. CEO not only has authority to create the overall cybersecurity strategy but also can supply executive guarantee for the strategy. It also helps staff to understand the significance of the training programs. The other C-suite members like CIO, or CISO bear primary accountability for implementing the educating procedures. In this manner, we take steps in building a culture of cybersecurity and increase cyber resilience in the organization. Furthermore, expanding monitoring capabilities and knowledge should be trained with the aim of receiving better cyber resilience performance.

A. *Measuring Cyber Resilience*

It should be an ultimate mission for organizations to concentrate on their cyber resilience capabilities and the actual influences emerging from the technical and the organizational security measures in order to evaluate the cybersecurity posture [44]. In other words, measuring and quantifying the state of cyber resilience are essential because leaders decide about additional security measures.

Traditional security metrics restrict vision about the real performance of cyber resilience provisions as they merely pay attention to existing security controls or completion of particular security necessities [45]. For instance, sometimes organizations measure the state of security awareness among employees through evaluating participation on mandatory security training course. However, completing an E-learning module will not necessarily assure to behave proper in case of a real security threat [46]. To correct such loss in the traditional security metrics model, some ability-metrics are needed to assess outcome of cyber resilience performance. A meaningful cyber resilience metrics model argues a spectrum of metrics includes ability to avert social engineering, ability to engage threat intelligence, ability to address vulnerabilities, ability to handle cyber incidents, ability to resist malware, ability to resist system intrusions, ability to resist DDoS attacks, ability to protect credentials, ability to protect key assets and ability to measure and minimize damage [9], and ability to assess insider threats. We believe in the predominance of evaluating the metrics model versus actually occurred attack scenarios in different industries, to check the degree of the avert ability in various stages of the attacks.

Each organization indicates its unique security risks. Therefore, there is no unique cyber resilience model which fits all imaginable features of risk [10]. Based on the described opinion above and in the literature, measuring cyber resilience can be accomplished by the following core guidelines with the aim of finding the breaches faster, fixing them faster and minimize their impact:

- Provide a centralized asset management system. Specify organizational valuable possession including hardware, software and data. Isolate backup data. Recognize critical potentialities that may act against the asset and the demanded organizational cyber resilience.
- Define the interlinkage between the organizational systems and find out how the interconnectivity makes the system vulnerable versus the actual attack scenarios. In this regard, ensure proper security monitoring for the organizational perimeter.
- Recognize the organizational characteristics, current organizational cyber resilience attitude; partner with peers, competitors and public entities to emphasize threat intelligence sharing among the organizational networks.
- Consider people hiring cycle and how to develop people's skills & behavior. Effective cyber resilience needs a strong cultural concentration driven by the organization's board and C-level management which reflects in the organization via wide programs to educate and increase cyber awareness of staff and third parties.
- Measure towards a culture of trust, organizational agility and continue to stakeholders trust and transparency at the same time.

VI. BUILDING CYBERSECUIRTY CULTURE BASED ON BEHAVIOR

Cybersecurity empowers organizational objectives and progressively provides competitive benefit [41]. Security culture is a set of security-based norms, values, attitudes and obligations within an organization. It especially focuses on the human related matters. Security culture adds value by evaluating shared opinions, customs, social behavior, adequate investment and management instruction for cybersecurity [15]. Improving security culture increases organizations security readiness [39]. It is a fact that the security culture is built top down. Building and maintaining a security culture notably leads to a higher security awareness among employees. As a result, employees will naturally behave as a proactive protective layer. It means, more attention to security culture gives greater likelihood that employees follow the security practices and consequently behave more securely. It finally causes overall reduction in the organizational risks. In general security culture is influenced by seven main dimensions: attitude, behavior, cognition, communication, compliance, norms and responsibility [41].

Attitude describes the feelings and beliefs that individuals propose to security protocols and security issues [14] [41]. Behavior refers to all activities of employees that have direct and indirect impact on security issues within an organization [40]. Behavior is defined as the combination of actions and habits in a situation, environment or stimulus [12]. Cognition discusses awareness, knowledge and employees' understanding of the security issues and related activities. Communication is about the quality of communication channels to share cybersecurity events, news and analysis of the security-related subjects. It encourages a real sense of belonging and helps solve security problems and incident reporting [41]. In a well-structured cybersecurity culture, leadership communicates the organizational security principles which should not be violated. These include procedural compliance, questioning attitude, integrity compliance, depth of knowledge, forceful backup and formality [23]. Compliance ensures knowledge about written security policies and determines security policies' scope which must be followed by employees. Norms talk about knowledge and commitment to unwritten management rules in organizations. Responsibility makes explicit how employees understand the significance of their role in supporting or threatening the security of their organization [41].

In constructing cybersecurity culture based on insiders' behavior, leadership also should train employees to listen to the internal alarms, search for causes and take right action. In addition, leadership should encourage procedural compliance and a questioning attitude among staff [15]. Employees with a questioning attitude usually perform double-and triple-check work, keep notifying for anomalies, and are never pleased with a less-than-complete response [23]. Moreover, compromising behavior which leads to security breaches, usually means breaches in the security principles [15]. For instance, imagine a system admin with fewer access limitations surfing the web and downloading an infected video clip. It clearly violates integrity and the procedural compliance. An employee who clicks on a malicious emailed link during online shopping is in phishing danger. It indicates lack of a questioning attitude, depth of knowledge and lack of procedural compliance. A beginner network administrator installs an update without consulting the implementation guide and with no supervision. Therefore, the former security upgrades are unpatched. In this case, depth of knowledge, procedural compliance, and forceful backup causes the problem. Think about a network help desk that resets a connection without exploring the reason for the deactivation. It might be an automated shutdown to prohibit an unauthorized access. It is again a type of breaking procedural compliance and a questioning attitude [23].

There is no conclusive method to establish a concrete cybersecurity culture but working actively on the behavior changing process. To achieve it, top-level management should specify the desired behavioral pattern and formulate how to reach goals and implement them. Improving security culture definitely provides more secure behavior from staffs' side. It consequently mitigates the general risks statistics within organizations. Below, we supply some points that can be beneficial in the way of improving the security culture into organizations:

- Set up periodic risk assessment and an ongoing monitoring solution for early discovering the organizational risks. Define human factor a serious matter in the risk assessment procedure.
- Define a human-related ability metric in the organizational cyber resilience metrics model. Measure the individuals' awareness and behavior with it.
- Expand a security-awareness culture; make aware employees about the desired behavior, unpleasant consequences and their responsibility in lack of compliance. Shape a strong security culture scheme by use of the seven main effective dimensions: attitude, behavior, cognition, communication, compliance, norms and responsibility.
- Create a positive cybersecurity culture by involving psychological methods into the security culture scheme, using novel "polymorphic" security warnings, rewarding and penalizing desired and undesired cyber behavior.
- Deploy automated awareness-training programs for a varied audience including all organizational departments and use unified communication tools and attack simulations. Define core organizational values and communicate the security-related leadership instructions clearly in a prescribed manner in a proper atmosphere without side descriptions which lead to inattention, faulty assumption and other errors.
- Take advantage of an analytical-driven security strategy by mobilizing an active messaging program across the organization, and develop a security community with peers to share knowledge and learn from them.

VII. CONCLUSION AND FUTURE WORK

The contribution of the paper resides in the multi-factoring CIS challenges to prevent the cybersecurity attacks in organizations, with a special focus on the complexity of human factors. To manage cybersecurity risks, it is inevitable promoting a people- and technology-centric comprehensive approach in organizations. We specify the importance of differentiating human errors and violations based on the individuals' attitudes and characteristics. In this manner, we highlight the significance of the interdependency among organizational components which may affect employees' general performance and actions. Improving cybersecurity culture is the main mission in this paper. We discuss how cybersecurity culture can increase organizations' cybersecurity readiness. We highlight the seven main components to improve a security culture model: attitude, behavior, cognition, communication, compliance, norms and responsibility. Thus, employees naturally behave as a proactive protective layer as defined in the cybersecurity culture model. The human-centric approach leads to overall reduction of cybersecurity risks in parallel with the technology-centric approach. As a result, cybersecurity resilience seriously restricts the scope of cybercrime in organizations. A mature cyber security resilience framework should include some ability-metrics for evaluation of the cybersecurity resilience performance. Future research could continue to explore the desired human behaviors that improve cybersecurity culture and accordingly form proper cybersecurity resilience. In addition, it should be investigated how an organization can achieve the desired behaviors from individuals.

REFERENCES

[1] Gregory Vial, Understanding digital transformation: A review and a research agenda, pp.4, 2019, https://doi.org/10.1016/j.jsis.2019.01.003.

[2] Patrick Katuruza, IT-OT Convergence: Managing the Cybersecurity Risks, 2021. Available from:https://gca.isa.org/blog/it-ot-convergence-managing-the-cybersecurity-risks.

[3] Richard Paes, David C Mazur, and Bruce K. Venne, A Guide to Securing Industrial Control Networks -IT/OT Convergence ,IEEE, Dec. 2019, pp.49-50. Electronic ISSN:1558-0598, https://doi.org/10.1109/MIAS.2019.2943630.

[4] Cybersecurity and Infrastructure Security Agency CISA, Insider Threat Mitigation Guide, pp. 20-21,2020.

[5] EU Data Protection Board, Examples Regarding Personal Data Breach Notification, pp. 15-16,2021.

[6] Pupillo Lorenzo, Fantin Stefano, Afonso Ferreira, and Polito Carolina, Artificial Intelligence and Cybersecurity Technology, Governance and Policy Challenges, pp. 40-41,2021.

[7] World Economic Forum with collaboration with Oxford University, Cybersecurity, Emerging Technology and Systemic Risk, pp. 44,2020.

[8] Alessandro Annarelli and Giulia Palombi, Digitalization Capabilities for Sustainable Cyber Resilience: A Conceptual Framework, pp.6,2021. https://doi.org/10.3390/su132313065.

[9] Participants in the Cyber Security Shared Research Program, Library of Cyber Resilience Metrics, pp.10,2017.

[10] Jim Alkove, Cyber security is no longer enough: businesses need cyber resilience, Available From:https://www.weforum.org/agenda/2021/11/why-move-cybersecurity-to-cyber-resilience/2021.

[11] Yuchong Liand Qinghui Liu, A comprehensive review study of cyber-attacks and cyber security; Emerging trends and recent developments, pp. 7-8, 2021.https://doi.org/10.1016/j.egyr.2021.08.126

[12] Keri Pearlson, Sean Sposito, Masha Arbismanand Josh A.Schwartz, How Yahoo Built a Culture of Cybersecurity,2021.

[13] Sivaram Chelakkara, CEH, CISSP, and GCISP, People, Processand Technology in Cybersecurity, pp. 4-6,2020.

[14] Check Point Software, Cyber Attack Trends, pp. 21-24,2021.

[15] Stjepan Groš, A Critical View on CIS Controls, pp. 3-5,2019.

[16] Nena Giandomenico and Juliana de Groot, Insider vs. Outsider Data Security Threats: What is the Greater Risk?, Available from:https://digitalguardian.com/blog/insider-outsider-data-security-threats,2020.

[17] Neetesh Saxena, Emma Hayes, Elisa Bertino, and Patrick Ojo, Impact and Key Challenges of Insider Threats on Organizations and Critical Businesses, pp. 16-17, 2020.doi:10.3390/electronics9091460

[18] Danny Murphy, Insider Threat Statistics, pp.6,2021.

[19] Martin Fishbein and Icek Ajzen, The Theory of Reasoned Actionof Fishbein and Ajzen, pp. 7-8,1975.

[20] Icek Ajzen, The Theory of Planned Behaviour, 1991.

[21] Regner Sabillon, Jeimy J. Cano M, Jordi Serra Ruiz, and Victor Cavaller, Cybercriminals, cyberattacks and cybercrime, pp.8,2016.

[22] Michael Swanagan, CISSO, CISA and CISM, Cyber Security Statistics The Ultimate List of Stats Data and Trends, pp.9,2022.

[23] Tashfiq Rahman, Rohani Rohan, Debajyoti Pal, and Prasert Kanthamanon, Human Factors in Cybersecurity: A Scoping Reviewpp. 8-9, 2021.doi:10.1145/3468784.3468789

[24] Alessandro Pollinietal, Leveraging human factors in cybersecurity: an integrated methodological approach, pp 11,2021.

[25] Edward Staddon, Valeria Loscri and Nathalie Mitton, Attack Categorisation for IoT Applications in Critical Infrastructures, pp. 14, 2021.https://doi.org/10.3390/app11167228.

[26] Moti Zwilling, Trends and Challenges Regarding Cyber Risk Mitigation by CISOs, A Systematic Literature and Experts' Opinion Review Based on Text Analytics, pp. 7,2022.

[27] Jongkil Jay Jeong, Joanne Mihelcic, Gillian Christina Oliver,andCarsten Rudolph, Towards an Improved Understanding of Human Factors in Cybersecurity,pp. 5-6, 2019. doi:10.1109/CIC48465.2019.00047.

[28] Lee Hadlington, Employees Attitude towards Cyber Security and Risky Online Behaviours: An Empirical Assessment in the United Kingdom,pp. 9,2018.

[29] Kristina Gyllensten and Marianne Torner, Therole of organizational and social factors for information security in a nuclear power industry, pp. 10-11,2021.

[30] Rao Faizan Ali, Dhanapal Durai Dominic Panneer Selvam, Emad Azhar, and Mobashar Rehman, Information Security Behavior and Information Security Policy Compliance: A Systematic Literature Review for Identifying the Transformation Process from Noncompliance to Compliance,pp. 17, 2021.doi:10.3390/app11083383

[31] Rick Wash, Prioritizing Security over Usability: Strategies for how people choose passwords, pp. 8, 2021.https://doi.org/10.1093/cybsec/tyab012

[32] Angela Sasseand Ivan Flechais, Usable Security: Why Do We Need It? How Do We Get It? PP. 4-5, 2005.

[33] Sylwia Agata Beczkowska and Iwona Grabarek, The Importance of the Human Factor in Safety for the Transport of Dangerous Goods, pp.13, 2021.

[34] John Soldatos, Security Risk Management for The Internet of Things Technologies and Techniques for IOT Security, Privacy and Data Protection, pp. 35-37,2020.

[35] Sebastian Hengstler and Natalya Pryazhnykova, Reviewing the Interrelation Between Information Security and Culture, pp. 7,2021.

[36] Jing Wanget al., Research Trend of the Unified Theory of Acceptance and Use of Technology Theory: A Bibliometric Analysis, pp. 14, 2022. doi:10.3390/su14010010.

[37] Judith de Groot and Linda Steg, Morality and Prosocial Behavior: The Role of Awareness, Responsibility, and Norms in the Norm Activation Model, pp. 4, 2009.https://doi.org/10.3200/SOCP.149.4.425-449.

[38] Linda Steg and Judith de Groot, Explaining Prosocial Intentions: Testing causal relationships in the norm activation model, pp. 8, 2010. doi:10.1348/014466609X477745.

[39] Accenture Security, Innovate for Cyber Resilience, pp. 27,2020.

[40] DanielA.SepúlvedaEstay,RishikeshSahay,MichaelB.Barfod,andChristian D.Jensen, A systematic review of cyber-resilience assessment frameworks, pp. 9-10, 2020.doi:10.1016/j.cose.2020.101996.

[41] Javvad Malik, How Security Culture Invokes Secure Behaviour, Available from:https://www.infosecurity-magazine.com/blogs/security-culture-invokes-secure/,2021.

[42] Thomas H.Llansó, Daniel A.Hedgecock, and J.Aaron Pendergrass, The State of Cyber Resilience: Now and in the Future, pp. 4,2021.

[43] lessandro Annarelli and Giulia Palombi, Digitalization Capabilities for Sustainable CyberResilience,2021. pp.4,https://doi.org/10.3390/su132313065.

[44] Aviram Zrahia, Threat intelligence sharing between cybersecurity vendors: Network, dyadic, and agent views, pp. 6-7, 2018.https://doi.org/10.1093/cybsec/tyy008.

[45] Reinder Wolthuis, Shared Research Program Cyber Security, pp.11- 12,2021.

[46] McKinsey, Cybersecurity in a Digital Era, pp. 44, 2020.

[47] Fortinet, Insider Threat Report, pp. 5,2019.

[48] Securonix, Insider Threat Report, pp. 8,2020.

[49] Nestor Gilbert, 31 Crucial Insider Statistics Latest Threat and Challenges, pp. 3, 2022.

Phishing Resistant Systems: A Literature Review

Jonathan Luckett
College of Business, Innovation, Leadership and Technology
Marymount University
Arlington, Virginia
Jonathan_luckett@marymount.edu

Abstract—**Phishing is one of the leading cyber attack vectors against businesses and consumers. President Biden signed an Executive Order on Improving the Nation's Cybersecurity in May of 2021. The Administration followed up with Memorandum M-22-09, which in addition to laying out a Zero Trust strategy for the federal government to follow, also provides special emphasis on phishing resistant systems such as MFA. This paper provides a literature review of phishing resistant systems and covers Microsoft solutions for the enterprise, eliminating passwords as specified in the Web Authentication API and FIDO 2 standards. Research into how threat actors accomplish phishing schemes is examined, along with email authentication (Sender Policy Framework, SPK; Domain Key Identified Mail (DKIM); and the Domain-Based Message Authentication, Reporting and Conformance (DMARC) standard). Browser-based detection systems are also reviewed, along with phishing intelligence databases that developers can integrate into their applications.**

Keywords—phishing; phishing-resistant; FIDO; SPK; DKIM; DMARC; Defender.

I. INTRODUCTION

On May 12th of 2021, President Biden signed EO 14208, Executive Order on Improving the Nation's Cybersecurity. The Executive Order directs federal agencies to enhance cybersecurity through several initiatives [1]. One of the specific initiatives spelled out in the EO is that within 180 days agencies must adopt Multi-factor Authentication (MFA). The White House followed up with Memorandum M-2209 in January of 2022, spelling out a Zero Trust strategy and placing special emphasis on the use of phishing-resistant MFA that protects users from cyberattacks [2]. The Memorandum defines phishing resistant authentication as "authentication processes designed to detect and prevent disclosure of authentication secrets and outputs to a website or application masquerading as a legitimate system,"[2]. The Memorandum notes that some MFA approaches do not protect against sophisticated attacks since they can spoof applications and interact dynamically with users. For example, users can be fooled into issuing a one-time code or responding to a security prompt that grants access to the attacker. The Federal Government's Personal Identity Verification (PIV) card protects against these types of attacks. The World Wide Web Consortium (W3C)'s web authentication standard is another approach that is effective that will be discussed later.

II. LITERATURE REVIEW

A. Discussion

The Anti-Phishing Working Group (APWG) noted in their Phishing Activity Trends Report for Q3, 2021 that webmail and Software-as-a-Service (SAAS) providers accounted for 29.1% of phishing attacks [3]. Figure 1 shows the most targeted industries [3].

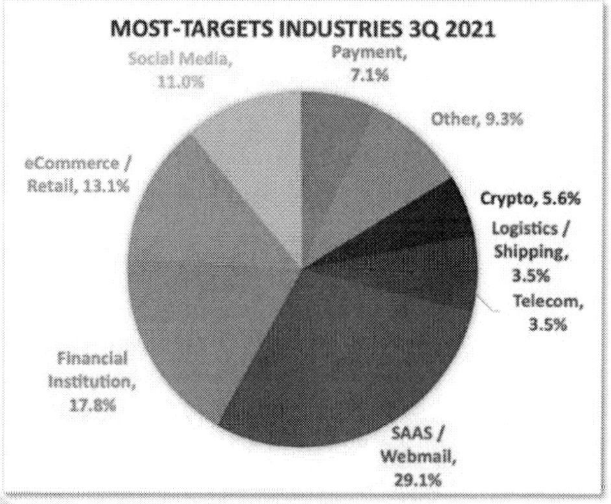

Fig 1. Most Targeted Industries, 3Q 2021 as originally published [3]

Younis and Musbah [4] note that smishing or SMS phishing is an attack that uses the SMS service that is an appealing attack vector for cybercriminals. Two-factor authentication (2FA) uses a hardware token, USB key, QR scan, one-time password, push notification, or contextual awareness to authenticate [5]. However, some 2FA approaches are vulnerable since they do not verify the webpage that the user is interacting with. In this attack, the user is tricked into entering the 2FA credentials into a counterfeit website. There are emerging protocols, such as FIDO (covered later) that help protect against this type of *runtime phishing*, which is where a user discloses their credentials and second factor codes to the adversary.

Phishing is the fraudulent practice of sending emails to lure you into providing credentials such as login information, passwords, and other sensitive information. This paper focuses primarily on phishing resistant techniques and technologies that provide a control against phishing emails. The paper also looks at technologies that can protect again malicious links or websites.

According to Dooremaal, et al. [6], phishing detection technologies that protect against fraudulent websites can be grouped into three categories: (1) list-based, (2) visual similarity-based, and (3) heuristic-based [6]. List-based approaches look at the URL of the website a user is visiting and compare that to a list of known phishing/malicious websites (called a block list) or a list of known legitimate websites (called an allow list). There are several anti-phishing websites such as, OpenPhish, PhishTank, and PhishStats. The main issue with list-based approaches is that they are not effective against zero-day attacks and these data sources need to be constantly updated to be useful. Han et al. found that some sites can take up to twenty days to add a site to their list [7]. Visual similarity-based alternatives utilize content on the website to determine its legitimacy. Techniques include examining the favicon (small image next to the website title), examining the logo or comparing screenshots of two websites to determine if one is trying to imitate the other. Heuristic-based approaches analyze features extracted from a website, such as the presence of an SSL certificate [7].

This research looks at a sampling of academic papers consisting of sixteen papers. The research did not take into consideration the number of surveys that have been conducted on phishing attacks. The papers were selected from cybersecurity databases such as Communications & Mass Media Complete, Telecommunications, ABI/INFORM Collection, ABI/INFORM Dateline, ACM Digital Library, and IEEE Computer Society. Keywords included phishing, phishing resistant, FIDO, authentication, MFA, 2FA, and others. Each paper was aligned to one of the four categories (compromised CSP, fraudulent website, stolen credentials and phishing emails) based on the discussion and results section of the paper.

B. *Microsoft Phishing Resistant Solutions*

There are configurations within Microsoft 365 and Exchange to enable anti-phishing settings [8]. Microsoft offers Microsoft Defender for Office 365 and Exchange Online Protection (EOP). EOP is a cloud-based filtering service that protects against spam, malware, and other threats [9]. EOP works by routing each message through filters that check for sender's reputation, malware, mail flow rules that the organization may have set up, and then delivered to the recipient, assuming no malicious content has been found. EOP utilizes the following [9]:

- URL block lists that help detect known malicious links within messages.
- List of domains that are known to send spam.
- Multiple anti-malware engines.
- Inspects the active payload in the message body and all message attachments for malware.

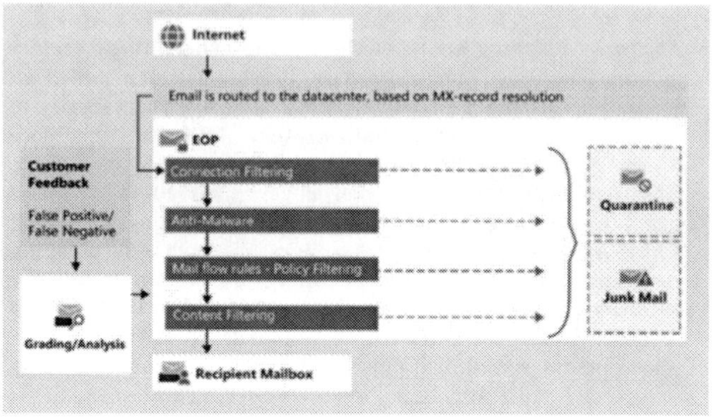

Fig 2. EOP Processing Email as originally published [8]

Microsoft Defender for Office 365 is a standalone product that builds on the protection afforded in EOP. Defender adds safe attachment scanning (for malware), URL scanning and real-time scanning of suspected links, anti-phishing protection (impersonation protection, protected users–specify email addresses that are protected from impersonation, and domain protection) [10]. Defender also adds post-breach investigation, hunting and response tools that allow administrators to see malware detected by the program, view phishing URLs, automate an investigation and response process, and investigate malicious emails [10]. It should be noted that the researcher did not test the effectiveness of these technical solutions.

C. *Eliminating Passwords*

One phishing resistant solution involves eliminating passwords. Passwords are a critical element in a phishing attack; so eliminating them goes a long way towards thwarting a phishing attack. The Web Authentication API, known as WebAuthn, is a specification developed by the World Wide Web Consortium (W3C) and the FIDO Alliance [11]. The API provides a mechanism for servers to register and authenticate users utilizing public key encryption instead of a password. It works with authentication systems that are built into devices such as Windows Hello and Apple's Touch ID. During registration a public/private key pair is created for a website. The user can use a FIDO Compliant authentication app or an external authenticator. The private key is stored securely on the device. Other sensitive information such as fingerprint and face ID data never leave the device. The server retains the user's public key and a randomly generated credential ID. The server uses the public key and credential ID to validate and authenticate a user to its services. The private key is never shared, and the public key is worthless without the corresponding private key [11]. Typically, a server would request a user ID and password from a user, which it would store online. A threat actor could seal the credentials from the server or with phishing, obtain the credentials from the user. Utilizing WebAuthn, when a user needs to access a web server, it sends a signature which is created with the private key. The server verifies the signature with the user's public key that was created during registration.

FIDO implementation comes in two forms: Platform authenticators are those that are embedded in a device such as a smartphone, tablet, or laptop. Many times, these devices have built-in biometric capabilities like Touch ID, Face ID and Windows Hello. FIDO supports Windows, Mac, Linux, Chrome OS, and Android. Cross-platform authenticators are external, physical devices that support USB, NFC, and Bluetooth [12]. FIDO supports biometrics including face, voice, iris, fingerprint, etc. [13]. FIDO keys include products from Yubico, Thetis, Google Titan, and Kensington, to name a few.

The FIDO Alliance is an industry association that is focused on reducing the reliance on passwords. FIDO stands for Fast Identity Online. FIDO has developed several specifications and standards, including FIDO and FIDO2. FIDO2 is the update to FIDO and was released in 2018. The main component of FIDO is WebAuthn. WebAuthn provides browser-based support for web authentication. FIDO2 also utilizes the Client-to Authenticator Protocol (CTAP), which allows for external authenticators, such as USB, NFC (Near Field Communication), or BLE (Bluetooth Low Energy) [14]. There is a growing number of companies that support FIDO including Apple, AWS, Coinbase, Dashlane, Dropbox, Ebay, Facebook, GitHub, GoDaddy, Google, Login.Gov, Microsoft, Oracle, Salesforce, Twitter, and Yahoo [14].

Miriam, et al. [15] researched how threat actors accomplish phishing schemes by posing as buyers in black-market services. They found five types of email lures: impersonating an associate, a stranger, a bank, Google, or a government authority. All of the services utilized domain squatting–registering and utilizing an internet domain name with the intent of profiting off of someone else's trademark (Nolo, n.d.). The threat actors were able to capture passwords in six out of nine attempts and immediately used the credentials to log in to the victim's account. Where 2FA was activated, the hackers sent subsequent phishing messages to victims asking for their phone number. Clicking on the link in the phishing message led to a fraudulent page that requested the 2FA code that was sent to the victim's phone. When the researchers inputted the 2FA code into the fraudulent page, the hackers were able to successfully log in [15]. The researchers noted that 2FA adds "friction" to attacks. Some dark web services noted that they could not access accounts without the victim's phone number and then had to add additional phishing messages to obtain the 2FA code, which added complexity to their attack [15].

MFA (and 2FA) are not without their flaws. Hendricks and Kettani [17] note that biometrics data is stored in a database and attackers could target those databases and use the biometrics to pass MFA. Further, threat actors have been successful in impersonating customers and resetting accounts and moving cell phone numbers to different SIM cards. Once that happens, the hacker can have the 2FA code sent to the new phone number [17]. Setting up an account PIN or some other form of identification is the best way to protect against this kind of vulnerability.

Razaq et al. [18] found that some threat actors mask fraudulent phone numbers by tricking victims into saving phone numbers as contacts so future calls from that number appear legitimate. Haworth defines Multi-factor authentication (MFA) fatigue as "the name given to a technique used by adversaries to flood a user's authentication app with push notifications in the hope they will accept and therefore enable an attacker to gain entry to an account or device," [19]. Threat actors have been observed using multiple authentication attempts in short succession against accounts that have MFA enabled. This technique, otherwise known as push notification spamming, works because users are often distracted or overwhelmed with notifications and will silence the authentication requests by approving the request [20]. Office 365 can limit these requests by configuring the default limits to the MFA service. Additionally, customers can utilize Microsoft Authenticator app, which works by providing a unique two-digit number that must be confirmed by inputting the number into the app. The authenticator app also supports industry standard time-based one-time passcodes (TOTP or OTP).

D. Email Authentication

By default, email headers and body are not encrypted or protected cryptographically. Thus, the sender's address is not a reliable verification of the sender's identity. There are, however, several methods that can be utilized to authenticate the sender [21]:

- The Sender Policy Framework (SPF) allows administrators to authorize hosts that are allowed to send mail.
- The Domain Key Identified Mail (DKIM) is a standard that provides outgoing email messages with a digital

signature. Recipients can use the signature to verify the validity of the sender.

- The Domain-Based Message Authentication, Reporting and Conformance (DMARC) standard builds on SPF and DKIM by providing a protocol for sender authentication and provides guidance on how to deal with a message that fails the SPF or DKIM test.

Adoption rates for these standards and protocols are low; Hu et al. [22] noted a 44.9% adoption rate in 2018 for SPF and 5.1% for DMARC. A 2019 study by 250ok found that 91.4% of non-profits have no DMARC policy in place despite holding a significant amount of PII [23]. Further, only 23% of Fortune 500 companies have some form of DMARC policy in place. Tatang et al. [23] noted that most email providers utilized some form of authentication. Their study revealed that out of 25 free email service providers, only one did not support SPF; DKIM was supported in 18 out of 25 service providers; and 14 out of 25 supported DMARC [24]. Hu et al. [22] noted a number of technical weaknesses with SPF, DKIM, and DMARC that impacted adoption of these standards and protocols. Table 1 displays these weaknesses.

TABLE I. SPF, DKIM, and DMARC TECHNICAL WEAKNESSES [22]

Protocol	Weakness	Problem Description
SPF	P1. Alignment	The SPF verified sender address can be different from the one displayed to users.
	P2. Mail forward	A forwarded email by default cannot pass the SPF test.
	P3. Mailing list	Emails sent to a mailing list by default cannot pass the SPF test.
DKIM	P4. Alignment	The sender domain that signed DKIM can be different from the one user sees.
	P5. Mailing list	Mailing lists often modify the email content, which will fail the DKIM test.
DMARC+SPF	P2. Mail forward	A forwarded email by default cannot pass the SPF test, and thus fails DMARC.
	P3. Mailing list	Emails sent to a mailing list cannot pass SPF and DMARC at the same time.
DMARC+DKIM	P5. Mailing list	Mailing lists often modify the email content, which will fail the DKIM test.
DMARC+SPF+DKIM	P5. Mailing list	SPF always fails; DIKM will fail if the mailing list modifies email content.

As noted in Table 1, the sender's domain can be different from what the end user sees. Figure 3 displays how SPF authentication focuses on the return-path domain, which can be different from what the user sees [22].

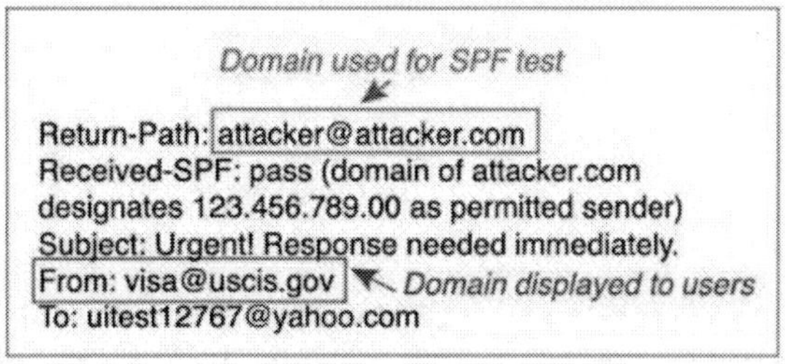

Fig 3. Return path Domain is Different that the Domain Displayed to User as originally published [22]

Additionally, the researchers found that administrators shared implementation challenges as well, such as, lack of control of their DNS servers [22].

E. Browser-Based Phishing Detection

Modern web browsers utilize safe browsing, which are a set of security measures that work to prevent unauthorized activity while an end user surfs the web. Safe browsing should protect against hackers, vulnerabilities, and online exploits. Google's Safe Browsing service that checks website URLs against a database of known malicious sites that is updated every 30 minutes [25]. Chrome actually samples a website's color profile and compares those to known phishing domains. Chrome counts basic colors in each pixel and stores the count in hashmaps. According to Google, image-based phishing is up to 50 times faster at the 50th percentile [25]. Apple's browser, Safari, also uses Google's Safe Browsing, as does Firefox, Chrome and Brave.

Some browsers offer third-party add-ons that provide anti-phishing toolbars and indicators to warn users of malicious sites. Research has shown, however, that these tools do not protect users against high-quality phishing attacks, and that users typically do not pay much attention to browser warnings [21]. Kaushik et al. [25] have found that hackers can take advantage of browser extensions to steal credentials, deliver malware, change browser settings, modify user interface elements, and substitute web content. The researchers noted that there are third-party applications that can scan an extension to see if it is legitimate or not. One such tool is Ext Analysis. While this tool can help prevent the installation of malicious extensions, they are time consuming to use and would need to be deployed on an enterprise level.

F. Phishing Intelligence Databases

There are several phishing intelligence databases that capture information on cloned websites. OpenPhish provides phishing feeds and has several developer plans that can get updates from 12 hours to (free) to five minutes (subscription) [27]. The site also offers an API that developers can use to integrate the searching of malicious URLs into a custom program. PhishTank is a collaborative clearing house for phishing data, which also provides an open API for developers to utilize [28]. PhishStats is a third dataset that is updated every 90 minutes. Developers can use an API as well [28]. All of these sites are useful but do not protect against zero day phishing exploits that have yet to be reported.

Figure 4 notes the top impersonated brands for December 2021 according to OpenPhish [30].

Brand	Industry	Hostnames
Facebook, Inc.	Social Networking	1992
Amazon.com Inc.	e-Commerce	1459
WhatsApp	Social Networking	1264
Office365	Online/Cloud Service	869
Outlook	Online/Cloud Service	624
Crypto/Wallet	Cryptocurrency	613
PayPal Inc.	Payment Service	358
Webmail Providers	Email Provider	344
Tencent	Online/Cloud Service	329
M & T Bank	Financial	295

Fig 4. Top 10 Impersonated Brands–December 2021 as originally published [30]

III. ANALYSIS

The intent is to identify new or variants of a tactic or technique as well as new or updated mitigation strategies. The sample of academic research consisted of sixteen papers. The papers were selected from cybersecurity databases such as Communications & Mass Media Complete, Telecommunications, ABI/INFORM Collection, ABI/INFORM Dateline, ACM Digital Library, and IEEE Computer Society. Keywords included phishing, phishing resistant, FIDO, authentication, MFA, 2FA, and others. Each paper was aligned to one of the four categories based on the discussion and results section of the paper.

70% of the academic papers reviewed fell into two of the four categories: fraudulent website and compromised credentials. 25% of the academic papers fell into the phishing email category.

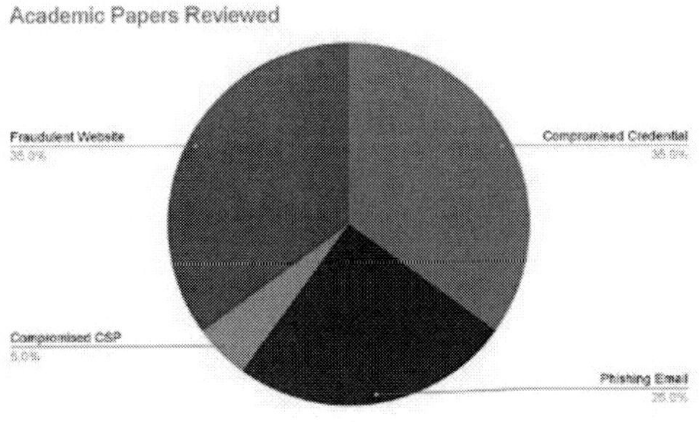

Fig 5. Academic Papers Reviewed.

IV. PASSWORDLESS AUTHENTICATION

Since the literature review of phishing resistant systems was completed, a new entrant is making its way to the market. As of September of 2022, passwordless authentication is being adopted by a number of vendors [5]. Passkeys are a fido authentication credential that provides passwordless entry to online systems [31]. Support for passkeys [6] has been announced by Apple, Google, and Microsoft. Passkeys utilize biometrics or a pin to authentication [32]. Apple integrates Touch ID or Face ID into passkeys and makes it simple to log into a website [7]. Passkeys are synced across user's Apple devices and are encrypted (even Apple [8] does not know that encryption password), [33]. Microsoft utilizes Microsoft Hello for Business, their Authenticator app [9], and fido2 security keys to implement passwordless authentication [10][34]. Google has also expressed support for fido passwordless authentication and will utilized passkeys stored on mobile phones and synced to the cloud for authentication [11] [35]

V. CONCLUSION

The purpose of this study was to review the literature of phishing resistant systems. The author reviewed 16 papers and categorized them into four categories: Fraudulent website, compromised credentials, Compromised CSP, and Phishing Emails. The literature review revealed that there is no single product that provides full protection against phishing attacks. This study is limited in some ways. The scope of the literature review only contained 16 papers. A future study could further expand the number of papers reviewed and map the literature review to the MITRE ATT&CK and D3FEND frameworks. The most exciting technology to prevent phishing is undoubtedly passwordless systems. With support from the fido Alliance, and the big three tech companies (Apple, Microsoft, and Google) the impact of passwordless authentication should significantly reduce phishing initiated attacks.

REFERENCES

[1] J. Biden, "Executive Order on Improving the Nation's Cybersecurity," *The White House*, May 12, 2021. https://www.whitehouse.gov/briefingroom/presidential-actions/2021/05/12/executive-order-on-improving-thenations-cybersecurity/ (accessed Mar. 08, 2022).

[2] S. Young, "M-22-09.pdf." Jan. 26, 2022. [Online]. Available: https://www.whitehouse.gov/wp-content/uploads/2022/01/M-22-09.pdf

[3] APWG, "Phishing Activity Trends Report, 3QTR, 2021." Nov. 22, 2021.

[4] Y. A. Younis and M. Musbah, "A Framework to Protect Against Phishing Attacks," in *Proceedings of the 6th International Conference on Engineering & MIS 2020*, Almaty Kazakhstan, Sep. 2020, pp. 1–6. doi: 10.1145/3410352.3410825.

[5] E. Ulqinaku, D. Lain, and S. Capkun, "2FA-PP: 2nd factor phishing prevention," in *Proceedings of the 12th Conference on Security and Privacy in Wireless and Mobile Networks*, Miami Florida, May 2019, pp. 60–70. doi: 10.1145/3317549.3323404.

[6] B. van Dooremaal, P. Burda, L. Allodi, and N. Zannone, "Combining Text and Visual Features to Improve the Identification

of Cloned Webpages for Early Phishing Detection," in *The 16th International Conference on Availability, Reliability and Security*, Vienna Austria, Aug. 2021, pp. 1–10. doi: 10.1145/3465481.3470112.

[7] X. Han, N. Kheir, and D. Balzarotti, "PhishEye: Live Monitoring of Sandboxed Phishing Kits," in *Proceedings of the 2016 ACM SIGSAC Conference on Computer and Communications Security*, Vienna Austria, Oct. 2016, pp. 1402–1413. doi: 10.1145/2976749.2978330.

[8] C. Davis, U. Gandhi, B. Shilpa, D. Hanson, and D. Coulter, "Anti-phishing policies - Office 365." https://docs.microsoft.com/en-us/microsoft365/security/office-365-security/set-up-anti-phishing-policies (accessed Jan. 30, 2022).

[9] C. Davis, "Exchange Online Protection (EOP) overview - Office 365," Feb. 17, 2022. https://docs.microsoft.com/en-us/microsoft-365/security/office-365security/exchange-online-protection-overview (accessed Mar. 08, 2022).

[10] MSFTTracyP, C. Davis, and D. Simpson, "Office 365 Security including Microsoft Defender for Office 365 and Exchange Online Protection - Office 365," Feb. 17, 2022. https://docs.microsoft.com/en-us/microsoft365/security/office-365-security/overview (accessed Mar. 08, 2022).

[11] Duo Security, "Guide to Web Authentication," *Guide to Web Authentication*. https://webauthn.guide (accessed Jan. 30, 2022).

[12] Hideez, "What is FIDO2 and how does it work? Passwordless Authentication Advantages & Disadvantages," *Hideez*, Jan. 31, 2022. https://hideez.com/blogs/news/fido2-explained (accessed Mar. 09, 2022).

[13] fido Alliance, "What is FIDO?," *FIDO Alliance*. https://fidoalliance.org/what-is-fido/ (accessed Jan. 30, 2022).

[14] S. Tzur-David, "Your Complete Guide to FIDO, FIDO2 and WebAuthn," *Secret double octopus*, Jun. 30, 2020. https://doubleoctopus.com/blog/biometrics/your-complete-guide-to-fido-fastidentity-online/ (accessed Mar. 09, 2022).

[15] A. Mirian, J. DeBlasio, S. Savage, G. M. Voelker, and K. Thomas, "Hack for Hire: Exploring the Emerging Market for Account Hijacking," in *The World Wide Web Conference on - WWW '19*, San Francisco, CA, USA, 2019, pp. 1279–1289. doi: 10.1145/3308558.3313489.

[16] Nolo, "Cybersquatting: What It Is and What Can Be Done About It," *www.nolo.com*. https://www.nolo.com/legal-encyclopedia/cybersquattingwhat-what-can-be-29778.html (accessed Mar. 10, 2022).

[17] A. Henricks and H. Kettani, "On Data Protection Using Multi-Factor Authentication," in *Proceedings of the 2019 International Conference on Information System and System Management*, Rabat Morocco, Oct. 2019, pp. 1–4. doi: 10.1145/3394788.3394789.

[18] L. Razaq, T. Ahmad, S. Ibtasam, U. Ramzan, and S. Mare, "'We Even Borrowed Money From Our Neighbor': Understanding Mobile-based Frauds Through Victims' Experiences," *Proc. ACM Hum.-Comput. Interact.*, vol. 5, no. CSCW1, pp. 1–30, Apr. 2021, doi: 10.1145/3449115.

[19] J. Haworth, "MFA fatigue attacks: Users tricked into allowing device access due to overload of push notifications," *The Daily Swig | Cybersecurity news and views*, Feb. 16, 2022. https://portswigger.net/daily-swig/mfa-fatigueattacks-users-tricked-into-allowing-device-access-due-to-overload-of-pushnotifications (accessed Feb. 18, 2022).

[20] L. Ubiedo, "Current MFA Fatigue Attack Campaign Targeting Microsoft Office 365 Users," *GoSecure*, Feb. 14, 2022. https://www.gosecure.net/blog/2022/02/14/current-mfa-fatigue-attackcampaign-targeting-microsoft-office-365-users/ (accessed Feb. 18, 2022).

[21] O. Wiese, J. Lausch, J. Bode, and V. Roth, "Beware the downgrading of secure electronic mail," in *Proceedings of the 8th Workshop on Socio-Technical Aspects in Security and Trust*, San Juan Puerto Rico, Dec. 2018, pp. 1–9. doi: 10.1145/3361331.3361332.

[22] H. Hu, P. Peng, and G. Wang, "Towards Understanding the Adoption of Anti-Spoofing Protocols in Email Systems," in *2018 IEEE Cybersecurity Development (SecDev)*, Cambridge, MA, Sep. 2018, pp. 94–101. doi: 10.1109/SecDev.2018.00020.

[23] D. Tatang, F. Zettl, and T. Holz, "The Evolution of DNS-based Email Authentication: Measuring Adoption and Finding Flaws," in *24th International Symposium on Research in Attacks, Intrusions and Defenses*, San Sebastian Spain, Oct. 2021, pp. 354–369. doi: 10.1145/3471621.3471842.

[24] A. Bannister, "Google supercharges Chrome's phishing detection mechanism," *The Daily Swig | Cybersecurity news and views*, Jul. 22, 2021. https://portswigger.net/daily-swig/google-supercharges-chromes-phishingdetection-mechanism (accessed Mar. 12, 2022).

[25] K. Kaushik, S. Aggarwal, S. Pandey, S. Mudgal, and S. Garg, "Investigating and Safeguarding the Web Browsers from Malicious Web Extensions," vol. 6, no. 10, p. 10, Sep. 2021.

[26] OpenPhish, "OpenPhish-Phishing Intelligence." https://openphish.com/index.html (accessed Mar. 12, 2022).

[27] PhishTank, "PhishTank | Join the fight against phishing." https://phishtank.org/index.php (accessed Mar. 12, 2022).

[29] PhishStats, "PhishStats." https://phishstats.info/ (accessed Mar. 12, 2022).

[30] OpenPhish, "Phishing Trends: December 2021 - OpenPhish," Jan. 26, 2022. https://openphish.com/blog/phishing-trends-dec2021.html (accessed Mar. 12, 2022).

[31] fido Alliance, "Passkeys (Passkey Authentication)," *FIDO Alliance*.https://fidoalliance.org/multi-device-fido-credentials/ (accessed Sep. 24, 2022).

[32] I. Mehta, "What is Apple Passkey, and how will it help you go passwordless?," *TechCrunch*, Sep. 12, 2022. https://techcrunch.com/2022/09/12/apple-passkey/ (accessed Sep. 24, 2022).

[33] Apple, "About the security of passkeys," *Apple Support*. https://support.apple.com/en-us/HT213305 (accessed Sep. 24, 2022).

[34] Microsoft, "Passwordless authentication | Microsoft Security." https://www.microsoft.com/en-us/security/business/solutions/passwordlessauthentication (accessed Sep. 24, 2022).

[35] S. Srinivas, "One step closer to a passwordless future," *Google*, May 05, 2022. https://blog.google/technology/safety-security/one-step-closer-to-apasswordless-future/ (accessed Sep. 24, 2022).

Advanced Access Control System for Mobility as a Service Platform

Anjali Rajith
Service Systems Innovation Center
Research and Development Group, Hitachi Ltd.
Yokohama, Japan
email: anjali.rajith.he@hitachi.com

Soki Sakurai
Service Systems Innovation Center
Research and Development Group, Hitachi Ltd.
Yokohama, Japan
email: soki.sakurai.mk@hitachi.com

***Abstract*—Mobility as a Service (MaaS) is a digital platform that integrates multiple transport and third-party providers into a single channel that enables customers to easily book and pay for services. Data misuse, accidental data leakage, and malicious services are the key threats to confidential customer and service provider data. To eliminate these threats, an advanced access control system is proposed for MaaS that utilizes a context based, customer-centric, hybrid fine-grained and quantitative trust computing approach. The eXtensible Access Control Language architecture is extended by adding a trust score computation module and policy update function. When a data request arrives, the data access context is determined, and the trust score of the data requester is computed based on selected trust parameters. Access to confidential information is subjected to trust score condition and fine-grained policy rules. Real-time policy updating and data masking are performed when personal data-sharing preferences are changed. Our model ensures a safe, reliable data flow and mitigates the security and privacy issues.**

Keywords-MaaS; access control; trust score; privacy; XACML.

I. INTRODUCTION

Mobility as a Service (MaaS) [1]–[3] is the integration of multiple transport providers and service providers into a single digital platform, accessible on demand. The integration and unification are undertaken by intermediaries who are between supply side and demand side as shown in Figure 1. The supply side is made up of Mobility Service Providers (MSPs), public or private organizations that own and manage transport services through transport service providers and other mobility-related services. The demand side is the customers or end-users who avail the MaaS service. A stack of services in the middle layer are required to coordinate the users and services of MaaS platform, such as payment services, ticketing services, recommendation services, etc. Therefore, the data in the MaaS platform belong to a plethora of services and customers.

In this work, MaaS architecture is proposed to be built on top of Lumada [4], the IoT platform of Hitachi, Figure 2. Lumada provides a stack of basic and solution functions, such as artificial intelligence, security, etc. required to build a business solution. It comprises: a Data Zone that captures and collects IT data from web applications and databases, and OT data from IoT data, such as weather data, information from Road Service Units (RSUs), and GPS data; Data Flow that acquires data from various sources; Data Processing Governance that governs the data processing, and Data understanding layer that provides several tools to understand the data. However,

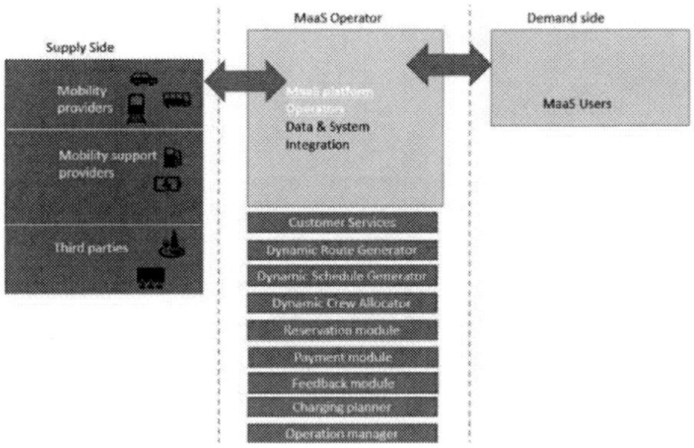

Figure. 1. Basic concept of MaaS.

the entire MaaS architecture is outside the scope of this work and only the Data Processing Governance Layer is considered that is related to technologies that handle the data management, policy handling, and access control. Stringent laws and regulations govern personal information, making data provenance and access monitoring imperative for keeping track of unauthorized access attempts on the MaaS platform. The Service Level Agreement (SLA) and access control policies in this layer help to prevent the invocation of services by unauthorized operators and prevent malicious services from accessing sensitive information.

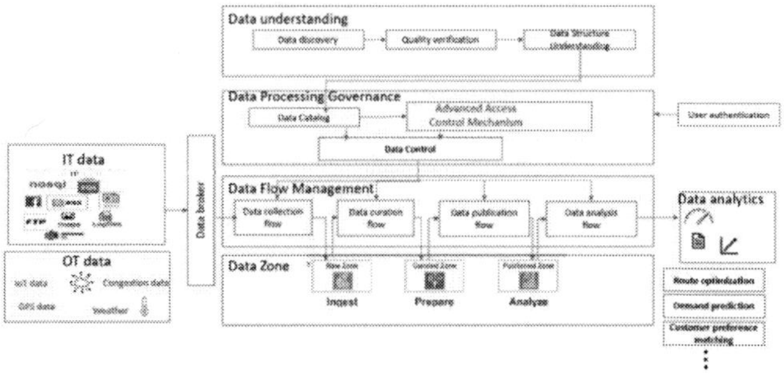

Figure. 2. Lumada-based Maas architecture.

A. *MaaS Security Challenges*

A large amount of Personally Identifiable Information (PII) and travel-related information of users and drivers are shared via the platform. Accidental or purposeful leakage of such information can breach users' privacy. MaaS also faces various realistic threats in which attackers gain access to GPS positioning of vehicles, steal data, and thereby gives undue advantages to competitors. There are also insider threats, such as misusing information for purposefully favouring or destroying one's business. Thus, we focus on three main security challenges faced by the MaaS platform [5]:

1) Misuse of personal information of customers: Sensitive personal information of the customers is utilized by third-parties without their knowledge. Power of consent doesn't always fall in the hands of the customers. Therefore, the first challenge is to ensure that the system complies with the personal information protection acts, as well as provides the power of consent revocation and right to determine who access their data to the customers.
2) Accidental data leakage: The service providers participating in the MaaS platform receive way too much information than that is actually required. So, the second challenge is to ensure that only minimum necessary information is provided to the services.
3) Threats from malicious services: There are chances that malicious insider services utilize the data for favouring their own business. The third challenge is to continuously monitor trust factor of the participating parties in a quantitative manner based on agreed SLAs.

B. Our Contributions

Our main contributions are as follows:

1) We propose a novel context based, customer-centric, hybrid fine-grained and quantitative trust computing access control approach such that the access approval to a particular data resource is determined based on the dynamic context of data access, access policy rules, and trust score of the data requester calculated at the time of access based on historic access log parameters.
2) A system architecture design with additional functionalities is proposed by extending the standard access control architecture to address the security challenges.

This paper is organized as follows: Section II explains related work on MaaS security threats and various access control systems. Section III explains conventional access control architecture and our system's approach. Section IV explains our system's architecture and details each component. Section V explains the implementation. Section VI concludes the paper and mentions future works on optimizing the system.

II. Related Work

There are different works that attempt to study the security threats faced by MaaS platforms. Callegati et. al [5], [6] focused on the insider threats in MaaS and followed a tiered architecture from individual operators to markets of federated MaaS providers to classify the threats of each tier, and proposed appropriate mitigation measures. These works point out the necessity of proper access control technologies and security loopholes caused due to inadequate policy definitions and indicate the necessity of adequate access logging and auditing facilities.

Some works address the security and privacy issues through access control approaches in cloud environments and blockchains. Toahchoodee et al. [7] proposed a trust-based access control approach for access control of pervasive computing systems, whereas P. K. Behera and P. M. Khilar [8] proposed a trust-based access control approach for cloud environment, in which the user request is passed through various sub-modules to make the authorization decision. However, this work is related to access of cloud resources where user should submit the QoS requirements, such as security, cost, computing power, etc., and the user authorization is made solely based on user trust value computed by a trust management module. A. Singh and K. Chatterjee [9] proposed a mutual trust based access control model for the healthcare system by modifying the conventional access control system by integrating the trust degree of communicating parties in the access control system. However, this system does not account for any dynamic changes in the data requesters and the environment. The access decision that is solely based on trust score of few parameters could make the system vulnerable to attacks that track the access decision pattern. Trust and reputation systems are widely used in e-commerce, social networks, search engines, and so on. User scoring is performed based on their activities in scoring systems of credit card agencies [10]. Works such as, A. Josang [11] and G. Zacharia and P.Maes [12] proposed trust and reputation systems in online environment by storing records of activities of users and calculating reputation score for users.

Works, such as Hogan et al. [13] used blockchain in MaaS for improving the transactional aspects and increasing the trust between various actors involved in MaaS. Guo et al. [14] also studied blockchain-based access control. However, blockchain is not considered in this work considering the high computation and gas cost. Ammar et al. [15] has implemented a semantic handler component for deciding the context of data access. In our work, we only consider two contexts, and hence do not implement a separate module for context evaluation.

None of the works have explicitly studied the access control paradigm for a cross-industrial collaboration system, such as MaaS, where the data providers and the data requesters change in a dynamic manner. The security preferences and data exchange between various operators, services, and end-users can change in an dynamic environment and that makes it very challenging.

III. Approach

This section explains the standard XACML architecture in sub-section III-A and proposed architecture in sub-section III-B.

A. Standard XACML Architecture

Access Control systems are trust infrastructures that allow or restrict access to protected resources through data authorization and access control. Role-Based Access Control (RBAC) [16] [17] system assigns access permissions to roles, and roles to subject. However, RBAC implements a static permission list and cannot scale into real-world dynamic environments. Attribute-Based Access Control (ABAC) [18]–[20] defines an attribute-based access control paradigm in which access rights are granted to users through eXtensible Access Control Language (XACML) [21]–[23] policies that combines the subject, object, action, and environment attributes. This approach is dynamic to an extent that access decision is based on attribute values at the time of access attempt. It comes with an architecture with the components, Policy Enforcement Point (PEP), Policy Decision Point (PDP), Policy Administration Point (PAP), and Policy Information Point (PIP). In the standard XACML engine, PEP wraps the data request into a XACML request and communicates it to the PDP. The PDP with the help of PIP, checks the attribute values and verifies the policies managed by PAP, makes an access decision, and communicates it back to PEP.

The fine-grained ABAC approach actualizes a dynamic access control technique, where only necessary information is passed on to the data requesters based on complex policies and rules. However, based on the studies in section II, implementing a conventional standalone access control system is insufficient for tackling the security challenges of a highly dynamic transaction environment, such as MaaS. Therefore, we devised a context-based hybrid access control approach that adds new functional modules to the standard access control system. In addition to pre-defined access rules and conditions stipulated through fine-grained policies, a separate module is necessary to modify and update conditions in the policy rules in a real-time manner. The conventional access control approach neither supports attribute logging nor quantitative computation. Logging the access attribute values and access decisions related to all data requesters helps to evaluate their reliability. The trust score computation approach calculates the trust score at the time of data request, based on the historic log data. It is to be noted that access log information is collected on a mutual consensus with participating parties. The trust score computation approach is critical in issuing security warnings to the admin user and the data requesters, restricting access to confidential customer information, and auditing. Since the system collects subjective trust parameters, such as user feedback, it can be used as a means to provide service provider recommendations to like-minded customers. Therefore, we implement new modules on top of the XACML architecture to incorporate additional functionalities.

B. Overview of Proposed System

MaaS is a highly dynamic data transaction environment involving multiple data providers and data requesters, with lot of security issues which are pointed out in sections I and II. In this paper, we propose a context based, customer-centric, hybrid access control approach for minimizing security issues faced by the MaaS platform. Our hybrid approach combines the fine-grained access control mechanism and quantitative trust computing approach on top of the XACML architecture. Trust score of the data requesters are computed at the time of data access request, based on selected trust parameters. The hybrid approach incorporates the trust score threshold condition into the XACML policies such that access to sensitive information could mandate to satisfy trust score criteria in the policy rules. In the MaaS platform, it is important to give more power to the user to make decision on the access of his/ her personal information. The customer-centric approach dynamically updates the access control policies based on real-time customer personal data access security preferences and dynamic trust threshold value changes. The context-based approach considers two contexts, normal and emergency; that is evaluated by the context handler in the gateway, based on access attributes. The data control flow is slightly altered in the emergency context, such that a risk threshold attribute is set and access control to sensitive customer information is passed to authorities for emergency evacuations. A data masking or data transformation function is incorporated such that even during the unfortunate event of accidental data leakage, sensitive information is protected.

IV. ARCHITECTURE DESIGN

Figure 3 represents the overall architecture and control flow of the proposed advanced access control system.

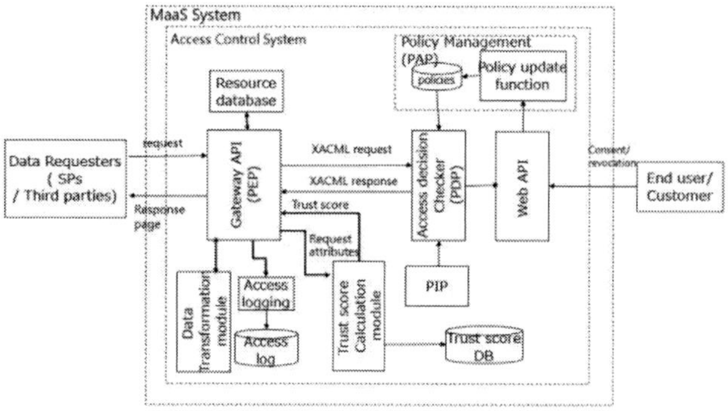

Figure. 3. System architecture to realize the proposed approach.

The main components are as follows:

1) Gateway API - Receives the data access request/ response and has a context evaluator function.
2) Web API - A user interface that allows customers/ end users to interact with the MaaS data management layer.
3) Policy Management (PAP) - Manages the policies and triggers the real-time policy update function upon changes.
4) Access Logging - Logs the access parameters of the data requesters for trust score calculation.
5) Trust calculation module - Calculates trust score of the data requesters and stores in trust score database.
6) Data Transformation Module - Masks the sensitive customer information.
7) Access decision checker (PDP) - Provides the access decision based on the policies defined.

In this work, WSO2 Identity Server [24], an open source software is used for access control, policy management, and configuration of PIP.

When an access request for a data resource arrives, the first step is to verify the credentials, which is performed by an identity authentication module. The details of this module will be skipped as it does not fall under the scope of this work. In the second step, data request attributes are extracted by the gateway API, the PEP. In standard XACML architecture, the PEP module generates the authorization request and sends it to the PDP module immediately. In our approach, the context evaluator function in the gateway API judges the data request context, which is a dynamic attribute with values `[normal, emergency]`. If the context value is `normal`, the request attributes are passed on to a trust calculation module. If the context value is `emergency`, step three is skipped. In step three, the trust calculation module performs the trust score calculation of the data requester based on historic access log data and communicates the trust score back.

As the fourth step, the PEP generates the XACML request based on the attributes and context. In the fifth step, the authorization request is passed on to the access decision checker, that checks the access request parameters against defined policies. Based on the access decision, access is permitted or denied to the data resource requested. In the sixth step, either the requested data fetched from resource database or an error message is delivered by the gateway to the data requester. The access request parameters and response parameters are logged accordingly for auditing and trust scoring purpose.

Definition 1. *The XACML data flow is as follows:*
Step 1: The gateway API receives the access request and the context value is determined based on $[subject_{real-time}, environment_{real-time}, action_{real-time}.]$
Step 2: If context value is `emergency`*, the request handler generates the XACML request with value of* `risk threshold` *attribute set as 1, and skip to step 4, else go to step 3.*
Step 3: The trust calculation module calculates the trust score of the data requester and sends back to gateway.
Step 4: The gateway generates the XACML request based on the values of access attributes, risk threshold, and trust score and communicates the request to access decision checker (PDP).
Step 5: The access decision checker evaluates the access request by checking additional attributes against PIP and access policies, provides response to gateway, which is either `permit` *or* `deny`*.*
Step 6: If the response is `permit`*, gateway executes obligation services and provides access to requested data to the data requester. Else, an authorization error message is returned. The response and access parameters are logged to access log database.*

A. Context Evaluation

In the context-based approach, data access context is determined by the context evaluator function in the gateway API module. In normal scenarios, the access control system prevents access to any unauthorized access attempts on sensitive end-user information, such as user location and sensitive driver information, such as driver GPS location, name, etc. Only users in the appropriate role can access this information. This is to prevent the insider misuse of information that is completely irrelevant to their purpose. However, in the emergency life-threatening situations, such as natural disasters, the location information of all users can be accessed by the admin user or city authorities for necessary actions. For this purpose, the dynamic context attribute is utilized. Based on the values of $[subject_{real-time}, action_{real-time}, environment_{real-time}]$ attributes, the context is determined as `[normal, emergency]`. The data flow handling is altered in the `emergency` context by skipping the trust computation based on agreed SLAs with end-users.

B. Customer-Centric Approach

In the customer-centric approach, the customers are given the power to control access to their personal information. This is realized through the policy management and the web API module. They can enable or disable access to their PII, as well as location and destination information to selected transport providers and third-party services by setting their security preferences through the web API.

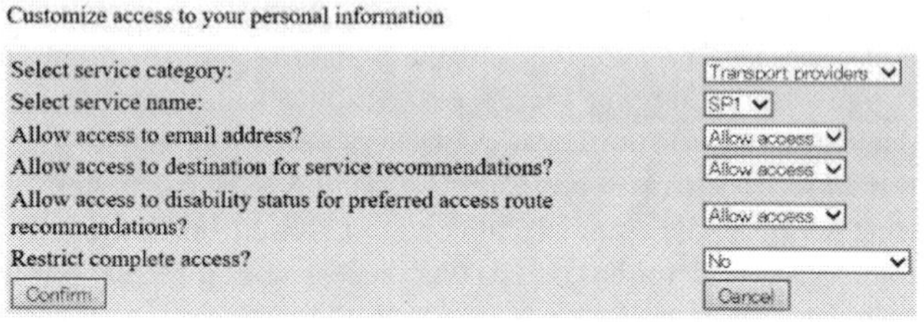

Figure. 4. User security preference form.

Figure 4 illustrates the user security preference form available to the MaaS users. It provides the option to restrict complete record access or column access to selected service categories and service providers. If an end-user allows/ restricts his information to be accessed by a third-party service through the provided web API, the access rules associated with the records of user in the respective location are updated real-time by calling an `update function`, that can update the attribute values in policy conditions and add or delete conditions to the policy rules. A XACML policy template is auto-generated with the new attribute values or conditions, and the corresponding customer policy is updated by invoking the policy administration APIs of WSO2 [25] tool. Once the policy is updated and deployed, the change in access permissions to concerned service providers are reflected.

Figure 5 illustrates the restricted column access, in which the data requester cannot access the columns, such as *disability status* of the customer. The values of selected columns by the customer are masked by calling a `mask function` offered by data transformation module.

Customer Name	Email address	Destination	Disability status	Smoking preference
sam	sam1@gmail.com	bokutho hosptial	N	not smoking
cathy	******@gmail.com	****	****	smoking
yamamoto	yamamoto99@gmail.com	bakurocho station	N	not smoking
suzuki	******@yahoo.com	****	****	not smoking
miura	******@hotmail.com	****	****	not smoking
akiko	akiko@gmail.com	sumida community center	N	not smoking

Figure. 5. Transformed data.

C. Access Logging

The access logging function logs the data request and response attributes associated to a data requester, such as authentication id, name, service category, access location, access time, action, resource id, and access decision to an access log database, which are used for the trust score computation and auditing purpose. The parameters associated with trust computation, which will be explained later in sub-section IV-D, are derived values from the log data. Any unfortunate incident of access by an unauthorized person is reported and prompts the admin for immediate policy definitions' review. This is very important because careless policy definitions can breach SLAs with customers and service providers.

D. Trust Scoring Approach

This section explains the trust scoring approach, parameters used, and trust score calculation. The trust scoring function is realized through the trust computation module. It calculates the trust score of the data requesters based on the trust parameters logged in the access log database, as well as from security monitoring system. The trust parameters under consideration are:

1) Invalid data access request rate: This parameter is calculated for the data requester based on the unauthorized access attempts obtained from the access history data logs. The invalid data access attempt rate, DAR is calculated as:

$$DAR = \frac{R_d}{R_t} \tag{1}$$

where, R_d is the number of unauthorized or failed access attempts made by the data requester and R_t is the total number of access attempts.

2) Access frequency rate: The ratio of number of access requests from a particular data requester to total number of access requests per unit time. Monitoring this parameter helps to detect Denial-of-Service(DOS) Attacks. Access frequency rate, AFR is calculated as:

$$AFR = \frac{R_t}{T_t} \tag{2}$$

where, R_t is the number of access attempts made by the data requester and T_t is the total number of access attempts per unit time.

3) Transaction rate: The number of successful transactions made by a service provider through the MaaS platform with respect to other service providers who belong to the same user category per unit time interval.
4) User satisfaction: This is a subjective parameter based on the user feedback about the service of particular service provider. This could be considering aspects, such as punctuality in the service, delay notifications, payment service, etc.
5) Network Protection: A weighted impact score calculated by security monitoring system of MaaS system on each collaborating service provider, based on data on network-related parameters, such as access measures (encryption measures), network environment (local or remote), and suspicious packet count.

The trust score of the data requester n, T^n is calculated as:

$$T^n = \sum_{w=i}^{j} w_i * p_i \tag{3}$$

where p_i are the j parameters used, and w_i are the weights of p_i parameters. The weights vary from 1 to 10 based on priority. Higher weights are assigned to high priority parameters, based on occurrence of security incidents. All new users are assigned a minimum trust score greater than 0. The calculated trust scores are stored in a trust database. The trust score, T^n is normalized such that T_{max}, T_{min} are the minimum and maximum trust scores and the direction of reliability is made similar:

$$NT^n = \frac{T^n - T_{min}}{T_{max} - T_{min}} \tag{4}$$

An access control criteria can be set such that such that trust score of the data requester calculated at time of access must be greater than defined score $NT^n >= NT^{th}$, where NT^{th} is the threshold value. NT^{th}, T_{max}, and T_{min} are selected based on the training dataset. The threshold is selected such that it maximizes the accuracy of trust decision. Some malicious users may attempt to take advantage of the system before their trust score drops. To handle this scenario, the weights associated with negative trust parameters are changed based on the user activity. Weights of positive parameters such as, transaction rate and user satisfaction are unchanged irrespective of user activity.

E. Access Decision Checker

The access decision checker is the PDP entitlement engine. Here, WSO2 identity server is used. The XACML request generated from the gateway contains the attribute values associated with the data requester. The access decision is made by PDP by checking the request against the attribute values obtained from PIP and policies. If response from PDP is `permit`, access is allowed. All PDP responses are logged and a `permit` decision to the data requester triggers an email to the admin user through XACML-obligation features. The hybrid approach formulates an access decision based on fine grained policy-based conditions such that the trust score based condition can be incorporated to policies in a flexible or optional manner.

V. Implementation

In this section, the implementation of proposed model in an experimental MaaS system is explained. To implement the system, Eclipse Integrated Development Environment (IDE) using Java programming language is used. Capturing of access parameters of the data requesters, customer feedback, and personal information preferences are also done in the same environment. As explained in section IV, WSO2 Identity Server is used as access decision engine. Gateway API (PEP) is implemented as Java servlets running on top of Tomcat server [26].

We have considered ten customers and four service providers (data requesters) in the test set. A dynamic trust threshold monitoring function updates the trust threshold variable in the policy, upon change in optimal threshold value based on past 'n' unit time. The WSO2 policy administration APIs are invoked to update the trust threshold value defined in the policies based on the output of this function. Meeting the trust threshold criteria can be used as a condition in policy rules to access customer records. This criteria can be applied to any confidential records. The customer preferences on their personal record access and trust threshold criteria are reflected in policy rules as shown below:

Definition 2. *rule Rule1* {
description: "Only service providers of category transport providers, with trust score greater than 0.6 are allowed by customer1 to read the data"
subject:"SP1"
action:read
object:"customer#1.data"
condition:"SP1.service_category==transport_provider && $SP1.trust\_score \geq 0.6$"
decision: permit}

Data access will be denied to the requesters who fail to satisfy the policy conditions. Figure 6 illustrates an example XACML policy where decision of the rule is permit, if trust score is greater than the set trust threshold value 0.6. The real-time trust score computation along with the other fine-grained policy rules based on attribute values at the access time provides a better approach when compared to standard models. Since the access decision does not solely depend on trust computation, it can be also be optionally removed as a policy criteria and can be only used for security monitoring purpose.

Figure 7 demonstrates the trust score of the service providers belonging to a selected category service using open-source Grafana dashboard [27].

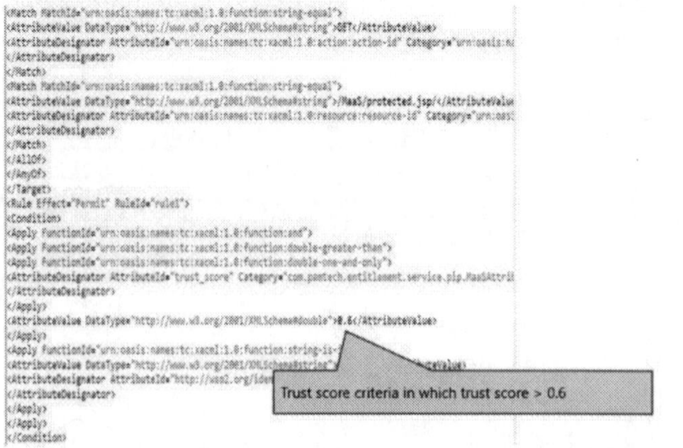

Figure. 6. XACML policy with real-time trust score condition.

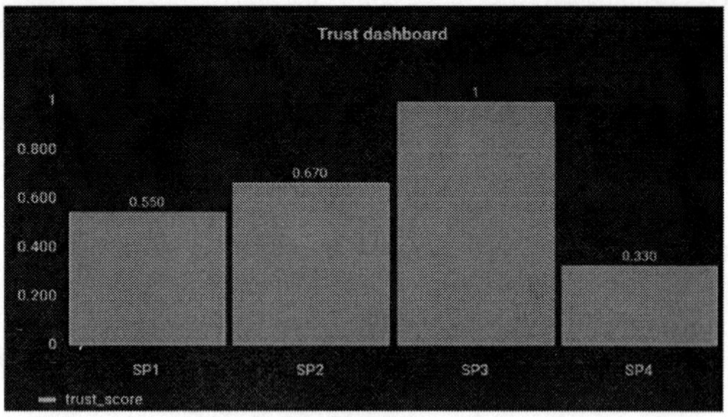

Figure. 7. Trust scores of service providers.

VI. Conclusion and Future Work

We implemented a context based, customer-centric, hybrid access control system for a MaaS platform to mitigate the MaaS security challenges, such as misuse of customer information, accidental leakage of sensitive information, and insider threats from malicious services. Our proposed system extends the XACML architecture to address problems caused by malicious users and services. We analyze historic access logs and security monitoring data to derive trust score of the data requesters. Confidential information access is only permitted if the trust score calculated at the time of access and other attribute values meet the stipulated policy rules. Therefore, the access decision made using the hybrid access control model is more reliable than the conventional models. The user-centric approach of this system gives complete power to the end-users in deciding how their personal data is utilized. Data masking and access policy updating are done real-time without affecting other processes in the system. The context-based approach classifies the data access into `normal` and `emergency` contexts. This module prioritizes safety over security by altering the data flow handling in the emergency context. The advanced access control system can be realized in any dynamic data collaboration platform similar to MaaS.

In future work, we will study the dynamic selection of trust parameters based on historical parameter data analysis. We will also study the system performance by analysing the number of concurrent users against the number of cores with respect to response time and computation cost. Furthermore, experiments will be performed for the empirical analysis of trust score to study rate of change of trust score, ideal trust score retention period, and effect of few suspicious transactions on a trust-worthy user.

ACKNOWLEDGMENT

This research is funded and supported by Hitachi Research and Development Group, and would like to thank them for providing support and technical advice.

REFERENCES

[1] "Maas https://smart-maas.eu/en/ (visited on 05/20/2021)."

[2] D. Sitányiová and S. Masarovicová, "Development status of sustainable urban mobility plans in european union new member states," *International Journal of Transport Development and Integration*, vol. 1, no. 1, pp. 16–27, 2016.

[3] E.-I. Europe, "Mobility as a service (maas) and sustainable urban mobility planning," *ERTICO–ITS Europe: Brussels, Belgium*, 2019.

[4] S. Hanaoka, Y. Taguchi, T. Nakamura, H. Kato, T. Kaji, H. Komi, N. Moriwaki, N. Kohinata, K. Wood, T. Hashimoto, *et al.*, "Iot platform that expands the social innovation business," *Hitachi Review*, vol. 65, no. 9, p. 439, 2016.

[5] F. Callegati, S. Giallorenzo, A. Melis, and M. Prandini, "Cloud-of-things meets mobility-as-a-service: An insider threat perspective," *Computers and Security*, vol. 74, 11 2017.

[6] F. Callegati, S. Giallorenzo, A. Melis, and M. Prandini, "Data security issues in maas-enabling platforms," in *2016 IEEE 2nd International Forum on Research and Technologies for Society and Industry Leveraging a better tomorrow (RTSI)*, pp. 1–5, 2016.

[7] M. Toahchoodee, R. Abdunabi, I. Ray, and I. Ray, "A trust-based access control model for pervasive computing applications," in *IFIP Annual Conference on Data and Applications Security and Privacy*, pp. 307–314, Springer, 2009.

[8] P. K. Behera and P. M. Khilar, "A novel trust based access control model for cloud environment," in *Proceedings of the international conference on signal, networks, computing, and systems*, pp. 285–295, Springer, 2017.

[9] A. Singh and K. Chatterjee, "A mutual trust based access control framework for securing electronic healthcare system," in *2017 14th IEEE India Council International Conference (INDICON)*, pp. 1–6, IEEE, 2017.

[10] "Ficoscore https://www.fico.com/ (visited on 11/02/2021)."

[11] A. Jøsang, "Trust and reputation systems," in *Foundations of security analysis and design IV*, pp. 209–245, Springer, 2007.

[12] G. Zacharia and P. Maes, "Trust management through reputation mechanisms," *Applied Artificial Intelligence*, vol. 14, no. 9, pp. 881–907, 2000.

[13] G. Hogan, S. Dolins, I. Senturk, I. Fyrogenis, Q. Fu, E. Murati, F. Costantini, and N. Thomopoulos, "Can a blockchain-based maas create business value?," vol. 28, p. 1, 10 2019.

[14] H. Guo, W. Li, M. Nejad, and C.-C. Shen, "Access control for electronic health records with hybrid blockchain-edge architecture," in *2019 IEEE International Conference on Blockchain (Blockchain)*, pp. 44–51, IEEE, 2019.

[15] N. Ammar, Z. Malik, E. Bertino, and A. Rezgui, "Xacml policy evaluation with dynamic context handling," *IEEE Transactions on Knowledge and Data Engineering*, vol. 27, no. 9, pp. 2575–2588, 2015.

[16] R. S. Sandhu, E. J. Coyne, H. L. Feinstein, and C. E. Youman, "Role-based access control models," *Computer*, vol. 29, no. 2, pp. 38–47, 1996.

[17] E. Coyne and T. R. Weil, "Abac and rbac: scalable, flexible, and auditable access management," *IT professional*, vol. 15, no. 03, pp. 14–16, 2013.

[18] E. Yuan and J. Tong, "Attributed based access control (abac) for web services," in *IEEE International Conference on Web Services (ICWS'05)*, IEEE, 2005.

[19] R. S. Sandhu, "Attribute-based access control models and beyond.," in *AsiaCCS*, p. 677, 2015.

[20] S. Quirolgico, V. Hu, T. Karygiannis, *et al.*, *Access Control for SAR Systems*. US Department of Commerce, National Institute of Standards and Technology, 2011.

[21] "Xacml https://en.wikipedia.org/wiki/XACML (visited on 08/02/2021)."

[22] Y. Keleta, J. Eloff, and H. Venter, "Proposing a secure xacml architecture ensuring privacy and trust," *Research in Progress Paper, University of Pretoria*, 2005.

[23] C. D. P. K. Ramli, H. R. Nielson, and F. Nielson, "The logic of xacml," *Science of Computer Programming*, vol. 83, pp. 80–105, 2014.

[24] "Wso2 identity server https://github.com/wso2/product-is (visited on 06/04/2021)."

[25] "Wso2 policy administration apis https://is.docs.wso2.com/en/latest/develop/entitlement-with-apis/ (visited on 06/04/2021)."

[26] "Apache tomcat server https://tomcat.apache.org/ (visited on 12/09/2020)."

[27] "Grafana https://grafana.com/ (visited on 07/08/2021)."

Secure and Flexible Establishment of Temporary WLAN Access

Steffen Fries, Rainer Falk
Corporate Technology
Siemens AG
Munich, Germany
e-mail: {steffen.fries|rainer.falk}@siemens.com

***Abstract*—Several use cases demand for the setup of a separate, dedicated communication channel that provides a specific quality of service, or to separate communications of different criticality. Different properties of communication channels are performance, latency, but may be also security related. In several cases, a reliable association to an already established communication channel is required. Specifically, if a first communication channel has been securely established, a cryptographic binding of a second communication channel to this first communication channel is needed. One example use case is the charging of electric vehicles. Besides the charging control, also value-added services like software updates for the infotainment system shall be provided. To avoid interfering with the charging-related control communications, a second, separate communication channel is established. The two communication channels require different quality of service. However, authorization to access value-added services and maybe also the billing of consumed value-added services shall be to bound to the user that has been authenticated in the setup of the first communication channel. The paper proposes a general solution that allows establishing arbitrary communication channels of different nature on the example of an electric vehicle and a charging station, all bound to the actual charging control session.**

Keywords–communication security; cryptographic channel binding; quality of service; industrial automation and control system; Internet of Things.

I. INTRODUCTION

In network communications, it is typically required to have distinct relations between communicating endpoints, which are defined by several parameters, like the addresses of the communicating endpoints, security credentials connected with the endpoints, but also by certain quality-of-service related features. Quality-of-service (QoS) features may relate to a specific throughput expected by the communication channel or a specific response time or latency of the communication, but also to specific security properties of the communication like integrity protection or combined integrity and confidentiality protection. These properties may be provided by the utilized transport protocol or application protocol, but may already be enforced by the network access. Network access may be achieved as wired access using a classic cable installation, but also using wireless access via wireless LAN (WLAN), 4G, or 5G mobile communications.

Specific QoS features are required for a variety of applications. Examples comprise electric vehicle charging, real-time control of, e.g., industrial control, voice-and-video conferences, or video streaming. Also, specific security applications may leverage a separate communication channel like the provisioning of credentials using a link with weak protection or general access authentication. If the setup of a communication channel with certain QoS features is based on a previously established communication relation, a binding of the two communication sessions can be leveraged in multiple ways.

The aim of this paper is to propose a solution for setting up a new wireless communication channel that utilizes a previously established communication channel. The initial target use case was provided by electric vehicle charging systems that, in addition to the actual charging, provide value-added services. These value-added services may relate to updates of the firmware, software, or map material for the infotainment system of an electric vehicle.

This paper is structured in the following way. Section II provides an overview about a potential target scenario, taking electric vehicle charging as example. Section III investigates existing approaches to provide distinct communication channels with distinct properties. Section IV describes a new approach, and section V analyzes its advantages. Section VI concludes the paper and provides and outlook to future work.

II. ELECTRIC VEHICLE CHARGING WITH VALUE ADDED SERVICES

The number of electric vehicles as bicycles, motorcycles, and cars has increased in the recent years significantly. They are connected to the Digital Smart Grid for charging. Developments are also ongoing for bidirectional charging, which allows to utilize electric vehicles as energy storage system and to feedback energy to the power grid when necessary. Depending on the charging interface between the electric vehicle and the infrastructure, the charging may be accomplished within minutes, or it may need up to several hours. While connected to a charging station, the vehicle exchanges constantly control data with the charging station to provide data like locally measured energy consumption on the vehicle side or charging commands with parameter adaptations from the charging station. This connection time may also be used to provide value-added services by utilizing the connection already established between the electric vehicle and the charging station.

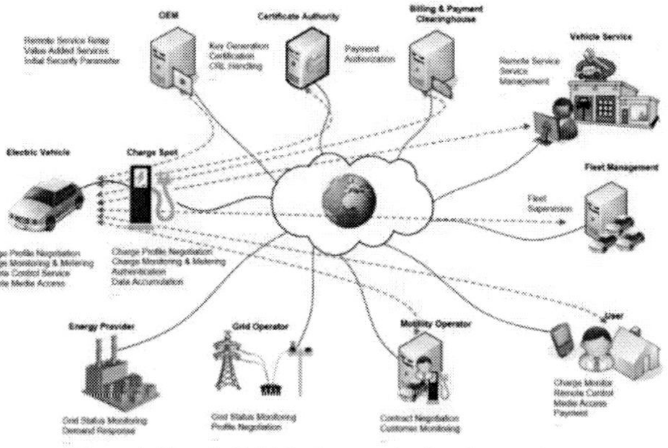

Figure 1. Electric Vehicle Communication Connections

As depicted in Figure 1, there is a multitude of potential communication options with different actors of the system. The communication channel established between the electric vehicle and the charging station may be setup using different standards like ISO/IEC 15118 [1] or CHaDemo [2]. The focus in this paper is placed on ISO/IEC 15118.

The communication may use power line communication when the vehicle is connected via a wired interface, or wireless using WLAN in case of inductive charging. In this case, the charging station provides a WLAN access point to facilitate the communication also in a wireless fashion. According to ISO/IEC 15118, access to the charging station is not protected on the WLAN access layer, but on higher communication layers. This avoids a specific WLAN access configuration of electrical vehicles for a specific charging station. The communication performed in the context of ISO/IEC 15118 allows to provide charging parameter information, billing relevant information, and also to perform mutual authentication of the electric vehicle and the charging station. The security of ISO/IEC 15118-2 has been studied from the early beginning of standardization (cf. for example [3]). Meanwhile, the standard has been completed, and a revision will be published soon as Edition 2.

The communication channel is part of the Digital Grid communication and the control network of an energy utility. Value-added service providers may utilize the communication channel as well, but are independent of the power system operator. The energy distribution network as critical infrastructure relies on the availability of the information infrastructure. Therefore, the information infrastructure must be managed and operated according to the same level of reliability as required for the stability of the power system infrastructure to prevent any type of outage or disturbance. The immediately apparent security needs target the prevention of financial fraud and ensure the reliable operation of the power grid. Especially the interaction between new market participants and value-added services has been investigated and is also addressed in ISO/IEC 15118.

Common to both editions of the standard ISO/IEC 15118 is the security approach and specifically the security setup between the electric vehicle and the charging infrastructure. It relies on the establishment of a secured communication channel based on Transport Layer Security (TLS, version 1.2 specified in IETF RFC 5246 [4], version 1.3 in IETF RFC 8446 [5]). It requires that the charging station authenticates towards the electric vehicle using an X.509 certificate during the TLS handshake. In turn, if the electric vehicle uses plug-and-charge, or if it wants to consume value-added services, it authenticates with an own X.509 certificate that is bound to the charging contract that the vehicle owner has established with his mobility operator. This allows for a seamless charging experience for the vehicle owner, and to access value-added services after connecting to the charging station.

The value-added service communication is performed separately from the control and measurement communication channel. This is to avoid any interference with the charging related control communication. ISO/IEC 15118 facilitates this by establishing a separate communication channel that is bound to the initial authentication of both peers and outlined in section III.C below.

The following section investigates different options of providing an authenticated channel that is bound to a mutual authentication between the electric vehicle and the charging station.

III. EXISTING APPROACHES

There exist different approaches for setting up a communication channel bound to another communication channel, which has certain cryptographic properties like the authentication of a single peer or of both peers. This section investigates known approaches.

A. *Socket Secure – SOCKS*

SOCKS [6] is an internet protocol that allows applications (client or server) to connect through proxies in an application layer independent way. This is done by using a SOCKS proxy that creates a TCP connection to the target server on behalf of the client. As SOCKS operates on layer 5, it can handle different application protocols like HTTP, SMTP, or FTP. It allows a client to open a connection from behind a firewall to an external server in an authenticated and authorized way. SOCKS5 allows for different authentication methods, in which the client authenticates towards the SOCKS server. It may also be used in conjunction with TLS. After authentication and authorization check by the SOCKS server, the application protocol is tunneled over the established connection and forwarded to the external target server.

The authentication is done between the requesting client and the SOCKS server, and the tunneling of the application protocol binds to this authentication. However, the server is not aware of this authentication and needs to authenticate the client by other means. As the tunnel is provided on an application base, multiple tunnels for different applications are necessary, all with an own, independent security setup.

B. Virtual LAN – VLAN

VLAN or virtual local area networks are defined in IEEE 802.1Q [7]. The standard defines a logical network and allows the separation of different communication channels on layer 2. Different properties may be assigned in addition to this virtual LAN like performance or throughput. To achieve this, infrastructure components like managed switches are used, supporting the differentiation of traffic according to VLANs. A peer sending information in this VLAN (unicast or multicast) will only reach other peers that are part of the same VLAN.

Two basic approaches exist for VLANs. The first approach is a port-based VLAN in which the association to a logical LAN is done by attaching the client to a dedicated physical port of a managed switch. The second approach is a tagged VLAN, in which the Ethernet frames are tagged with a specific VLAN identifier (VLAN ID). Based on this VLAN tag, a switch can forward the Ethernet frame according to its configuration.

With this, VLANs themselves provide a way to separate traffic, which is also a step towards improved security. The definition of this separation is not done on cryptographic means, as stated before. Therefore, it is recommended to provide additional protection of the communication. Examples are IEEE 802.1X [8], providing port-based access control. With this, a client authenticates to the infrastructure (typically a RADIUS or DIAMETER server) via the infrastructure access network switch using different means, e.g., based on the Extensible Authentication Protocol (EAP) [9]. EAP allows for authentication with username and password, but also for a certificate-based authentication employing a client's X.509 certificate. In addition, MAC security (MACSec), specified in IEEE 802.1AE [8], can be used to provide integrity and/or confidentiality protection for the traffic between the device and the network switch in a hop-by-hop fashion.

Security for VLAN can be provided using additional security means like IEEE 802.1X as outlined. If associated to a dedicated VLAN, quality of service parameter may be assigned.

C. Transport Layer Security Features

Transport Layer Security (TLS) is a protocol defined in IETF RFC 5246 as version 1.2 [4]. Meanwhile, it evolved to version 1.3 in IETF RFC 8446 [5]. While version 1.3 is being increasingly adopted [14], version 1.2 is still widely used. TLS is probably the most commonly used security protocol to protect TCP-based communications. Prominent applications are protection of web-based communication over http. Also, other TCP-based protocols leverage the bump in the wire properties of TLS, like ISO/IEC 15118. ISO/IEC 15118-20 mandates the support of TLS v1.3, while TLSv1.2 may still be used.

TLSv1.3 features a re-designed handshake, which is not backward compatible to TLSv1.2. The version handling in TLS allows to fall back to TLSv1.2, if TLSv1.3 is not supported yet. The handshake is encrypted, except for the very first message, to better protect the privacy of client certificate information that is thereby already send encrypted. Moreover, the handshake may already transmit application data, which can accelerate the communication setup. This feature is called 0-RTT (zero round-trip time), but the use requires careful review.

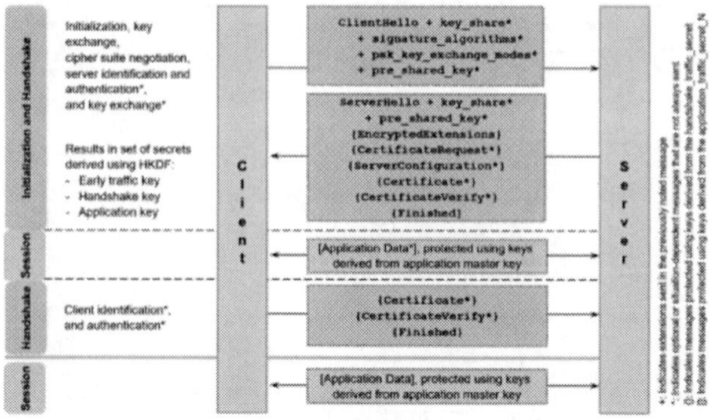

Figure 2. TLS v1.3 Session Establishment with full handshake

The full handshake of TLSv1.3 is depicted in Figure 2. TLS supports different authentication options:

- server-side authentication (mainly used in web traffic) using X.509 certificates;
- mutual authentication involves the client to authenticate using an X.509 certificate in addition to server authentication;
- authentication based on a pre-shared key, which is applied also within TLS as described below;
- authentication based on raw public keys.

Besides the peer authentication, the TLS handshake is used to negotiate further session parameters like the cipher suite for protecting communication integrity and confidentiality.

TLS with mutual authentication is applied in ISO/IEC 15118-20 for plug-and-charge and for access to value-added services. This ensures that billing-relevant charging and service consumption can be associated with a dedicated account.

Besides the establishment of a protected channel, TLS defines further operations for the management of this secured channel, beyond them the update of session parameters during an ongoing session, like the utilized cryptographic key. One important functionality is the so-called session resumption. Session resumption allows a previously established and closed session to be resumed, based on the security parameters negotiated in the initial session. This saves the asymmetric cryptographic operations during the TLS handshake, and it utilizes a pre-shared key included in a ticket from the initial handshake. Note that there is a timely limitation how long a closed session may be resumed, depending on the TLS version. While TLSv1.2 recommends 24 hours, TLSv1.3 limits the validity time in the tickets used for resumption to seven days.

Besides the re-establishment of a closed connection, TLS session resumption may also be used to "clone" an existing session. This can be achieved by opening a TLS connection to a different port on the target host than the original one used and referencing the existing session. Using this, a separate TLS-protected TCP communication channel is established.

As the second communication channel relies on the security parameters of the first one and thus is cryptographically bound to it, it also provides the assurance of mutual authentication to both participants.

ISO/IEC 15118 utilizes this feature to allow the establishment of value-added service communication channels. Note that these are currently restricted to TCP-based communications. There also exists a TLS-like protocol with Datagram Transport Layer Security protocol (DTLS, IETF RFC 9147, [11]) that provides a similar functionality as TLS, but for UDP-based communications. It could be used to protect, e.g., media traffic, which is often transmitted via UDP. Note that interactions between both (TLS and DTLS) are not considered in ISO/IEC 15118, as the protection of the actual value-added service data is left to the value-added service itself.

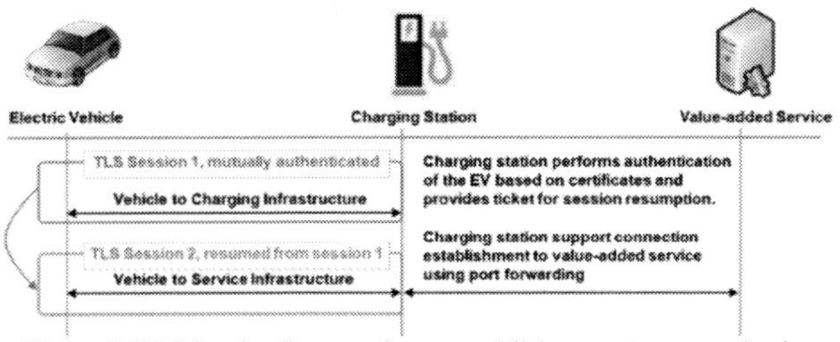

Figure 3. TLS Session Resumption to establish second communication channel

As shown in Figure 3, a second session is opened between the electric vehicle and the charging station using TLS session resumption. This saves communication overhead and provides a binding to the TLS channel protecting the ongoing charging session. Note that while TLSv1.3 has specific optimizations like sending application data already in the resumed handshake (called 0-RTT), this feature is not allowed in ISO/IEC 15118 to avoid replay attacks of application data.

Port forwarding is used at the charging station to forward the traffic to the intended value-added service provider. The security of the communication channel to the value-added service provider is out of scope of ISO/IEC 15118 and needs to be defined and setup by the value-added service separately. For protecting UDP-based traffic between the electric vehicle and the charging station, OpenVPN is mentioned.

D. TLS Channel Binding

IETF RFC 5929 [12] describes a binding of a higher layer communication protocol to a negotiated TLS channel. Different approaches are specified. The most versatile is the definition of the *tls-unique* value. The *tls-unique* value is essentially the first "Finish Message" sent in the latest TLS handshake. The finish message contains a hash over all messages exchanged in the handshake phase.

This definition makes this parameter specific to a session. When a session is resumed or renegotiated (only for TLS 1.2), the *tls-unique* value will change accordingly. This has to be obeyed by the applying application. Using *tls-unique* in an application provides a direct linkage to the properties of the TLS handshake.

An example is the application in the context of Enrollment over Secure Transport (EST, IETF RFC 7030, [13]), a certificate enrollment protocol executed over TLS. In this protocol, the client sends a certification request to enroll a new client certificate. The certification request is signed with the private key of the freshly generated key pair. This provides a proof-of-possession to the receiver, that the sender, i.e., the client, knows the private key corresponding to the contained public key. Part of the certification request can be a *tls-unique* value. As the TLS handshake is performed with mutual authentication, the receiver gets in addition a proof-of-identity of the client, due to the link to the utilized client certificate in the TLS handshake. This is enabled through the inclusion of the *tls-unique* value.

IV. Solution Proposal

As discussed in section I, the aim is to propose a solution for setting up an additional wireless communication channel that utilizes a previously established communication channel. The existing solutions discussed in section III provide elements that are used in the approach.

The following description takes the electric vehicle charging as example as in section II and provides an alternative solution. This described solution specifically allows for multiple connections between a value-added service provider and an electric vehicle, which are all bound to an existing charging session. These multiple channels may be of different nature like TCP/IP or UDP/IP traffic.

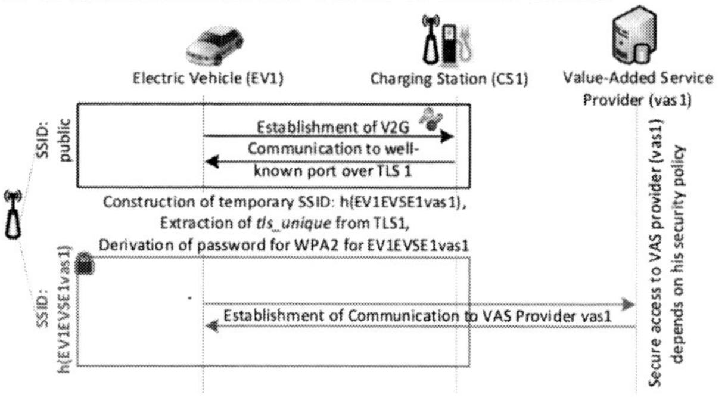

Figure 4. Application of *tls-unique* to protect second WLAN

Figure 4 provides an overview of the solution. According to ISO/IEC 15118-20, a TLS connection is established between the electric vehicle *EV1* and the charging station *CS1* via a well-known service-set identifier (SSID) of the charging station. The well-known SSID may be either preconfigured, or it may be broadcasted using Bluetooth beacons in the vicinity of the charging station. The connection is established based on the authentication of CS1 as server towards EV1. The EV1 authentication can be carried out over the already TLS protected link to protect the identity information of EV1. The client-side authentication may be done based on an X.509 certificate but also using other methods on application layer like HTTP digest authentication or based on a token. Specific for the electric vehicle charging, the owner of the EV may also authenticate directly towards the charging station, avoiding any information to be transmitted over the communication link. In each case, a binding to the originally established TLS connection is required.

To achieve this, the *tls-unique* value is extracted, which is intended as means to provide the binding to the originally established TLS channel for further connections to be opened. This extraction equals to the TLS channel binding described in section III.D.

Over the established TLS channel, an information is provided to the electric vehicle regarding available value-added services via the charging station, which can be consumed during the charging period. These value-added services may be software updates for the infotainment system, normal web access, gaming, or videos to bridge the charging time.

While in section II the additional communication channel for value-added services is opened using TLS session resumption on a different port than the one for the charging communication, the following describes an alternative, which can be used for different types of data exchange.

When the EV selects a value-added service, it will receive the additional configuration information for setting up a second, temporary WLAN access to the charging station for the electric vehicle. The configuration information shall be specific to the charging session between EV1 and CS1 and a specific value-added service provider vas1. This allows for correct billing of consumed services, based on the association.

For setting up a temporary access point, a second network access policy needs to be provided, which may comprise information regarding protection means or quality of service parameter. In case of WLAN, a temporary network name (SSID) and a pre-shared key for access protection to the temporary WLAN are also required to utilize WPA2 and WPA3 for access protection to the temporary WLAN.

Instead of providing this information directly. it can be derived locally on the communication peers based on the already existing charging control communication session as following:

Temporary SSID = Hash (EV ID | CS ID | VAS ID)

In the example in Figure 4, this will result in the hashed value of *"EV1CS1vas1"*. Depending on the utilized hash function the result can be truncated to, e.g., 20 Bytes. With the goal to bind the temporary WLAN to the already existing charging session, the temporary WLAN access credentials in terms of a shared secret are derived incorporating the *tls-unique* value of the initial TLS session as following:

Temp. SSID PW = Hash (tls-unique | EV ID | VAS ID)

The derivation may consist of further parameter besides the EV identifier and the VAS identifier. Depending on the security policy of the charging station operator, the temporary WLAN access for the value-added services may be terminated as soon as the charging session ends. There may be cases for leaving the session open for a grace period, e.g., for ending a specific transaction. This option may also be part of the contract a customer has with a specific charging station operator.

As described, the approach can be generalized to provide the binding also to other network access methods like 4G or 5G. It may also be leveraged to setup further VLANs for separate communication, utilizing derived parameter for VLAN name and access credentials.

V. Evaluation

The evaluation of the proposed solution is done based on the concept only, as it has not been implemented, yet. In general, the security of an industrial system is evaluated in practice in various approaches and stages of the system's lifecycle:

- A Threat and Risk Analysis (TRA, also abbreviated as TARA) is typically conducted at the beginning of the concept definition, as for ISO/IEC 15118, product design or system development, and updated after major design changes, or to address a changed threat landscape. In a TRA, possible attacks (threats) on the system are identified. The impact that would be caused by a successful attack and the probability that the attack happens are evaluated to determine the risk of the identified threats. The risk evaluation allows to prioritize the threats, focusing on the most relevant risks and to define corresponding security measures. Security measures can target to reduce the probability of an attack by preventing it, or by reducing the impact.
- Security checks can be performed during operation or during maintenance windows to determine key performance indicators (e.g., check compliance of device configurations) and to verified that the defined security measures are in fact in place.
- Security testing (penetration testing, also called pentesting for short) can be performed for a system that has been built, but that is currently not in operation. A pentest can usually not be performed on an operational automation and control system, as the pentest could affect the reliable operation auf the system. Pentesting can be performed during a maintenance window when the physical system is in a safe state or using a separate test system.

As long as the solution proposed in the paper has not been proven in a real-world operational setting, it can be evaluated conceptually by analyzing the impact that the additional security measure would have on the identified residual risks as determined by a TRA. The main objective is to determine the specific benefits that are relevant for the selection of a suitable protection approach. The main aspects relevant for the evaluation of the proposed solution are:

a. The level of isolation of different types of communications (charging control communication; value added services communication);
b. the scope of protection, i.e., what exactly is protected concerning integrity and or confidentiality, and
c. the flexibility to use it for various protocols used by different value-added services.

These aspects can be evaluated qualitatively as follows:

a. The control communication for charging control and the communication of value-added services are taking place on separate layer 1 / layer 2 communication links. While a reliable traffic isolation can be implemented also on a logical level, the isolation realized by having separate layer 1 / layer 2 communication links ensures by design a strong isolation, avoiding logical interference between these different types of communications. Moreover, this separation offers the option to not only provide different protection options for the communication links, but also to assign different quality of services classes to ensure for instance a dedicated throughput or latency.

b. The proposed solution protects all communications, including, e.g., dynamic host configuration by DHCP or IPv6 auto configuration, or DNS requests. Thereby, also user privacy protection is increased, as meta-data of communication as, e.g., network addresses, cannot be intercepted as all communication is protected on layer 2. Also, active manipulations by 3rd parties, e.g., injected false DNS responses, can be avoided.

c. The solution can be used with any types of communication, including UDP datagram communication. So, it can be flexibly applied also for value-added services using UDP-based communications (e.g., multi-media communications based on RTP).

VI. Conclusion

This paper provides a new generic approach for setting up a separate temporary network access channel allowing to assign specific quality of service parameter to the new network access, which is cryptographically bound to an already established communication channel. The approach is discussed in the context of electric vehicle charging combined with value-added services.

The advantage of the proposed approach is the ability to be applied in an application layer protocol independent way by preserving the privacy of user credentials for observers of the network. This is especially important for wireless communication as the exchanged communication can be easily accessed.

The proposed approach is available as concept and needs to be implemented a proof of concept, which would be a future intended step. Such a proof of concept can leverage already specified base mechanisms like *tls-unique* extraction.

References

[1] ISO/IEC 15118-20: Road vehicles — Vehicle-to-Grid Communication Interface — Part 20: Network and application protocol requirements, Work in Progress

[2] CHAdeMO, https://www.chademo.com/, [retrieved: July, 2022]

[3] R. Falk and S. Fries, "Electric Vehicle Charging Infrastructure – Security Considerations and Approaches", Internet 2012, June 2012, ISBN: 978-1-61208-204-2, pp.58-64

[4] T. Dierks and E. Rescorla, IETF RFC 5246, "Transport Layer Security (TLS) Protocol v1.2, 08/2008, https://tools.ietf.org/html/rfc5246, [retrieved: July, 2022]

[5] E. Rescorla, IETF RFC 8446, "Transport Layer Security (TLS) Protocol v1.3", 08/2018, https://tools.ietf.org/html/rfc8446, [retrieved: July, 2022]

[6] M. Leech et al., IETF RFC 1928, „SOCKS Protocol Version 5, 03/1996, https://tools.ietf.org/html/rfc1928, [retrieved: July, 2022]

[7] IEEE 802.1Q, "IEEE Standard for Local and Metropolitan Area Networks – Bridges and Bridged Networks", 2018, https://standards.ieee.org/ieee/802.1Q/6844/, [retrieved: July, 2022]

[8] IEEE 802.1X, "IEEE Standard for Local and Metropolitan Area Networks – Port-Based Access Control", 2020, https://ieeexplore.ieee.org/document/9018454, [retrieved: July, 2022]

[9] B. Aboba, L. Blunk, J. Vollbrecht, J. Carlson, and H.Levkowetz., IETF RFC 3748, "Extensible Authentication protocol (EAP)", 06/2004, https://tools.ietf.org/html/rfc3748, [retrieved: July, 2022]

[10] IEEE 802.1AE "IEEE Standard for Local and Metropolitan Area Networks – Media Access Control (MAC) Security", 2018, https://ieeexplore.ieee.org/document/8585421, [retrieved: July, 2022]

[11] E. Rescorla, H. Tschofenig, and N. Modadugu, IETF RFC 9147, "The Datagram Transport Layer Security (DTLS) Protocol Version 1.3", April 2022 https://datatracker.ietf.org/doc/html/rfc9147, [retrieved: July, 2022]

[12] J. Altman and N. Williams, IETF RFC 5929, TLS channel binding, July 2010, https://tools.ietf.org/html/rfc5929, [retrieved: July, 2022]

[13] M. Pritikin, P. Yee, and D. Harkins, IETF RFC 7030, "Enrollment over Secure Transport ", 10/2013, https://tools.ietf.org/html/rfc7030, [retrieved: July, 2022]

[14] SSL Puls: TLS Dashboard, continuously updated, https://www.ssllabs.com/ssl-pulse/, [retrieved: July, 2022]

Longitudinal Study of Persistence Vectors (PVs) in Windows Malware: Evolution, Complexity, and Stealthiness

Nicholas Phillips
Department of Computer and Information Sciences
Towson University
nphill5@students.towson.edu

Aisha Ali-Gombe
Division of Computer Science and Engineering
Louisiana State University
aaligombe@lsu.edu

***Abstract*—Malware is the driving force for most cyber-attacks and, in recent years, has continued to be one of the most challenging threats facing our cyber infrastructure. Modern malware's adaptive design often leverages complex and evolving technologies to overcome various detection and preventive security tools. One of these techniques is Persistence - an ability to survive on victim systems past the current power cycle. The persistence vector allows the malware to live on host machines without detection. Thus, this paper conducts a longitudinal study and characterization of Windows malware Persistence Vectors (PVs) across more than 1000 malware samples. We explored the evolution, complexity, and stealthiness of persistence vectors in modern Windows malware families using the combination of static and dynamic analysis. The result of our study indicated that security tools and analysts could utilize PVs as decoys to strengthen malware defensive strategies.**

Keywords: Malware, Persistence Vectors, System Security, Reverse Engineering

I. INTRODUCTION

Malware is an ever-evolving threat against cyber infrastructure. With nearly one billion malware attacks in 2021, and predictions show that, with the rise in remote work, this number is forecasted to increase a minimum of ten percent over the next year, making the ever-growing threat more daunting [7]. Current defensive measures are predominately positioned at the perimeter of networks and scanning the system attempting to stop potential malware infections [1]. However, they have an extensive blind spot in dealing with malware once it obtains a foothold on the system. New generation malware, especially the Rootkit class, leverages variable stealth and mutation strategies to persist after infection. With these advantages, coupled with vulnerabilities present on the system and those introduced via users, security is constantly on the back foot in the endless cycle of attack and defense. Therefore, the practice of identifying, extracting, and utilizing the persistence mechanisms in defensive measures is one massive step towards leveling the field.

The rest of the paper is organized as follows: Section 2 presents the problem statement; Section 3 provides an analysis of the current research into malware; Sections 4 presents a delve into the background of persistence vectors in malware; Section 5 and 6 presents our data collection and analysis of persistence vectors, respectively; and Section 7 presents future works and concludes the paper.

II. PROBLEM STATEMENT

As security works to develop methodologies to stop malicious threats from obtaining access, malware authors deploy new methods, such as those presented via zero days [4] [5] [6] [13] . In 2021, record numbers of zero days utilized, 64 confirmed, and untold number unconfirmed [31]. This cycle resets with malicious actors constantly holding the edge by only needing one compromise to be victorious. Even major advancements, such as Secure Boot have proven insufficient and susceptible to compromise. Theoretical and wild bootkits have generated means around this improvement, such as forged certificates or enabling their loading prior to the safe image Security Boot loads [16]. Attention primarily focused on the exterior surface with attempts to stop malware from infecting the system. Only a small amount of focus has been paid to internal areas where the attacks land. Persistence vectors, while not deeply diverse as developed attack vectors, have undergone a constant evolution, and remained unanalyzed. Thus, we present a longitudinal analysis on the evolution of Windows malware persistence vectors providing new insight into their complexity and stealthiness. The objective of our study is to provide a new direction for malware defensive capabilities leveraging persistence vectors rather than the traditional payload and infection vector scanning.

III. RELATED WORK

Literature dealing with malware persistence is limited in content, which is presented below. Gittins and Soltys conducted one of the few pieces of research into malware persistence mechanisms. They analyzed the more common currently used malware persistence elements, and some are believed to be utilized by Nation State actors through a showing of independent samples for each of the presented persistence mechanisms [2]. While the illustrated persistence vectors are accurate, the sample base shown is only five samples deep, leaving it only as an overview, not in-depth. Rana et al. presented research into persistence mechanisms in conjunction with obfuscation techniques. Based on the solar wind attack, they cover various persistence utilized on Windows systems, with proposed solutions to attempt to minimize the effects of persistence vectors identified [3]. While the persistence vectors covered are extensive and the suggested solutions can help mitigate malware persistence, there is a shortcoming in that malware continues to evolve and tend to avoid detection using different obfuscation techniques. Khushali presented research into the subsection of malware titled fileless malware. This malware often does not write to the persistent storage, making them harder to detect [29]. Although very stealthy, fileless malware remain present on a victim system until the next power cycle. While these types of malware are useful for small campaigns, persistence is still vital for more prolonged operations generally utilized by nation-state actors and more extensive malware campaigns. Kohout and Pevný used persistence implanted web traffic as means of identifying long-placed malware [30]. While this does provide an effective means of identifying infected systems, it is limited to targeting the web traffic and not dealing with the various other persistence mechanisms. Our study presents a deeper analysis, utilizing a more comprehensive sample base than previously used and including means of relating persistence to stealth measures as well.

The remaining literature referencing persistence is focused on two main categories of research: (1) Research into malware's functionality, such as anti-analysis techniques, API modifications, or evasion techniques, and (2) Deeper analysis into a specific malware family/sample. Maffia [24], Mills [23], and Galloro [22] researched into the evolution of malware evasion techniques over the years. Mills developed a sandbox modification tool titled MORRIGU, which is utilized to subvert the malware evasion techniques, specifically those that prevent malware from executing in an analysis environment [23]. Analysis tools such as this, and some of its predecessors such as HookMe, Cuckoo Sandbox, and PyREBox, are excellent at dealing with defensive measures that malware deploys to prevent its analysis [25]. However, they are designed with extensive implementation and configuration changes, making them difficult to configure. These analysis environments are also designed to detect malware behavior mostly from a payload standpoint. However, they quickly become obsolete because modern malware evolves and employs sophisticated obfuscation techniques. Galloro et al. study the history and development of various evasion techniques. By completing the analysis comparison, they produced listings of evasion techniques only utilized via malware [22]. Maffia also conducted research along similar lines. The authors proposed PEPPER - a Pintool designed to defeat standard malware evasion techniques, such as Anti-VM [24]. Both provide excellent detailing of evasion techniques; however, as with the analysis environments, they detect from the payload standpoint. These analysis tools may provide false negatives if the evasion techniques have changed.

IV. Background on Persistence Vectors

Persistence vectors are sections of code built within software packages (both legitimate and malicious) that allow programs to survive system restart, switching between users, and similar system start-up functionality. In general, persistence is achieved by modifying certain sections of the system or kernel data structure. This section will enumerate and discuss the most commonly used persistence vectors. The complete listing of known Windows persistence vectors can be found in the MITRE ATT&CK framework® [15].

A. Common Persistence Vectors

1) Registry modification : Registry modifications are the most common persistence mechanisms utilized by malicious code [28]. By adding a value to a specific registry key, malicious code can ensure either it is loaded upon start, it is utilized before legitimate files, or it is reinstalled after being deleted. An example of this is the entry of a modification in the *run* key. These values can be set under *HKCU\SOFTWARE\Microsoft\Windows\CurrentVersion* or *HKLM\SOFTWARE\Microsoft\Windows\CurrentVersion* for the following keys:

- *HKCU\....\Run*
- *HKCU\....\RunOnce*
- *HKLM\....\CurrentVersion \Run*
- *HKLM\....\RunOnce*
- *HKLM\.... \PoliciesExplorer\Run*

2) DLL Replacement/Reorder : The next common persistence method is Dynamic Link Library (DLL) Hijacking. This vector works with modification or complete replacement of vulnerable DLLs with malicious code. When the modified DLL is called the malicious code is loaded and executed. A secondary method utilizing DLLs is through the DLL search order hijacking, where the original DLL remains intact but is dropped in priority for the malicious version placed on the system.

3) Startup Keys : Start-up key and service modification vectors utilize a combination of the above two techniques by setting the malicious code into a priority slot in boot order. Once loaded the malicious code is restarted on the system, maintaining the infection.

Files under the startup directory can have a shortcut created to the location pointed by subkey of startup. If this value is present then the service will launch during a system reboot. These values can be set under *HKCU\SOFTWARE\Microsoft\Windows\CurrentVersion* or *HKLM\SOFTWARE\Microsoft\Windows\CurrentVersion* for the following keys:

- *HKCU\....\Explorer\ShellFolders*
- *HKCU\....\Explorer\User\ShellFolders*
- *HKLM\....\Explorer\ShellFolders*
- *HKLM\....\Explorer\User\ShellFolders*

B. Services

Several Windows services are required to be started at boot for the system to run properly. By placing any malware keys in this startup folder it is able to execute at startup as other services. Additionally, because alternative services can be started if another fails to load, a malware author can append these failed states to launch the malware.

1) Boot Modifications : Bootkits and other malware have begun utilizing a type of alteration called boot key modifications. In persistence technique, the smss.exe launches before the Windows subsystem, calling the configuration subsystem to load the hive present at *HKLM\SYSTEM \CurrentControlSet\Controlhivelist*. Any value that contains the *BootExecute* key will be launched at system boot by the smss.exe via the *HKLM\ControlSet002\ControlSession Manager* [27]. A normal system should only have the value of autocheck or autochk*.

2) Shortcut Creation/Modification : Shortcut hijacking obtains persistence via rewriting of saved icons of applications that users commonly use. This is created through either replacing the direct calling program with a compromised version or a wholly malicious one.

3) Event Trigger Execution : One of the oldest forms of persistence is the event-triggered execution technique. This method achieves persistence on a system via the setting of time-trigger automation, such as CHRON to launch upon the system restart or through program infection when another program is launched, a redirect to the malware code is present, restarting it.

4) Kernel Module Changes : Although much more challenging to implement, malware can leverage changes in the kernel module to achieve persistence. In this technique, the malware hides its presence by loading modules from the default order to include the malware as a high-value loaded item, either as a change to the BIOS load order or through appending BOOTSTRAP code. While this is often not as pervasive as the other techniques discussed due to the possibility of a system crash, it is nonetheless one of the most effective persistence vectors.

V. Data Collection and Analysis

As stated in the introduction, this paper aims to systematize knowledge for Windows malware persistence vectors in a longitudinal study. We will analyze the persistence vector's characterization, complexity, and stealthiness. The overarching goal is to drive new knowledge in understanding the metamorphosis of persistence vectors that will help design new malware defensive strategies. Thus, for the data collection, we downloaded a total of one thousand malicious software from virus repositories VirusShare and VirusTotal [26]. All are samples from within the past ten years, yielding a solid base for the evolution of malware over time, and were selected to run the spectrum of malware families. Each sample was manually processed via static and dynamic malware analysis to extract APIs, data, and metadata. Then the sample is passed to IDA Pro for the actual persistence vector extraction. Finally, a detailed code reconstitution is performed.

1) Environment Setup: The PV extraction process is carried out on Windows 7 and 10 Virtual Machines (VMs), with two copies of each: one for dynamic analysis and one for static analysis. Each machine has two 2.4 GHz cores and 4 GB RAM. Additional steps were taken using Hidetoolz to minimize the effect of Anti-VM and Anti-Reversing during the analysis [10]. Configuration settings were then modified through the utilization of the Vbox info modifier capability. This allowed for the default options, such as the system utilized and system manufacturer searched for via VM aware malware, to be changed. Additional VM capabilities, such as the Addons, were removed and the sub-keys in the registry deleted. Commonly installed user software were added, attempting to give the appearance of a real system instead of a virtual one.

2) Static Analysis: Static analysis is defined by collecting information about the binary, precisely a malware sample in this case, without executing or creating a runtime memory space [12]. Before analysis, the first step is to collect a file hash in the form of MD5 and/or SHA256. This step ensures that the file downloaded matches the one presented by the collection sites of VirusTotal and Malshare. We utilized the Powershell command - *get-filehash* to accomplish the hashing process. Next, for each target malware, we ran it against an unpacker to remove any possible common packers and cryptors, leaving behind the bare-bones malware code that the analysis tools would evaluate. For this we utilized PEId to identify and remove the common packers and compression utilized by the malware samples. In the static analysis of the Rovnix bootkit for instance, we found the hash to be 7CFC801458D64EF92E210A41B97993B0, and PEID identified that two packers were used in the initial sample.

Immediately after unpacking, a target sample is then executed against the *Strings* utility. This utility allows for ASCII and Unicode string identification. In this task, we are looking for specific Windows API calls which can be tied back to the potential persistence modifications and additional files created, which could contain remaining malicious payloads. The sample is also loaded into Dependencies, a modern rewriting of Dependency Walker, which identifies utilized DLLs for the executable. This tool also determines the potential persistence vectors utilized via DLL replacements, and those utilizing the creation of files. In the Rovnix bootkit sample, the strings showed indications of file creation, such as the *CREATE* and *FILEACCESS APIs*, while Dependencies showed access to kernel-level modules, kernel32.dl and ntdll.dll. These match the boot modifications, driver deployment, and registry changes, along with the items needed to generate the malicious Volume Boot Record (VBR).

3) Dynamic Analysis: Dynamic analysis is completed by collecting binary elements while executing the file on the system. Before launching an executable, we first run a suite of malware analysis tools: ProcWatch, CaptureBatch, and RegShot. These tools create baseline analysis to compare modifications made by the malware sample in processes, batch files, and registry. After removing standard system processes, we can notice the unique ones created by the malware and registry modifications, if any. These creations are the specific items we targeted as the persistence functions of the malware as they show the specific files, DLLs, and registry keys that the malware implants to obtain persistence.

For Rovnix, we identified the file creations for the modified VBR and malicious DLLs. Additionally we found the registry modifications generating the boot changes, consisting of the backup copies of the malware code and the independent ones used to restart these backups if other elements were removed.

4) Persistence Identification and Extraction: The persistence vectors of the sample base are identified from this two tiered reverse engineering process. From here the process of removing these code segments is conducted. The samples are loaded in IDA Pro Disassembler, with the information gathered from analysis used to target the specific functions completing the persistence modifications. These functions are exported utilizing the inbuilt exporting capability in the HexRays loaded with IDA. Data like this can then be exported as raw text or as set variables or segments of C code. These individual identified persistence vectors are saved with the naming convention of "persistence vector-file hash". Each PV was then saved into a folder named by file type to be utilized in the follow on code reconstitution.

Identified in the Rovnix sample were the following persistence mechanisms:

- Construction of malicious VBR in conjunction with compressed original one
- Injection of polymorphic bootstrap code;
- Generation of new malicious DLL, titled BKSetup.dll;
- Multiple registry changes across multiple hives;
- Implanting of unsigned driver at end of file system data;
- Hidden partition with backup copies of malware code at end of file system data;

Presented below in Figure 1 is the generation of the boot loader and registry modifications for persistence. In this sample, several persistence creations spawned from a singular source function with the individual modifications completed in their unique functions.

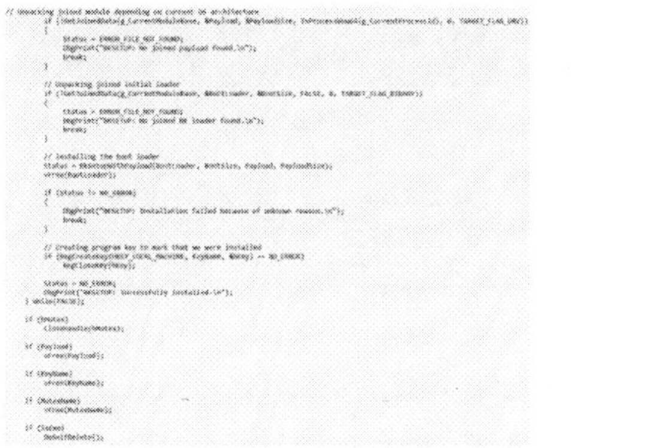

Fig. 1. Rovnix Registry Bootloader

A. Code Reconstitution

Code reconstitution has two phases: (1) Code identification and (2) Code matching and merging.

1) Code Identification and Conversion: Code identification and conversion involves turning this persistence mechanism from the assembly code found in the analysis into source code. The first means to resolve this is by deep searching for the sample's source code. Approximately twenty percent of the identified persistence mechanisms had source code available. These entries had their code segments that performed the system change for persistence removed, generally consisting of only one or two functions. The code was parred down, removing any repetitive PV value. These code segments were also used as base forms for samples lacking publicly available source code.

A complete comparison was performed against those extracted from the available source code samples, identifying code segments with the same structure. For example, samples within the same family often triggered fifty percent of searches. This allowed the values to be appended together instead of multiple individual entries. Those that do not have a matching structure are marked as new. New entries then have sections of code generated to house the persistence mechanism starting from one of three default templates. One specifically designed for registry changes, with an option presented for the main areas targeted, the second for changes to DLL ordering, and the last for the remainder of system changes.

2) Code Matching and Merging: Once each PV is generated into a code snippet, the elements were pushed into an element of code standardization. Each snippet was labeled via code comments on the type of sample it was extracted from, specifically labeled with sample name and hash. Samples with similar areas of persistence were grouped and sorted to ensure that each value was unique. Duplicates were removed. The process generated a series of white listings containing 800 unique persistence vectors.

VI. Evaluation

We analyzed the collected and reconstituted persistence vectors above and examine their evolution, complexity, and stealthiness. For evolution, we examined the vectors based on their familial characterization, (e.g., Rootkit, Trojan, Adware, etc). For complexity, we evaluated each sample's type and the number of persistence mechanisms. Finally, for stealthiness, we assessed their use of obfuscation, such as ease of detection, junk code insertion, and/or the use of encryption.

A. PV Familial Characterization

The largest among the families of the samples was bootkits/rootkits, with just under twenty-five percent of the total samples. The second largest typing was ransomware, with twenty-one percent. Adware was the next largest typing with twenty percent of the total samples. This is due to the transition to tele-networking in recent years, bringing Adware back from among the smallest types to most consistent from 2020. Backdoors and Trojans tied for the third largest typing amongst the samples, each having around fifteen percent of the samples. Worms, hackertool, and spyware had the lowest percentages with around one percent each, with more of the samples coming from farther back in history, late 1990 to early 2000. Figure 2 shows this breakdown.

B. PV Type and Complexity

From all the samples, the PVs utilized followed a two fold progression. As the samples grew more modern both the number of persistence and the type changes, thus increasing their complexity. Older samples, up to 2010, generally worked

Malware Families	Percentage of Total Samples
Bootkit/Rootkit	25%
Ransomware	22%
Adware	20%
Backdoors	15%
Trojans	15%
Spyware	2%
Worms	1%
HackerTools	1%

Fig. 2. PV Family Characterization

with one established PV per sample. This is most likely due to the limitations of security tools to properly identify the infections on systems. From this they did not require the newer means to ensure their persistence on the system. Modern samples and those dating back to as early as 2017, have started to utilized multiple contingent persistence vectors, allowing for protection of the persistence on the system even if one or two of these is identified. An example of this is the Haxdor-Gen rootkit. As a modular based malware sample, the author is able to tailor the deployment, were included in, as of writing, twelve different persistence vectors. These include generated registry keys, root services, and start up scripts, to name the most common. Included in the source code are commands to reinstall any deleted or removed persistence from the surviving, such as the start up service with code to reinstall an additional copy of the scheduled tasks and to redeploy the virus code into a secure region of the system.

The most common persistence methods utilized by malware are: Registry modification, DLL Replacement/Reorder, startup Keys, Services, and boot modifications [9]. Of the 1000 malware samples studied, all utilized one or multiple of these to establish persistence. We found Registry modifications in most of samples, which was to be expected due to the straightforward ability to generate change. Boot modifications were the next largest of the PVs found amongst the sample base. Consistently, these were found in the more modern malware, as this placed the persistence in areas that are not checked by security tools or are able to start prior and bypass. A small percentage of the older samples did contain this PV, but this was very selective, and found exclusively within the bootkit and ransomware families.

DLL order modifications and startup key were in approximately half of the sample base. However, we noticed none of the hackertools and the spyware families included this PV. Broken down even further, the DLL modifications were a two-to-one in regards to order modifications versus DLL replacement. The more modern malware leaned more on the replacement of the DLL, placing instead its code wrapped in a legitimate version of the DLL. Services were the next largest percentage of the PVs from the sample base. Of the samples there was the common theme that majority were generated

Persistence Mechanisms	Percentage of Total Samples
Registry Modifications	90%
Boot Modifications	75%
DLL Order	50%
Startup Keys	45%
Services	44%
Event Triggers	25%
Shortcut Modifications	22%

Fig. 3. Trend Pattern of PV Type and Complexity

at the Windows system level. Only five percent generated services at the user level, paired with other persistence methods, to launch higher privilege execution. Services PVs were found across majority of malware families, however the largest concentration came from the ransomware, adware, spyware, and rootkit families.

Event triggers were the most diverse PVs, fitting only together based upon the requirement of an action to cause the triggering. Triggers involved various programs being executed, certain accounts being logged in, a specific interrupt, user key inputs, and even screen saver launching. The largest family utilizing event triggers were Trojans with roughly sixty percent implementing at least one event trigger. Least amongst the identified PVs in the sample base was the shortcut modifications. These modifications were generally found in only twenty-two percent of the samples, specifically more in the Trojans, the hacker tool, and portions of the adware. Figure 3 shows a breakdown of all the samples based upon their persistence vectors.

As the age of the samples evolved, the complexity of the malware persistence methodologies improved. Early pieces were only able to manage and maintain one persistence method within their code base. More modern samples, such as our example of Rovnix, can support multiple persistence vectors. These allow for the piece to regain persistence even if one of its vectors is identified and removed.

C. PV Stealth Factor Categorization

In this analysis, we examined the security elements utilized by our samples' persistence mechanisms. Inverse to the commonality, registry key modification is proven easiest to detect. Multiple tools, such as Regshot which was partly used to identify persistence vectors, could isolate these changes. However, there is the caveat to this detection in the commonality of false positives and negatives. Limited listings show these modifications made from the malware and those made by more legitimate programs. The most challenging persistence modification to identify was the boot modifications, generally the changes created by Rootkit/Bootkits and certain types of Ransomware. These are difficult for both the user and analyst due to their execution prior to most of the OS functionality. One example is Nemsis bootkit, which contained multiple changes to the core operating system elements. One of the key persistence mechanisms is the rewriting of the VBR, which allows it to start before loading the basic operating system elements. The changes reach the point where the bootkit can reapply itself once the hard drive is changed. Finding and cataloging all these changes proved a substantial challenge. Due to their loading prior to the operating system, several took extended static analysis to identify as dynamic analysis could not be relied upon.

Anti Reversing is one of the elements under consistent evolution, with the complexity increasing nearly exponentially as time progresses. Samples with the dates of late 1990s and the early 2000s generally are lacking in complexity of defensive measures. These samples generally had their code as is, due to the lack of diverse options with security tools and the limited knowledge of detecting these samples. These covered the majority of the hackertools and worms. Security improved across the samples with the next section involving masking the sample type within the legitimate functionality. The majority of Trojans and roughly a quarter of the adware samples were predominant in this category. These PVs were masked with generally legitimate changes that would be made to the system, such as with one sample that installed a playable game in conjunction with its malicious payload. While this was a drastic move forward regarding security, the PVs were still straightforward. As with the standard code PVs discussed previously, simple analysis can locate and identify these. Continued progression led to the next level of defensive measures deployed via malware to obfuscate their PVs, covering another twenty-five percent of the adware and roughly fifty percent of the spyware. Segmentation was one of the methodologies in many of the newer samples. Through this process, only a portion of the malicious code is involved in the initially executed malware. Additional elements were requested via system resources once the initial infection was complete. Without a malicious payload, scans of the current code would yield a non-malicious identification.

The final category of defensive measure, predominately found in the newer malware samples, minimizes the items generated to the system's hard drive. This malware evolution has the samples run exclusively on system volatile memory, removing itself once the system is restarted and making it much harder to collect a sample for analysis. None of the samples utilized for the evaluation was this type. Presented in Figure 4 is a breakdown of the stealth functionalities that were found in the sample base. Similar to the complexity of the persistence vectors, the stealth factors evolved exponentially. This stealth is reflexive of the enhancements to security tools designed to catch the common malware attempting to compromise the system.

VII. Conclusion and Future Works

This study examines how persistence vectors evolve in complexity and stealthiness over time. It explores the differences in the adaptation of PVs by the different classes of malware, thus paving the way for potential new advancements in malware defense. By shifting focus to these targeted areas for defensive measures, scanning can reduce time, and processor utilization [14]. While not infallible, these persistence scanning elements could be added as an additional layer or decoy in a fully deployed defense-in-depth methodology. Scanning through more diverse operating systems, such as the various ones on Linux and mobile platforms, would be helpful to gain more diverse areas of persistence. Based on this study, our evaluation showed a directed trend in the classification/family of malware away from simple samples like common viruses and evolved into complex multi-module bootkits. Also, we found an exponential trend for complexity and stealthiness, with samples only becoming more adapted to overcome the security tools in place to protect systems. In conclusion, malware is already a significant threat, only increased by persistence, allowing it to remain on the system to perform further malicious activities. Further study of the persistence vectors present across other operating systems could yield similar results. As a recommendation and for future work, persistence utilization can serve as another strong layer for malware prevention in a properly deployed defense in depth.

Obfuscation Technique	Percentage of Total Samples
Polymorphic Code	36%
Masking/Junk Instructions	30%
Boot Modifications	50%
API Hooking	55%
Anti-RE Techniques	15%

Fig. 4. Trend Pattern of PV Stealthiness

References

[1] M. Abhijit, and S. Anoop. "Persistence Mechanisms." In Malware Analysis and Detection Engineering, pp. 213-236. Apress, Berkeley, CA, 2020.

[2] Z. Gittins, and M. Soltys. "Malware persistence mechanisms." Procedia Computer Science vol. 176, pg 88-97, 2020.

[3] M. U. Rana, M. Ali-Shah, and O. Ellahi. "Malware Persistence and Obfuscation: An Analysis on Concealed Strategies." In 2021 26th International Conference on Automation and Computing (ICAC), pp. 1-6. IEEE, 2021.

[4] R. Brewer. "Ransomware attacks: detection, prevention and cure." Network security 2016, no. 9, pg 5-9, 2016.

[5] M. Abhijit, and S. Anoop. Malware Analysis and Detection Engineering: A Comprehensive Approach to Detect and Analyze Modern Malware. Apress, 2020.

[6] N. Virvilis, and D. Gritzalis. "The big four-what we did wrong in advanced persistent threat detection?." In 2013 international conference on availability, reliability and security, pp. 248-254. IEEE, 2013.

[7] R. Anusmita , , and N. Asoke. "Introduction to Malware and Malware Analysis: A brief overview." International Journal 4, no. 10, 2016.

[8] M. O'Leary, and McDermott. Cyber Operations. Apress, 2019.

[9] I. Kirillov, D. Beck, P. Chase, and R. Martin. "Malware attribute enumeration and characterization." The MITRE Corporation, 2011.

[10] L. Zeltser. "Reverse engineering malware.", 2010.

[11] W. Yan, Z. Zhang, and A. Nirwan. "Revealing packed malware." ieee seCurity PrivaCy 6, no. 5. Pg 65-69. 2008.

[12] S. Megira, A. R. Pangesti, and F. W. Wibowo. "Malware analysis and detection using reverse engineering technique." In Journal of Physics: Conference Series, vol. 1140, no. 1, p. 012042. IOP Publishing, 2018.

[13] P. Vinod, R. Jaipur, V. Laxmi, and M. Gaur. "Survey on malware detection methods." In Proceedings of the 3rd Hackers' Workshop on computer and internet security (IITKHACK'09), pp. 74-79. 2009.

[14] R. Tian, I. Rafiqul, L. Batten, and S. Versteeg. "Differentiating malware from cleanware using behavioural analysis." In 2010 5th international conference on malicious and unwanted software, pp. 23-30. Ieee, 2010.
[15] R. Al-Shaer, J. M. Spring, and E. Christou. "Learning the associations of mitre att ck adversarial techniques." In 2020 IEEE Conference on Communications and Network Security (CNS), pp. 1-9. IEEE, 2020.
[16] C. Kallenberg, S. Cornwell, X. Kovah, and J. Butterworth. "Setup for failure: defeating secure boot." In The Symposium on Security for Asia Network (SyScan)(April 2014). 2014.
[17] P. Black, and J. Opacki. "Anti-analysis trends in banking malware." In 2016 11th International Conference on Malicious and Unwanted Software (MALWARE), pp. 1-7. IEEE, 2016.
[18] B. Min, V. Varadharajan, U. Tupakula, and M. Hitchens. "Antivirus security: naked during updates." Software: Practice and Experience 44, no. 10, pg 1201-1222, 2014.
[19] J. Mankin. "Classification of malware persistence mechanisms using low-artifact disk instrumentation." PhD diss., Northeastern University, 2013.
[20] M. S. Webb. "Evaluating tool based automated malware analysis through persistence mechanism detection." PhD diss., Kansas State University, 2018.
[21] R. Tahir. "A study on malware and malware detection techniques." International Journal of Education and Management Engineering 8, no. 2, vol 20, 2018.
[22] N. Galloro, M. Polino, M. Carminati, A. Continella, and S. Zanero. "A Systematical and longitudinal study of evasive behaviors in windows malware." Computers Security vol 113, 2022.
[23] A. Mills, and P. Legg. "Investigating anti-evasion malware triggers using automated sandbox reconfiguration techniques." Journal of Cybersecurity and Privacy 1, vol. 1, pg 19-39, 2020.
[24] L. Maffia, D. Nisi, P. Kotzias, G. Lagorio, S. Aonzo, and D. Balzarotti. "Longitudinal Study of the Prevalence of Malware Evasive Techniques." arXiv preprint arXiv:2112.11289, 2021.
[25] J. Rutkowska. "System virginity verifier: Defining the roadmap for malware detection on windows systems." In Hack in the box security conference. 2005.
[26] Total, V. (2012). Virustotal-free online virus, malware and url scanner. Online: https://www. virustotal. com/en, 2.
[27] J. A. Halderman, S. D. Schoen, N. Heninger, W. Clarkson, W. Paul, J. A. Calandrino, A. J. Feldman, J. Appelbaum, and E. W. Felten. "Lest we remember: cold-boot attacks on encryption keys." Communications of the ACM 52, vol 5, pg 91-98, 2009.
[28] G. Cabau, M. Buhu, and C. P. Oprisa. "Malware classification based on dynamic behavior." In 2016 18th International Symposium on Symbolic and Numeric Algorithms for Scientific Computing (SYNASC), pp. 315-318. IEEE, 2016.
[29] V. Khushali. "A Review on Fileless Malware Analysis Techniques." vol 9, pg. 46-49, 2020.
[30] J. Kohout, and T. Pevný. "Unsupervised detection of malware in persistent web traffic." In 2015 IEEE International Conference on Acoustics, Speech and Signal Processing (ICASSP), pp. 1757-1761. IEEE, 2015.
[31] M. Guo, G. Wang, H. Hata, and M. A. Babar. "Revenue maximizing markets for zero-day exploits." Autonomous Agents and Multi-Agent Systems 35, no.2. pg 1-29. 2021.

Efficient Consensus Between Multiple Controllers in Software Defined Networks (SDN)

Stavroula Lalou
Department of Digital Systems
University of Piraeus
Piraeus, Greece
slalou@unipi.gr

Georgios Spathoulas
Dept. of Inform. Sec. and Comm. Techn.
NTNU
Gjøvik, Norway
georgios.spathoulas@ntnu.no

Sokratis Katsikas
Dept. of Inform. Sec. and Comm. Techn.
NTNU
Gjøvik, Norway
sokratis.katsikas@ntnu.no

***Abstract*—Software Defined Networking (SDN) has emerged as a popular paradigm for managing large scale networks. The traditional single controller architecture has limitations in managing the entire network: it can become a bottleneck when it comes to exchanging large volumes of data and it implies overhead as the number of user increases. Additionally, the single controller acts as a single point of failure because all the forwarding decisions depend directly on the controller. Once the SDN controller or the switches-to-controller links fail, the entire network may collapse. Therefore, scalability, reliability, interoperability, and fault tolerance remain as challenges in centralized network architectures. On the other hand, multiple controller architectures exhibit faster response and a more flexible network structure. Additionally, they can improve scalability and they avoid a single point of failure. In order to synchronize the network state between different controllers, a consensus protocol is required. In this paper, we propose a consensus mechanism, based on the Raft algorithm, which provides a stable, consistent, and efficient network in which all the controllers have the same network state. The proposed mechanism supports high throughput, dynamic view changes, fault tolerance, and controller synchronization. The performance of the proposed mechanism has been experimentally assessed and found to be very satisfactory compared to existing alternatives.**

Index Terms*—*Software Defined Networking; multiple controllers; Consensus Algorithm; fault-tolerance.

I. Introduction

Single controller approaches are the main paradigm used to support SDN networks, but it fails to serve a number of critical domain requirements. Firstly, the efficiency of such centralized approaches is limited upon the resources of the single controller. Scalability is an issue, as is high availability, and security is of high importance as, if an attacker compromises the controller, management capability over the network is completely lost. Redundancy is one of the most significant aspects of any design. One controller could fail at anytime and, leave the network without a control plane. Multiple controllers can minimize the consequences of such a situation. Controllers operating normally could even collaborate to detect that another one is misbehaving and even isolate it from the network. Thus, having multiple controllers running at the same time and collaborating with each other enables the network to improve in terms of scalability, persistency, workload sharing and availability.

Consensus is the central protocol behind services replicated for fault tolerance. Consensus protocols are the foundation for building many fault tolerant distributed systems and services. A number of solutions have been proposed in this context.

In this paper, we introduce a novel mechanism that supports the operation of multiple controllers in an SDN network. The mechanism achieves network flexibility and enhances network management; it also synchronizes the network state between different controllers, while addressing single point of failure, fault tolerance and scalability issues. To demonstrate the practicality of the proposal, we present an implementation with the Raft algorithm [1] for state machine replication, whose performance we evaluated and compared to that of an existing alternative by means of experimentation.

The contribution of this paper is:

- The analysis of the existing mechanisms and protocols for SDN networks
- The definition of the consensus problem for distributed SDN controllers.
- The introduction of a mechanism that supports high throughput, dynamic view changes, fault tolerance, and controller synchronization in multiple SDN controllers setups.

The remaining of the paper is structured as follows: In section II, we briefly review necessary background knowledge on SDN and on the Raft consensus algorithm. In section III, we discuss related work. In section IV, we present our proposal for a mechanism supporting multi-controller SDN architectures. In section V, we present the experimental setup that we used for evaluating the performance of the proposal and we discuss the results. Finally, section VI summarizes our conclusions.

II. Background

This section presents a review of the architecture of SDN and Raft Algorithm.

A. *SDN Architecture*

SDN has emerged as a new networking paradigm for implementing flexible network management solutions. Figure 1 depicts SDN architecture [2]. SDN is a network architecture where the forwarding state in the data plane is managed by a remote control plane decoupled from the former. The key principle of SDN is the separation of the control and data planes. The control plane is logically centralized and provides programmable application programming interfaces (APIs) for managing the physical layer. The data plane specializes in forwarding packets according to the instructions received from the controllers. In SDN, the controllers enable flexible management and unified control via programmable interfaces with a global view of the network status.

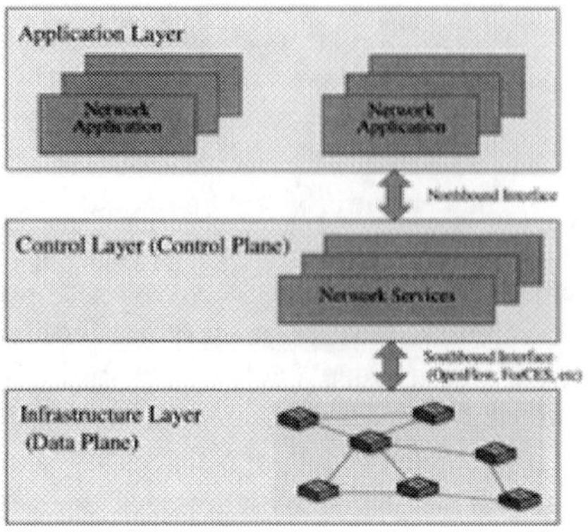

Fig. 1. Software Defined Networking.

The SDN is also defined as a network architecture:

- The control and data planes are decoupled. Control functionality is removed from network devices that will become simple (packet) forwarding elements.
- Forwarding decisions are flow-based, instead of destination-based. A flow is broadly defined by a set of packet field values acting as a match (filter) criterion and a set of actions (instructions). In the SDN/OpenFlow context, a flow is a sequence of packets between a source and a destination. [2].
- Control logic is moved to an external entity, the so-called *SDN controller* or *Network Operating System (NOS)*. The NOS is a software platform that runs on commodity server technology and provides the essential resources and abstractions to facilitate the programming of forwarding devices based on a logically centralized, abstract network view. It is similar to that of a traditional operating system [2]. The network is programmable through software applications running on top of the NOS, that interacts with the underlying data plane devices. This is a fundamental characteristic of SDN, and is considered to be its main value proposition.
- The network is programmable through software applications running on top of the NOS that interacts with the underlying data plane devices. This is a fundamental characteristic of SDN, considered as its main value proposition.

B. *Raft Algorithm*

Consensus is a fundamental problem for distributed systems. It pertains to getting a group of participants to reliably agree on some value used for a computation. Several protocols have been proposed to solve the consensus problem [3], and these protocols are the foundation for building fault tolerant systems, including the core infrastructure of data centers [1]. For example, consensus protocols are the basis for state machine replication [4], which is used to implement key services.

The Raft algorithm, depicted in Figure 2 [1] is a significant consensus algorithm for managing a replicated log. At the core of Raft lies a replicated log that is managed by a leader. Writes are funneled to the log and replicated throughout the cluster, through the leader. A leader election algorithm is integrated into the Raft algorithm to ensure consistency.

Raft separates the key elements of consensus, such as leader election, log replication, and safety, and it enforces a stronger degree of coherency to reduce the number of states that have to be considered in order to reach consensus. It also includes a mechanism for changing the cluster membership, which uses overlapping majorities to guarantee safety. There are three different node states, namely *leader*, *candidate*, and *follower*. Raft divides time into *terms* with arbitrary duration. Terms are monotonically increasing integers, where each term begins with an election. If a candidate wins an election, it serves as the leader for the rest of the term. Terms allow Raft servers to detect obsolete information such as stale leaders. Current terms are exchanged whenever servers communicate. When a leader or a candidate learns that its current term is out of date, then it immediately reverts to the follower state. Servers reject vote requests from the leader and replicated log entries with a stale term number.

A leader sends periodical heartbeats to all followers. If a follower receives no heartbeat messages over a predefined period of time (election timeout), it assumes there is no leader and starts a new election. It increments its current term, votes for itself, and moves to candidate state. Then, it sends request-to-vote RPCs to other servers. If it receives votes from a majority, it sends heartbeats to all servers to prevent new elections and establish its authority for its term. While waiting for votes, the candidate server may receive a heartbeat message from another server claiming to be the leader.

Raft is typically used to model replicated state machines. Leaders receive state machine commands and write them to a local log which is then replicated to followers in a batching approach. Once a command submitted to a leader has been logged and replicated to a majority of nodes of the cluster, the command is considered committed, and the leader applies the command to its own state machine and responds to the client with the logs. In the event of a server restart, the server replays the committed entries in its logs to rebuild the state of the server state machine.

According to the Raft algorithm a set of nodes can maintain a consistent shared data record. Each node can be a Master or a Candidate, and it sends messages to system nodes. If the Master fails, a new Master controller is chosen, following the process prescribed by Raft. Data records are funneled to the memory and then replicated throughout the cluster, and then through the leader. The leader checks all the data records

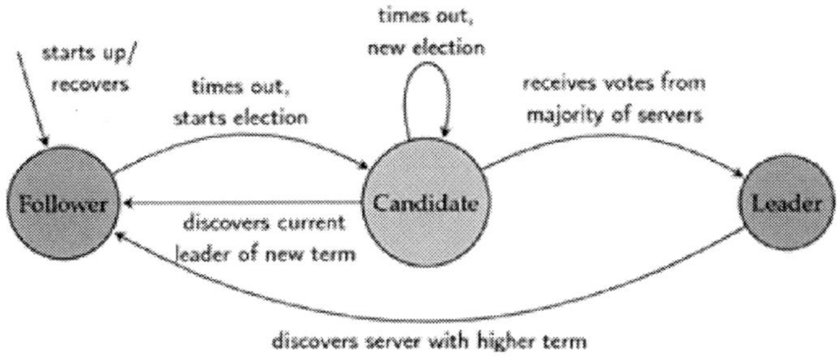

Fig. 2. Raft Consensus Algorithm.

and uses the election algorithm to ensure consistency.In our network we use Raft, so each node has a role either Master, Controller or Worker.

III. Related Work

The use of a single SDN controller offers flexibility and efficiency in network management, but leads to problems such as single points of failure and scalability issues. Existing studies propose multiple SDN controller architectures to address the above issues. The synchronization of the network state information among controllers is a critical problem, known as the controller consensus problem. To synchronize the network information between controllers, a proper consistency model should be chosen. *Strong consistency* and *eventual consistency* are two consistency models commonly used in distributed systems.

Many papers have proposed systems for SDN. The authors of [5] introduce a multicontroller SDN architecture, which employs a Fast Paxos based Consensus (FPC) algorithm to handle the consensus between multiple SDN controllers. The concept of leader election is also supported, as three roles, namely *Listener*, *Proposer*, and *Chairman* are applied to different controllers. The proposal was tested on a small-scale multicontroller architecture. In this research the evaluation of the performance was conducted in an ODL (OpenDaylight) Clustering on 3-node clustering. The FPC is composed of four phases, namely *Propose*, *Accept*, *Update*, and *Adjust*. A controller maintains a table that records its current controller state.

Hyperflow [6], [7] is described as a flat design. It is a distributed event-based control plane for OpenFlow. HyperFlow is logically centralized but physically distributed: it provides scalability while keeping the benefits of network control centralization. By passively synchronizing network-wide views of OpenFlow controllers, HyperFlow localizes decision making to individual controllers, thus minimizing the control plane's response time to data plane requests. HyperFlow is resilient to network partitioning and component failures. It also enables interconnecting independently managed OpenFlow networks, an essential feature missing in current OpenFlow deployments. The network is structured into several domains, where each domain is controlled by a controller situated within its own local network view. Controllers communicate with others through their east-westbound interfaces to get the global view of the network. Each controller only processes flow requests sent from the switches that belong to its local domain. Network events (e.g., flow information, routing information) are transmitted based on specific publish/subscribe mode among controllers [6].

Onix uses Paxos Consensus [8]. It is a multiple SDN controller architecture that provides a control application with a set of general APIs to facilitate access to the network state. It adopts a distributed architecture approach to offer the programmatic interface for the upper control logic and uses Network Information Base (NIB) to maintain the global network state. In Onix, the controller stores network information in key value pairs by utilizing the NIB, which is the core element of the model. It synchronizes the network state by reading and writing to the NIB, thus it provides scalability and resilience by replicating and distributing the NIB across multiple NIB instances. Once a change of a NIB on one Onix node occurs, the change will be propagated to other NIBs to maintain the consistency of the network.

ONOS [9] stands for Open Network Operating System. It uses Raft, it provides the control plane for a SDN, managing network components such as switches and links, and running software programs or modules to provide communication services to end hosts and neighboring networks. ONOS applications and use cases often consist of customized communication routing, management, or monitoring services for SDNs. [9].

Kandoo [10] is a typical hierarchical controller structure. The root controller communicates with multiple domain controllers to get the domain information, but the domain controllers do not contact each other.

DISCO (DIStributed multi-domain SDN COntroller) [11] is a distributed SDN controller scheme, implemented on top of Floodlight. It was introduced to partition a wide area network (WAN) into constrained overlay networks. A DISCO controller manages its own domain and communicates with other controllers via a lightweight and manageable control channel to provide end-to-end network services.

Akka [12] is a toolkit used in ODL Clustering and is responsible for communication and notification among controllers. In the default clustering scheme, switches connect to all controllers, and these controllers coordinate among themselves to choose a master controller. The ODL uses the Raft algorithm to reach controller consistency [2]. The Raft consensus algorithm periodically elects a controller as a leader controller, and all data changes will be sent to the leader controller to handle the update.

As observed from the existing distributed controller architectures, the problem of single point of failure of the SDN controller was solved using multiple distributed controllers. The Copycat project is an advanced, feature-complete implementation of the Raft consensus algorithm that diverges from recommendations. For instance, Raft dictates that all reads and writes are executed through the Master Controller (node), but Copycat's Raft implementation supports per-request consistency levels that allow clients to sacrifice linearizability and read from followers. Similarly, the Raft literature recommends snapshots as the simplest approach to log compaction, but Copycat prefers an incremental log compaction approach to promote more consistent performance throughout the lifetime of a cluster. Copycat's Raft implementation extends the concept of sessions to allow server state machines to publish events to clients.

IV. Our proposal

The proposed mechanism implements a novel network of multiple controllers using the Raft consensus algorithm. It supports the connection and coordination of multiple distributed SDN controllers to serve as backup controllers in case of a failure. Moreover, multiple controllers allow data load sharing when a single controller is overwhelmed with numerous flow requests. In general, our approach can reduce latency, increase scalability, and fault tolerance, and provides enhanced availability in SDN deployments.

The proposed mechanism, as shown in Figure 3, consists of a set of independent controllers (nodes), each one of which stores the required data in its memory. Each controller (node) is assigned with a unique id. In our implementation and test scenario we used a number of nodes in different states. Each one can be in one of three different states, namely *Master*, *Candidate* or *Worker*. In the *Master* state the node manages and controls the network while it can also process data and send update information to the other controllers. In the *Candidate* state the node can send and receive data to/from the other nodes. A Candidate node with the updated data can potentially transit to Master state if the current Master node fails. Finally in the *Worker* state the node passively receives data from Master or Candidate nodes.

If a Master node fails, the Raft election process is initiated to elect a new Master node and avoid single point of failure effects. In this process a node in Candidate state will be elected and will act as Master node, while the previous Master node will switch to Candidate state. Through this process the system maintains its stability and fault tolerance.

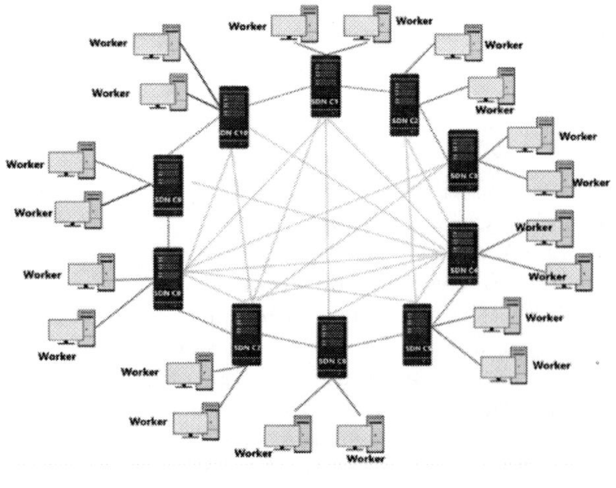

Fig. 3. Proposed mechanism.

Inputs are introduced to the SDN multiple controllers network by clients (nodes). When new data are introduced in the mechanism by a node, according to the Raft protocol, such data is forwarded to the Master Controller. Once the Master Controller receives a series of information, it logs and replicates these to all the mechanism controllers, which store such data in their memory.

When the Master Controller receives a series of data, a broadcast process is initiated to send such data to all nodes in the network and update information in all controllers accordingly. Information is stored in the memory of the Master controller and its initial state is defined as not read. The Master node sends data to all Candidate nodes and the latter forward such data to their neighboring Worker nodes. The Master node monitors if all Candidate nodes have received and stores the new data to ensure that all of them have an updated memory. Each Candidate node makes sure that it records newly sent data, while it also monitors data records to avoid duplicate ones. Consequently, each Candidate node sends data to attached Worker nodes. During this process the same approach is followed to ensure successful delivery of data to all nodes.

When all nodes have successfully forwarded all data, the mechanism transits to an "OK" state when all controllers have the same data stored in memory. If a controller receives new data, then it stops being in the "OK" state and data shall be sent to the other controllers and workers (neighbor nodes) of the mechanism according to the procedure which has been described previously.

In the proposed mechanism the main entity is the Raft node which shall be deployed along with each SDN controller in an SDN setup. Each node keeps in its memory a set of records which adhere to the structure *record (data, send)*. The variable *data* holds the information to be exchanged and the variable *send* is Boolean and is used to flag whether a specific record has been successfully forwarded to the network. Nodes are identified by a unique id.

The Raft consensus algorithm is used to coordinate the sharing of information between nodes. It defines the creation of a group of controllers (candidates) and the required processes to elect one leader the Master controller. The Master is the one who manages the data flow in the mechanism and leads the group if it is active.

If the Master node fails, then a new Master node must be elected through the mechanism process. Specifically, a time is defined in which the Master sends a message to the other controllers. If the message does not arrive in time, a Controller node sends a message requesting to become the Master node. In this case the other controllers respond, and the specific node is designated as the Master node.

The main processes that nodes operate upon to maintain consistency, stability, and availability are the following:

- The *read* process, that reads from the mechanism memory and checks records and if those have been successfully distributed to others.
- The *send* process that sends data to other controllers.

- The *send-to-all* process, that is responsible for iteratively sending data to all neighboring controllers.

V. PERFORMANCE EVALUATION

To evaluate the performance of the proposed mechanism we conducted a network simulation. Also we compare it with other mechanisms in terms of consensus time, distribution time, data access time and presenting test results.

A. Experimental Setup

Table II shows the main simulation parameters.The system on which the simulation was performed was based on an AMD Ryzen 5, 4500 U CPU and the goal was to evaluate the time required for the main functionalities of the proposed design.

TABLE I
SIMULATION PARAMETERS

Parameters	Value
Consensus algorithm	Raft
Data	In all node types
Number of controllers	10
Number of Workers per Controller	2
Test environment	Windows 10
Hardware	AMD Ryzen 5, 4500 U
Compiler	NetBeans 8.2
Code	Java

To evaluate the proposed approach, we have run an periment to assess the time response of the algorithm. first run an experimental simulation of a failure scenaric which the proposed algorithm is executed for 100 sec fc mechanism with 30 controllers, 10 of which run as Ma: nodes and 20 run as Worker nodes. We check that dat: being transferred correctly between nodes. In this scenario assume that at a specific time point, around 20 sec after start, the master node fails. The main objective is to maint mechanism stability at all times and avoid the effects o single point of failure.

To extend the initial scenario, another test was also e cuted, in which the newly elected Master nodes drop at ti points around 20 sec, 30 sec and 60 sec respectively. All no have been monitored to test the read and write performa in each node (in Master, Controller or Worker states).

In the tests, all the nodes except those of the original Master node and the Worker nodes connected to it have the same data after the initially set Master node crashes. Another node is elected as the new Master node. This is repeated a number of times during the execution of the experiment.

The proposed mechanism reduces the network overhead. Moreover, it maintains the proper network operation, even when there is a controller failure. Moreover, it offers controller synchronization, as all network controllers have the same data. In addition, it preserves it's reliability, scalability, fault tolerance, and interoperability. In the event of Master node failure, a new master controller would be selected to take the control of the network. The mechanism of choosing a new master is through the Raft consensus algorithm process, so the proposed mechanism enjoys high availability rates. The conducted experiment simulates the operation of a distributed mechanism consisting of remote computers or systems.

B. Results

During the tests we compare the proposed mechanism and the Paxos-based mechanism [8], in terms of consensus time, distribution of normalized consensus time, and data access time. The consensus time is the time that elapses from when a transaction is created to when the transaction is committed.According to the research these are closest to our approach and are implemented according to distributed SDN multiple controller architecture and consensus algorithms.

TABLE II
COMPARISON OF PROTOCOLS/ALGORITHMS

Feature	Proposed	CopyCat Raft	Paxos
Consensus algorithm	Raft	Raft	Paxos
Controllers	10	1	3
Workers	2/controller	1 client	6 End Users
Time to read data	10 ms	0.20 s	6.425 ms
Time to write/send data	10.4 ms	0.40 s	17.814 ms
Time to elect a Master	10.06 ms	0.060 s	28 ms

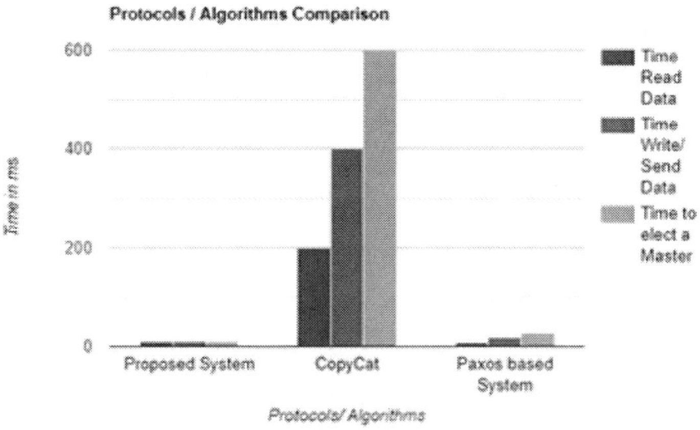

Fig. 4. Comparison of Protocols/ Algorithms.

Table II shows the basic features of the proposed mechanism in comparison to the CopyCat project and a Paxos-based system [8], that we have tested. All models are using consensus algorithms and a distributed SDN multiple controller architecture. As is shown in Table II, through the comparison between the Copycat project and the proposed mechanism it is clear that Copycat requires more computing resources than the proposed mechanism and this makes Copycat less reliable for large scale networks. Also, the time required for reading, writing and sending data is higher than the other two mechanisms. The average time that the Copycat system needs to start and elect a Master Controller is 23.23 seconds.

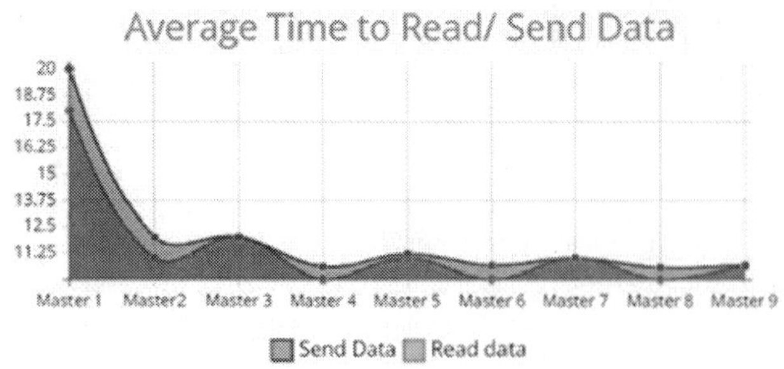

Fig. 5. Read and Write Average Time.

The consensus time of the proposed mechanism is stable. Also, the Write/ Send Data time is stable and low (see Figure 5); the proposed protocol needs 10.4 ms. Low and stable times for reading and sending data can improve the mechanism performance and offer a stable and functional mechanism architecture. Furthermore, all controllers had the same data even after a controller drop in our simulation environment of 100 seconds; the network maintains its stability.

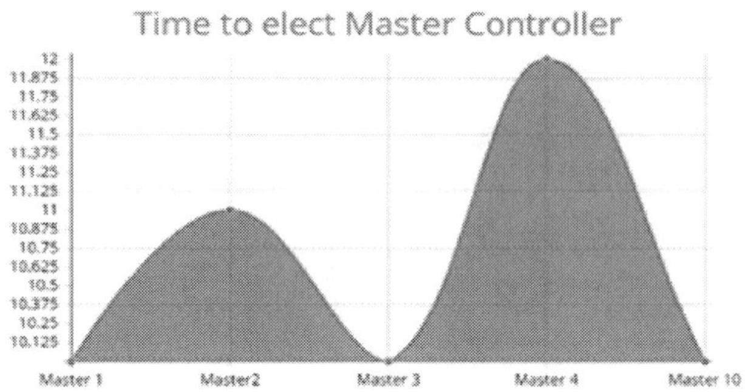

Fig. 6. Controller election Time with Raft.

The test results have shown that for the proposed mechanism the average required time for Master node election is 10.06 ms (see Figure 6). It is stable and low, as shown in Fig. 4 and described in Table II.

VI. Conclusion

SDN is a promising paradigm for network management because of its centralized network intelligence. However, the centralized control architecture of SDNs raises challenges regarding reliability, scalability, fault tolerance and interoperability. The existing solutions which were analyzed in literature are not offering high-throughput, fault-tolerance, and controller synchronization. We proposed a novel implementation, based on the Raft algorithm, that can efficiently synchronize the network state information among multiple nodes, thus ensuring good performance at all times irrespective of the traffic dynamics. Further, the proposed mechanism supports high-throughput, fault-tolerance, and controller synchronization. Our simulation results have shown that the proposed mechanism can support Multiple Controllers, as it maintains stability (all nodes have the same data, after a Master node failure) and the average required times are low. The average time it takes to read, write in memory, and send data to neighbor controllers is low and stable. Also, the time it takes to elect a new controller is also low. In our proposal, multiple controllers maintain a consistent global view of the network. This is achieved by employing the Raft consensus protocol to ensure consistency among the replicated network states maintained by each controller.

Acknowledgments

This work has been partly supported by the University of Piraeus Research Center and also was funded in part by the Research Council of Norway under project nr. 310105 "Norwegian Centre for Cybersecurity in Critical Sectors".

References

[1] D. Ongaro and J. Ousterhout, "In search of an understandable consensus algorithm", in Proceedings of the 2014 USENIX conference on USENIX Annual Technical Conference (USENIX ATC'14), USENIX Association, USA, 2014, pp. 305--320.

[2] D. Kreutz, et al., "Software-Defined Networking: A Comprehensive Survey", in Proceedings of the IEEE, vol. 103, no. 1, pp. 14-76, Jan. 2015, doi: 10.1109/JPROC.2014.2371999.

[3] L. Lamport, "The part-time parliament", ACM Trans. Comput. Syst., vol. 16, no. 2, pp. 133--169, May 1998, https://doi.org/10.1145/279227.279229.

[4] A. Abdelaziz et al, "Distributed controller clustering in software defined networks", PLoS ONE, Vol. 12, no. 4: e0174715, April 2017, https://doi.org/10.1371/journal.pone.0174715(2017).

[5] C. -C. Ho, K. Wang and Y. -H. Hsu, "A fast consensus algorithm for multiple controllers in software-defined networks," 2016 18th International Conference on Advanced Communication Technology (ICACT), pp. 1–1, 2016, doi: 10.1109/ICACT.2016.7423293.

[6] D. Dotan and R. Y. Pinter, "HyperFlow: an integrated visual query and dataflow language for end-user information analysis", 2005 IEEE Symposium on Visual Languages and Human-Centric Computing (VL/HCC'05), 2005, pp. 27–34, doi: 10.1109/VLHCC.2005.45.

[7] A. Tootoonchian and Y. Ganjali, "HyperFlow: a distributed control plane for OpenFlow", in Proceedings of the 2010 internet network management conference on Research on enterprise networking (INM/WREN'10), USENIX Association, USA, 2010.

[8] R. Y. Shtykh and T. Suzuki, "Distributed Data Stream Processing with Onix," 2014 IEEE Fourth International Conference on Big Data and Cloud Computing, 2014, pp. 267–268, doi: 10.1109/BDCloud.2014.54.

[9] P. Berde et al, "ONOS: towards an open, distributed SDN OS", in Proceedings of the third workshop on Hot topics in software defined networking (HotSDN '14), Association for Computing Machinery, New York, NY, USA, pp. 1--6, 2014, https://doi.org/10.1145/2620728.2620744.

[10] S. H. Yeganeh and Y. Ganjali, "Kandoo: a framework for efficient and scalable offloading of control applications", in Proceedings of the first workshop on Hot topics in software defined networks (HotSDN '12), Association for Computing Machinery, New York, NY, USA, 19--24, 2012, https://doi.org/10.1145/2342441.2342446.

[11] K. Phemius, M. Bouet and J. Leguay, "DISCO: Distributed multi-domain SDN controllers", 2014 IEEE Network Operations and Management Symposium (NOMS), 2014, pp. 1–4, doi: 10.1109/NOMS.2014.6838330.

[12] W. Xia, Y. Wen, C. H. Foh, D. Niyato and H. Xie, "A Survey on Software-Defined Networking", in IEEE Communications Surveys & Tutorials, vol. 17, no. 1, pp. 27-51, Firstquarter 2015, doi: 10.1109/COMST.2014.2330903.

Unsupervised Graph Contrastive Learning with Data Augmentation for Malware Classification

Yun Gao
Graduate School of Informatics
Nagoya University
Nagoya, Japan
email:gaoyun@net.itc.nagoya-u.ac.jp

Hirokazu Hasegawa
Center for Strategic Cyber Resilience
Research and Development
National Institute of Informatics
Tokyo, Japan
email:hasegawa@nii.ac.jp

Yukiko Yamaguchi
Information Technology Center
Nagoya University
Nagoya, Japan
email:yamaguchi@itc.nagoya-u.ac.jp

Hajime Shimada
Information Technology Center
Nagoya University
Nagoya, Japan
email:shimada@itc.nagoya-u.ac.jp

***Abstract*—Traditional malware detection methods struggle to quickly and effectively keep up with the massive amount of newly created malware. Based on the features of samples, machine learning is a promising method for the detection and classification of large-scale, newly created malware. The current research trend uses machine-learning technologies to rapidly and accurately learn newly created malware. In this paper, we propose a malware classification framework based on Graph Contrastive Learning (GraphCL) with data augmentation. We first extract the Control-Flow Graph (CFG) from portable executable (PE) files and simultaneously generate node feature vectors from the disassembly code of each basic block through MiniLM, a large-scale pre-trained language model. Then four different data augmentation methods are used to expand the graph data, and the final graph representation is generated by the GraphCL model. These representations can be directly applied to downstream tasks. For our classification task, we use C-Support Vector Classification (SVC) as a classification model. To evaluate our approach, we made a CFG-based malware classification dataset from the PE files of the BODMAS Malware Dataset, which we call the Malware Geometric Multi-Class Dataset (MGD-MULTI), and collected the results. The evaluation results show that our proposal achieved Micro-F1 scores of 0.9975 and Macro-F1 scores of 0.9976. According to our experimental evaluation, the unsupervised learning approach outperformed the supervised learning approach in Graph Neural Networks based on malware classification.**

Keywords*—*malware classification; graph contrastive learning; data augmentation; unsupervised learning

I. Introduction

Fueled by the progress of software technology and the internet's development, thousands of malware are created every day due to the proliferation of malware creation and obfuscation tools. Such a massive flood of data poses a considerable challenge to malware analysts and security response centers (SOCs). Traditional malware detection methods cannot continue to quickly and effectively detect such a massive amount of newly created malware. In past decades, machine learning has played an important role in information security, especially in malware detection and classification tasks. It is also a promising method to detect and classify large-scale newly created malware using the features of samples.

In the field of static malware detection, the feature extraction method of portable executable (PE) files used in the Endgame Malware Benchmark for Research (EMBER) dataset [1] has been widely applied. This feature extraction method directly provides consistent feature vectors to researchers, allowing individuals in the same field to compare their respective proposed methods. The information related to software structure, such as the Control-Flow Graph (CFG), is rarely extracted, and most methods are based on surface analysis for extracting statistical information as features. In addition, in most malware detection and classification scenarios, the model is supervised for end-to-end training.

Supervised learning requires manual labeling of a large amount of data, and the model effect depends on the quality of the labels. Therefore, the future research trend, which is exploring unsupervised learning methods, is critical for malware detection and classification. In recent years, Graph Neural Networks (GNNs) have made remarkable progress. We can exploit their powerful representation ability to better represent malware and improve the effectiveness of its detection and classification. However, one remaining difficulty is how to represent malware in graphical form. Since CFG is a natural graph structure, we can generate the graph structure data of malware by extracting CFG. Therefore, we seek to classify malware by constructing a graph dataset and using unsupervised learning. Since no publicly available graph classification dataset exists for malware classification, we started by creating such a dataset.

Our contributions can be summarized as follows:

- We propose a malware classification framework based on graph contrastive learning under unsupervised learning.
- We retain the structural information of the samples extracted from CFG and embed the text features of each

node with a pre-trained language model.

- We create a special graph dataset for malware classification that can be used directly on GNNs.
- Our pre-trained model can effectively perform a low-dimensional representation of malware with which a variety of downstream tasks can be performed. We have achieved good results on malware family classification tasks.

The remainder of this paper is organized as follows. Section II reviews related researches and highlights their methodological differences. In Section III, we discuss the principles of our proposed data augmented GraphCL-based static malware PE classification system and its application to malware classification. In Section IV, we briefly discuss the implementation details of our proposal. In Section V, we describe the corresponding experiments and evaluate their feasibility as well as the advantages and limitations of our proposal. Finally, we discuss our conclusion and describe future work in Section VI.

II. Related Work

Static malware detection allows a sample to be classified as malicious or benign without executing it. In contrast, dynamic malware detection is based on its runtime behavior and as well as its analysis, including time-dependent system call sequences [2]–[4]. Although static detection is not generally deterministic [5], its advantages are also evident over dynamic detection, which can identify malicious files before the samples are executed. Since 1995, various machine-learning-based methods for static PE malware detection have been proposed [6]–[8].

A. Supervised-learning-based Methods

Saxe used histograms through byte-entropy values as input features and multilayer neural networks for classification [7]. Raff et al. showed that fully connected and recursive networks can be applied to malware detection problems [9]. They also used the raw bytes of PE files and built end-to-end deep learning networks [8]. Chen proposed robust PDF malware classifiers with verifiable robustness properties [10]. Coull explored malware detection byte-based deep neural network models to learn more about malware and examined the learned features at multiple levels of resolution, from individual byte embeddings to the end-to-end analysis of models [11]. Rudd proposed ALOHA, which uses multiple additional optimization objectives to enhance the model, including multi-source malicious/benign loss, count loss on multi-source detections, and semantic malware attribute tag loss [12].

B. Supervised Graph Classification

Graph classification assigns a label to each graph to map the graph to the vector space. A graph kernel is dominant in history. It uses the kernel function to measure the similarity between graph pairs and maps graphs to a vector space with a mapping function. In the context of graph classification, GNNs often employ readout operations to obtain a compact representation at the graph level. GNNs have attracted a lot of attention and demonstrated amazing results in this task.

The Dynamic Graph Convolutional Neural Network [13] (DGCNN) uses K nearest neighbors (KNN), builds a subgraph for each node based on the node's features, and applies a graph convolution to the reconstructed graph. The Graph Isomorphism Network (GIN) [14] presents a GIN that adjusts the weights of the central nodes by learning, theoretically analyzes the GIN's expressiveness better than such GNN structures as the Graph Convolutional Network (GCN), and achieves state-of-the-art accuracy on multiple tasks.

C. Unsupervised Graph Classification

Graph2vec [15] uses a set of all the rooted subgraphs around each node as its vocabulary through a skip-gram training process. Infograph [16] applies contrastive learning to graph learning, which is carried out in an unsupervised manner by maximizing the mutual information between graph-level and node-level representations.

Recently, contrast learning has received much attention. It has also been applied in the field of malware detection and classification. Yang presented a novel system called CADE, which can detect drifting samples that deviate from existing classes, and explained detected drift [17]. EVOLIoT [18] is a novel approach that combats "concept drift" and the limitations of inter-family IoT malware classification by detecting drifting IoT malware families and examining their diverse evolutionary trajectories. This robust and effective contrastive method learns and compares semantically meaningful representations of IoT malware binaries and codes without expensive target labels.

III. Proposed Data Augmented GraphCL-Based Static Malware PE Classification

Our proposal is a data augmented GraphCL-based static malware PE classification framework, which can obtain a graph-level representation from malware. We directly extract malware CFG from PE files and through graph contrastive learning obtain a representation of the malware with a vector notation. Finally, malware representations can be performed downstream for various tasks. Graph-level representation shows good performance on malware classification tasks. Next we scrutinize the framework.

A. Raw Graph Generation

To train the GNNs, we need to produce graph datasets, and the main task of this module is to convert PE files into raw graphs. The overview of raw graph generation is shown in Fig. 1.

1) CFG Structure and Disassembly Code: First, the CFG information is extracted from the original PE file samples, the structure information of the basic blocks is retained, and the disassembly code of each basic block is extracted. Each basic block of CFG has a corresponding disassembly code, and the relationship between each basic block is directional. Disassembly codes need to be transformed into feature vectors of specific dimensions to train GNNs. Since the malware CFG

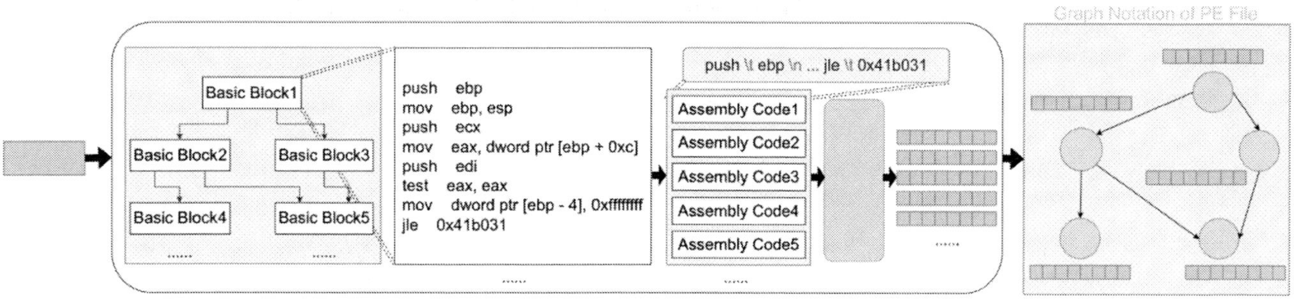

Figure 1. Raw graph generation for proposal

is usually a very large graph, extracting the CFG is very time consuming. Since the disassembly code in each basic block of CFG contains rich semantic information, we need to completely exploit that information and suitably embed it, for example, using a large pre-trained language model.

2) Pre-trained Language Model MiniLM: MiniLM is a method released by Microsoft based on reducing large-scale transformer pre-trained models into smaller models [19]. This Deep Self-Attention Distillation (DSAD) method uses large-scale data for pre-training. The model we use is called "all-MiniLM-L12-v2," which has a 1-billion-sized training set and is designed as a general-purpose model. MiniLM model is a 12-layer transformer with a 384 hidden size and 12 attention heads that contain about 33 M parameters. It maps sentences and paragraphs to a 384-dimensional dense vector space and can be used for tasks like clustering or semantic search. This model is the fastest generation of related studies and still provides good quality. In this step, a 384-dimensional dense vector is generated for each CFG node using the pre-trained model. This vector is added to the corresponding nodes of the directed graph to generate complete graph data with node feature vectors. These directed graphs are used as our raw graph data.

B. Data Augmentation for Graphs

We used the following four data augmentation methods. As shown in Fig. 2, our proposal uses two of them. The best combination is explored in Section 5.

1) Node Dropping: Randomly discard some parts of the vertex and its connections. The missing parts of the vertices do not affect the semantic meaning of the graph, and so the learned representation is consistent under the disturbance of nodes. The dropping probability of each node follows a default Bernoulli uniform distribution (or any other distribution).

2) Edge Perturbation: Randomly add or remove a certain ratio of edges so that the learned representation is consistent under edge perturbation. The prior information of the representation is that adding or removing some edges does not affect the semantics of the graph. The dropping probability of each node follows a default Bernoulli uniform distribution. We only used Edge Removing in this evaluation.

3) Attribute Masking: Randomly removing the attribute information of some nodes motivates the model to use other information to reconstruct the masked node attributes. The masking probability of each node feature dimension follows a default uniform distribution. We only used simple Feature Masking.

4) Subgraph Sampling: Use random walk subgraph sampling [20] to extract subgraphs from the original graph. The basic assumption is that a graph's semantic information can be preserved in its local structure.

Table I overviews the data augmentation for graphs. The default augmentation (dropping, perturbation, masking) ratio is set to 0.1, and the walk length is set to 10.

TABLE I. OVERVIEW OF DATA AUGMENTATION FOR GRAPHS

Data Augmentation	Type	Default Setting
Node Dropping	Nodes, edges	Bernoulli distribution (ratio = 0.1)
Edge Perturbation	Edges	Bernoulli distribution (ratio = 0.1)
Attribute Masking	Nodes	Uniform distribution (ratio = 0.1)
Subgraph Sampling	Nodes, edges	Random Walk (length = 10)

C. Graph Contrastive Learning

Motivated by recent developments in graph contrast learning, we propose a graph contrast learning framework for malware classification. As shown in Fig. 2, in graph contrast learning, pre-training is performed by maximizing the agreement between two augmented views of the same graph by contrast loss in the potential space. The framework consists of the following four main components:

1) Graph Data Augmentation: Throughout the GraphCL framework, given graph data G, two related augmented graphs, $\hat{G}_i, \hat{G}_j$, are generated as positive sample pairs by data augmentation.

2) GIN-based Encoder: GIN-based encoder $f(\cdot)$ is used to generate graph-level vector representation. There are three layers in the GIN-based encoder, and the hidden layer has 64 dimensions. Through the readout function, the embedding of all the nodes is summed to obtain initial graph representation h_i, h_j for augmented graphs $\hat{G}_i, \hat{G}_j$. Graph contrast learning does not apply any constraint to the GIN-based encoder.

3) Projection Head: Nonlinear transformation $g(\cdot)$, called a projection head, maps the augmented representations to another latent space. Contrast loss is computed in the latent space, and z_i, z_j are obtained by applying a two-layer perceptron (MLP).

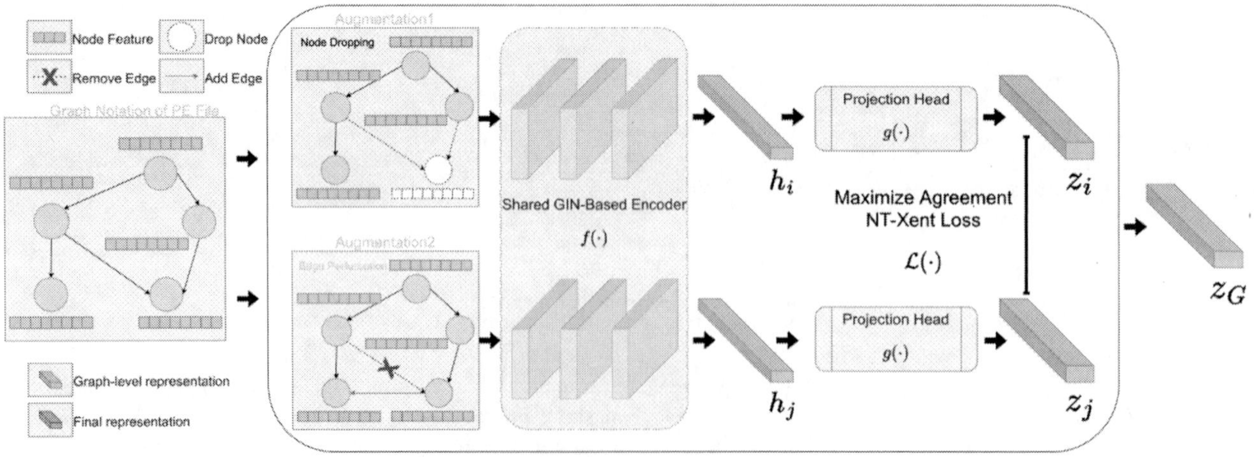

Figure 2. Proposed malware graph contrastive learning framework for graph representation generation

4) Contrastive Loss Function: Contrastive loss function $\mathcal{L}(\cdot)$ is defined to enforce the maximum consistency between positive pairs z_i, z_j and negative pairs. Here we exploit the normalized temperature-scale cross-entropy loss (NT-Xent) [21] [22] and obtain a graph-level final representation of z_G.

D. Graph Classification

By pre-training with GraphCL, we can obtain a valid graph representation z_G. To further verify the effectiveness of our method, different classification models can be chosen for the process, such as random forest, logistic regression, SVM, etc. We chose C-Support Vector Classification (SVC) as the algorithm to validate our pre-trained model's effectiveness.

IV. Implementation Details

We verified the effectiveness of our proposed contrastive learning framework by implementing it with open-source libraries. The implementation details are introduced in this section.

A. Malware Geometric Multi-Class Dataset

1) PE Files Source: Our PE file sample was obtained from the BODMAS Malware Dataset [23]. The software types of all the PE file samples used in our dataset are executable files under an x86-architecture Windows platform without any Dynamic Link Library (DLL) type.

2) Dataset Description: From the BODMAS dataset, we selected eight families of malware and took 500 samples from each family, for a total of 4000 samples in our dataset. Our dataset is named MGD-MULTI. The malware family distribution information is shown in Table II.

TABLE II. MALWARE FAMILY DISTRIBUTION OF MGD-MULTI

Family Name	Category Name	Origin Count	Selected Count	Graph Data Size
sfone	worm	4729	500	3.2 GB
upatre	trojan	3901	500	879.4MB
wabot	backdoor	3673	500	4.1 GB
benjamin	worm	1071	500	263.1MB
musecador	trojan	1054	500	1.5 GB
padodor	backdoor	655	500	2.9 GB
gandcrab	ransomware	617	500	6.6 GB
dinwod	dropper	509	500	3.3 GB
Total	-	16209	4000	22.7 GB

Due to the difficulty of collecting benign samples and the imbalanced data problem, we did not include white samples in our multi-class dataset. In our previous malware detection work [24], the MGD-BINARY dataset contained benign samples. We used almost the same GIN model to represent the PE samples, with a slightly different operation of the READOUT layer this time compared to the GIN model in our previous work, giving the final representation a higher vector dimensionality. Based on our previous research, we believe that the GIN model can effectively distinguish benign samples from malicious ones. In future work, we will add benign samples to our dataset.

Among the different types of malware, we chose families that are more common and have a relatively large number in BODMAS. Due to some limitations of the CFG extraction tool for the PE files we used, many samples couldn't be recognized, causing extraction failure. In addition, for large PE file samples, the process of extracting CFG is very time-consuming. Since the extraction of some samples will fail, we selected a family with more than 500 samples in BODMAS and relatively small original PE files. We further improved the efficiency by only selecting successful samples whose total extraction time is less than 20 seconds in which the total extraction time includes the time of the feature vectors generated by the pre-trained language model. We finally got our MGD-MULTI whose extracted graph data statistical information is shown in Table III.

TABLE III. GRAPH STATISTICS OF MGD-MULTI

Dataset	# Graphs	#Classes	#Features	Avg. #Nodes	Avg. #Edges
MGD-MULTI	4000	8	384	3861.75	5494.82

3) Dataset Splitting: We split 4000 pieces of data in MGD-MULTI into training, validation, and testing sets of 50%, 20%, and 30%, respectively. Since the results of the validation set and the test are similar, only the test set results are shown.

4) Pre-trained Language Model MiniLM: SentenceTransformers is a python framework for state-of-the-art sentence, text, and image embeddings. The initial work was described in a paper from the Sentence-Bidirectional Encoder Representations from Transformers (Sentence-BERT) [25]. We used the MiniLM model provided by the SentenceTransformers library with the model name, all-MiniLM-L6-v2. The model details used in this paper are shown in Table IV.

TABLE IV. PRE-TRAINED MINILM MODEL DETAILS

Name	all-MiniLM-L12-v2
Base Model	microsoft/MiniLM-L12-H384-uncased
Max Sequence Length	256
Dimensions	384
Normalized Embeddings	true
Size	120 MB
Pooling	Mean Pooling
Training Data	1B+ training pairs

5) Graph Contrastive Learning: PyGCL [26] is a PyTorch-based open-source Graph Contrastive Learning (GCL) library, which features modularized GCL components from published papers, standardized evaluation, and experiment management. The batch_size of all the experiments is 128, and the optimizer is Adam with a learning rate of 0.0001.

V. Evaluation and Discussion

In this section, we apply the GraphCL model and discuss the experiment results and limitations of our method.

A. Evaluation Metric

We used the following evaluation metrics to assess the performance of our proposed models:

- **The Micro-averaged F1 score** is defined as the harmonic mean of the precision and recall:

$$MicroF1\text{-}score = 2 \times \frac{\text{Micro-Precision} \times \text{Micro-Recall}}{\text{Micro-Precision} + \text{Micro-Recall}}$$

- **The Macro-averaged F1 score** is defined as the mean of the class-wise/label-wise F1-scores:

$$MacroF1\text{-}score = \frac{1}{N}\sum_{N}^{i=0} F1\text{-}score_i$$

where i is the class/label index and N is the number of classes/labels.

B. Evaluation Results

Next we apply the GraphCL model and discuss the experiment results of our method.

1) Different Data Augmentation Combination Results: We selected five different data augmentation methods: Identical (I), Edge Removing (ER), Node Dropping (ND), Feature Masking (FM), and Random Walk Subgraph (RWS). To compare the different data augmentation approaches on the GraphCL model, we used both data augmentation approaches for the input graph itself (Identical + Identical) as the GraphCL model baseline. We also tried different combinations of data augmentation, such as ER and ND, FM and ND, FM and ER, RWS and ER, RWS and ND, and RWS and FM. The experimental results are shown in Table V. The best two data augmentation combinations were RWS and FM. We obtained the best Micro-F1 (0.9958) and Macro-F1 (0.9959).

TABLE V. DIFFERENT AUGMENTATION COMBINATIONS

Method (+SVC)	Augmentation[1]	Micro-F1	Macro-F1
GraphCL	I + I	0.9883	0.9883
GraphCL	ER + ND	0.9925	0.9924
GraphCL	FM + ND	0.9942	0.9942
GraphCL	FM + ER	0.9942	0.9942
GraphCL	RWS[2]+ ER	0.9950	0.9949
GraphCL	RWS + ND	0.9950	0.9949
GraphCL	RWS + FM	0.9958	0.9959

[1] Default ratio setting is 0.1.
[2] RWS uses a default walk length setting of 10.

2) Best Combination with Different Ratio Results: In the previous set of experiments, we found that the best data augmentation combination is RWS + FM. Based on this combination, we also investigated the results on different ratios on the FM side, and the FM results on different ratios are shown in Table VI.

TABLE VI. BEST COMBINATION WITH DIFFERENT RATIO RESULTS

Method (+SVC)	Augmentation (Ratio)	Micro F1	Macro F1
GraphCL	RWS[1]+ FM (0.1)	0.9958	0.9959
GraphCL	RWS + FM (0.2)	0.9967	0.9967
GraphCL	RWS + FM (0.3)	0.9975	0.9976
GraphCL	RWS + FM (0.4)	0.9958	0.9958
GraphCL	RWS + FM (0.5)	0.9942	0.9941

[1] RWS uses a default walk length setting of 10.

3) Comparison of Different Methods: Our previous studies focused on supervised learning. This study is a graph contrastive learning method in an unsupervised setting. Baseline 1 is a direct graph-level encoding of an input graph using GIN as an encoder, and then the embedding effect is evaluated using SVC. Baseline 2 is data augmentation using the input graph itself. Baseline 3 is our previous work [24] on graph classification, trained using the GIN model in a supervised setting, with a two-layer MLP directly connected after the readout layer for direct classification. A comparison of different methods is shown in Table VII. GraphCL with a setting of RWS + FM (0.3) achieved the best classification results.

TABLE VII. COMPARISON OF DIFFERENT METHODS

Name	Method	Type	Micro-F1	Macro-F1
Baseline 1	GIN-Encoder + SVC	U[1]	0.9617	0.9620
Baseline 2	GraphCL (I + I) + SVC	U	0.9883	0.9883
Baseline 3	GIN + MLP (Previous work [24])	S[2]	0.9958	0.9957
Proposal	GraphCL (RWS + FM_0.3) + SVC	U	0.9975	0.9976

[1] U denotes unsupervised learning.
[2] S denotes supervised learning.

We used t-SNE technology to visualize the embedding of Baseline 1 and our proposed method. As shown in Fig. 3, the method of Baseline 1 has already clustered some

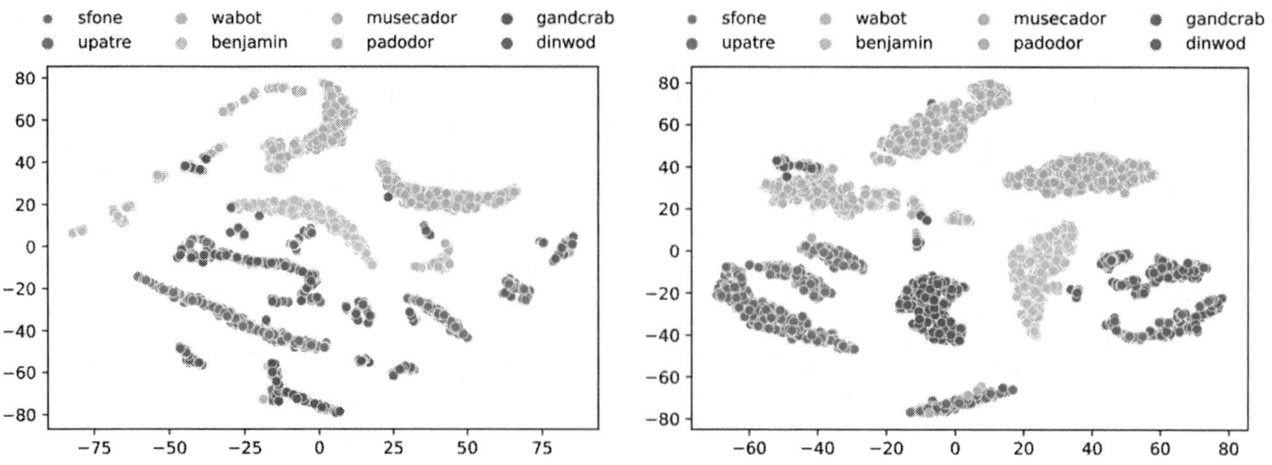

(a) Baseline 1: GIN-Encoder + SVC

(b) Proposal: GraphCL (SS+FM_0.3)

Figure 3. t-SNE visualization of Baseline 1 and Proposal

categories, such as the malware of the "padodor" family, but it cannot cluster the "gandcrab" family well. On the other hand, our comparative learning model proposal can better cluster different categories in the eight classes, and a large distance between different categories is maintained.

C. Current Limitations

GraphCL (I + I) is a combination of two Identical, and the effect is equivalent to turning a training set of N samples into 2N samples. The same data model is learned twice for the same data, so the obtained result naturally outperforms GIN-Encoder. The RWS + FM method is most effective because neither method changes the structural information of the original graph. The RWS method samples a subgraph that is smaller than the structure of the original graph, but still retains most of the original graph's structure. For the FM method, the original graph structure is not changed at all, but the values of some dimensions of the node feature vectors are masked, which makes the node features more robust. On the contrary, the other two methods (ER and ND) change the original graph structure more, so the results are lowered.

Because of the relatively large graph structure we extracted from the PE file and the high dimensionality of the nodes in each graph (384 dimensions), our result still leads to a slow training of the GraphCL model even though the dataset size is not too large, only 4000 pieces of data.

The training stage requires around ten minutes with GeForce RTX 3090. We desire a better way to generate node features, such as a lower dimensional in a method that retains its effectiveness.

VI. Conclusion

We proposed the unsupervised learning of different families of malware using graph comparison learning and the multi-classification of learned vectors using SVC and obtained good results. We extracted the CFG of the malware, embedded the disassembly code in a basic block through a large pre-trained language model MiniLM, and obtained a directed graph with node features. The advantage of a directed graph is that it contains the call structure information of the sample in addition to the features of each node. We also produced a multi-classification dataset: MDG-MULTI. Unsupervised GraphCL-based malware classification methods have surpassed graph-based supervised learning methods, such as the Graph Isomorphism Network (GIN) for graph classification. In future work, we will shift our focus to unsupervised learning.

Acknowledgments

This research was partially supported by MEXT/JSPS KAKENHI, Grant Numbers JP19H04108 and 19K11961, and financially supported by JST SPRING, Grant Number JP-MJSP2125. We also thank the "Interdisciplinary Frontier Next-Generation Researcher Program of the Tokai Higher Education and Research System."

References

[1] H. S. Anderson and P. Roth, "EMBER: an open dataset for training static PE malware machine learning models," *CoRR*, vol. abs/1804.04637, pp. 1–8, 2018.

[2] B. Athiwaratkun and J. W. Stokes, "Malware classification with LSTM and GRU language models and a character-level CNN," *ICASSP 2017*, pp. 2482–2486, 2017.

[3] G. E. Dahl, J. W. Stokes, L. Deng, and D. Yu, "Large-scale malware classification using random projections and neural networks," *ICASSP 2013*, pp. 3422–3426, 2013.

[4] R. Pascanu, J. W. Stokes, H. Sanossian, M. Marinescu, and A. Thomas, "Malware classification with recurrent networks," *ICASSP 2015*, pp. 1916–1920, 2015.

[5] F. Cohen, "Computer Viruses: Theory and Experiments," *Computers & security, Vol. 6, No. 1*, pp. 22–35, 1987.

[6] J. O. Kephart, G. B. Sorkin, W. C. Arnold, D. M. Chess, G. Tesauro, and S. R. White, "Biologically Inspired Defenses Against Computer Viruses," *IJCAI 1995, Vol. 2*, pp. 985–996, 1995.

[7] J. Saxe and K. Berlin, "Deep neural network based malware detection using two dimensional binary program features," *MALWARE 2015*, pp. 11–20, 2015.

[8] E. Raff, J. Barker, J. Sylvester, R. Brandon, B. Catanzaro, and C. K. Nicholas, "Malware Detection by Eating a Whole EXE," *AAAI Workshops 2018*, pp. 268–276, 2018.

[9] E. Raff, J. Sylvester, and C. Nicholas, "Learning the PE Header, Malware Detection with Minimal Domain Knowledge," *AISec@CCS 2017*, pp. 121–132, 2017.

[10] Y. Chen, S. Wang, D. She, and S. Jana, "On Training Robust PDF Malware Classifiers," *USENIX Security 2020*, pp. 2343–2360, 2020.

[11] S. E. Coull and C. Gardner, "Activation Analysis of a Byte-Based Deep Neural Network for Malware Classification," *SP Workshops 2019*, pp. 21–27, 2019.

[12] E. M. Rudd, F. N. Ducau, C. Wild, K. Berlin, and R. E. Harang, "ALOHA: Auxiliary Loss Optimization for Hypothesis Augmentation," *USENIX Security 2019*, pp. 303–320, 2019.

[13] Y. Wang, Y. Sun, Z. Liu, S. E. Sarma, M. M. Bronstein, and J. M. Solomon, "Dynamic Graph CNN for Learning on Point Clouds," *ACM Transactions on Graphics (TOG), Vol. 38, Issue 5*, pp. 1–12, 2019.

[14] K. Xu, W. Hu, J. Leskovec, and S. Jegelka, "How powerful are graph neural networks?," in *Proceedings of the 7th International Conference on Learning Representations (ICLR 2019)*, pp. 1–17, 2019.

[15] A. Narayanan, M. Chandramohan, R. Venkatesan, L. Chen, Y. Liu, and S. Jaiswal, "graph2vec: Learning Distributed Representations of Graphs," *CoRR*, vol. abs/1707.05005, pp. 1–8, 2017.

[16] F. Sun, J. Hoffmann, V. Verma, and J. Tang, "Infograph: Unsupervised and semi-supervised graph-level representation learning via mutual information maximization," in *Proceedings of the 8th International Conference on Learning Representations (ICLR 2020)*, pp. 1–16, 2020.

[17] L. Yang, W. Guo, Q. Hao, A. Ciptadi, A. Ahmadzadeh, X. Xing, and G. Wang, "CADE: Detecting and Explaining Concept Drift Samples for Security Applications," *USENIX Security 2021*, pp. 2327–2344, 2021.

[18] M. Dib, S. Torabi, E. Bou-Harb, N. Bouguila, and C. Assi, "Evoliot: A self-supervised contrastive learning framework for detecting and characterizing evolving iot malware variants," in *Proceedings of ASIA CCS '22: ACM Asia Conference on Computer and Communications Security*, pp. 452–466, 2022.

[19] W. Wang, F. Wei, L. Dong, H. Bao, N. Yang, and M. Zhou, "MiniLM: Deep Self-Attention Distillation for Task-Agnostic Compression of Pre-Trained Transformers," *CoRR*, vol. abs/2002.10957, pp. 1–15, 2020.

[20] A. Grover and J. Leskovec, "node2vec: Scalable feature learning for networks," in *Proceedings of the 22nd ACM SIGKDD International Conference on Knowledge Discovery and Data Mining*, pp. 855–864, 2016.

[21] A. van den Oord, Y. Li, and O. Vinyals, "Representation learning with contrastive predictive coding," *CoRR*, vol. abs/1807.03748, pp. 1–13, 2018.

[22] Y. You, T. Chen, Y. Sui, T. Chen, Z. Wang, and Y. Shen, "Graph contrastive learning with augmentations," *CoRR*, vol. abs/2010.13902, pp. 1–12, 2020.

[23] L. Yang, A. Ciptadi, I. Laziuk, A. Ahmadzadeh, and G. Wang, "BODMAS: An Open Dataset for Learning based Temporal Analysis of PE Malware," *DLS 2021*, pp. 78–84, 2021.

[24] Y. Gao, H. Hasegawa, Y. Yamaguchi, and H. Shimada, "Malware detection using attributed cfg generated by pre-trained language model with graph isomorphism network," in *Proceedings of the 12th IEEE International Workshop on Network Technologies for Security, Administration and Protection (NETSAP 2022)*, pp. 1495–1501, 2022.

[25] N. Reimers and I. Gurevych, "Sentence-BERT: Sentence Embeddings using Siamese BERT-Networks," *CoRR*, vol. abs/1908.10084, pp. 1–11, 2019.

[26] Y. Zhu, Y. Xu, Q. Liu, and S. Wu, "An empirical study of graph contrastive learning," *CoRR*, vol. abs/2109.01116, pp. 1–25, 2021.

IDE Plugins for Secure Android Applications Development: Analysis & Classification Study

Mohammed El Amin TEBIB
Mariem Graa
Oum-El-Kheir Aktouf
Univ. Grenoble Alpes, Grenoble INP, LCIS lab., 26000 Valence,France*
**Institute of Engineering Univ. Grenoble Alpes*
email: mohammed-el-amin.tebib@univ-grenoble-alpes.fr
email: mariem.graa@univ-grenoble-alpes.fr
email: oum-el-kheir.aktouf@univ-grenoble-alpes.fr

Pascal Andre
LS2N
University of Nantes France
email: pascal.andre@ls2n.fr

***Abstract*—In order to increase the security of Android applications, much effort is realised to assist developers in building secure code that is robust against security attacks. In fact, more attention is given to secure the development life-cycle, from requirement analysis to design, coding to test, and every step of the development process. Many security Integrated Development Environment (IDE) plug-ins have been proposed to assist developers in building secure applications. However, as far as we know, there is no study reviewing the existing tools and their effectiveness in detecting known vulnerabilities. The objective of this paper is to close this gap. We developed a classification framework of the current existing security IDE plug-ins in the context of Android application development. This classification framework allows to highlight salient features about 14 selected tools such as: (i) the analysis-based approach, (ii) the vulnerabilities checks coverage, and (iii) the development stage on which these tools could be employed. Obtained results allowed to establish an overview of secure Android applications development. Limits such as: tools unavailability, benchmarks incompleteness, and the need of dynamic analysis approaches are among the significant findings of this study. We believe this work provides useful information for future research on IDE plug-ins for detecting Android related vulnerabilities.**

Keywords*—*Android; Secure Coding; Classification Framework; IDE Plugins.

I. INTRODUCTION

Mobile applications have become an integral part of our daily life. Android operating systems maintain a leading position with the most significant market share *"70 percent on Feb. 2022"* [1]. In order to address Android users' expectations, the development of Android applications has been growing at a high rate. As a result, Android applications have become an ideal target for attackers to exploit users private data. According to the official MITRE organisation data-source for Android vulnerabilities [2], recent years witnessed the most significant increase of Android security threats, *"1034 vulnerabilities the last couple years"*. And it continues to increase with *"34 vulnerabilities for only the two first months of 2022"*. These vulnerabilities could be exploited to create harmful actions, such as creating malwares and stealing users private information.

In exploratory studies [3][4], Android developers practices are pointed out as the main reason for security vulnerabilities: considering security as a third party activity; lacking awareness about security measures; and making decision in an ad-hoc manner are among the main reasons for considering developers as the first creators of security vulnerabilities. To deal with these issues, both industry and academia have started recently to integrate security into the software development life-cycle, shifting *from* just ensuring the development speed with letting the security checks to external stakeholders, *to* employing new software development paradigms such as **DevSecOps** [5]. In these paradigms, developers are forced to adhere a secure development process by means of training sessions and analysis tools. In this context, it becomes essential to provide Android developers with an overview of existing security analysis plugins. This is the main contribution of our paper. After selecting a sample of open source IDE tools, we proposed a classification framework based on three dimensions: 1) the analysis based approach (static or dynamic); 2) the covered security vulnerabilities by each tool; and 3) the development stage on which these tools could be employed. To limit the scope of our study, the following factors are considered:

- We consider only tools integrated in the IDE environment,
- For industrial tools, we select only free and available ones,
- For academic tools, if the tool is not available, our analysis will be performed through reading the corresponding published paper.

The rest of the paper is organised as follows. Section II introduces material to understand the context and the comparison methodology. Section III summarises the existing related works reviewing the IDE plugins used for securing Android applications development. Section IV presents our proposed classification frameworks. Based on this framework, we present the results of our search and the analysis phases in section V. We give a set of resulting observations in Section VI. Finally, Section VII concludes the paper and provides tracks for future work.

II. BACKGROUND

Android provides a layered software stack composed of native libraries and a framework as an environment for running Android applications. Developers implement different types of applications: (i) **natives**, that restrict their access to Application Programming Interfaces (APIs) provided by the framework and, (ii) **hybrids**, that could also be web applications. Since considering the security of hybrid applications should cover a wide range of potential security issues coming from the web, our study covers only native applications. These applications are built using four types of components: *activities*, *services*, *broadcast receivers* and *content providers*.

Each Android application runs within its own sandbox, which is an isolation mechanism during runtime. Consequently, applications cannot communicate without having proper permissions. Thus, permission system restricts the access to applications, to its components and to system resources (contacts, locations, images, etc) to those having the *required permissions*. Permissions are declared by developers in the manifest file. Their manipulation is shown in many studies as the source of many security issues[6]: privilege escalation resulting from the over declaration of permissions [7], communication issues resulting from the use of undocumented message types of intents [8], etc.

We focus on security vulnerabilities **(Vi)** that could be mistakenly introduced by developers and exploited to craft attacks **(Ai)**. Based on the existing benchmarks such as *Ghera*[9] that contains open source applications implementing vulnerabilities, we started by considering a not exhaustive list of vulnerabilities that belong to the following class of attacks (we intend to extend this list in the future).

1) **A1**. Privilege escalation **(PE)**: this attack occurs when an application with less permissions gains access to the components of a higher privileged application by exploiting one of the following vulnerabilities: *Pending Intent* with empty *base action* (**A1.V1**); Fragments Dynamic Load (**A1.V2**); privileged component export (**A1.V3**); permissions over-privilege (**A1.V4**) or weak permissions checking (**A1.V5**).
2) **A2**. Data Injection: It consists of a malicious manipulation of data to gain control over the system by exploiting Ordered Broadcasts (**A2.V1**); Sticky Broadcasts (**A2.V2**); Components use *call(args)* to invoke provider-defined method (**A2.V3**) or External Storage (**A2.V4**)
3) **A3**. Code Injection: consists of injecting potentially malicious code that is then interpreted/executed by the application using Dynamic code loading without verifying the integrity and authenticity of the loaded code (**A3.V1**)
4) **A4**. Information leaks: they occur when an application private data are accessed by unauthorised applications using Block Cipher algorithm in ECB mode (**A4.V1**) or CBC mode (**A4.V2**) or encryption key stored in the source code (**A4.V3**) or loading files from internal to external storage (**A4.V4**)
5) **A5**. Android components hijack by exploiting Activities that start in a new task (**A5.V1**); Applications with low priority activities (**A5.V2**) or Pending Intent with implicit base intent (**A5.V3**).

Note that for sake of space, more details of each vulnerability are provided in Appendix [10].

The effectiveness of an analysis tool in detecting known vulnerabilities is closely related to the analysis method used by the tool. Analysis approaches are generally classified into 3 groups: (i) Static analysis, which inspects the program without running it to identify coding flaws. It is performed over the Abstract Syntax Tree (AST) that represents the syntax of a programming language as a hierarchical tree-like structure. Furthermore, formal verification can be used to identify errors in code design. (ii) Dynamic analysis, which evaluates the behaviour of the program while it is running based on different methods among them: (1) bytecode Instrumentation to determine how information flows in the program; and (ii) software testing techniques such as Fuzzing to find unknown vulnerabilities. Finally, (iii) Hybrid analysis combines both static and dynamic analysis to improve analysis results.

III. RELATED WORKS

Recent works [11][12] present a general review of existing tools for mobile applications. They list salient features such as their supported IDEs, applicable languages and their abilities to detect security vulnerabilities. However, they do not focus on the Android ecosystem. We focus on Android, and provide a more consistent analysis and finer applicability assets.

Mejía et al. [13] conducted a systematic review to establish the state of the art of secure mobile development. They found seven solutions for assisting secure development. These solutions are classified based on: 1) the type of the use (methodologies, models, standards or strategies); and 2) the related security concern (authentication, authorisation, data storage, data access and data transfer). After analysing the results of this research, we consider that the number of solutions is limited regarding the real existing ones in the literature. In addition, we found that none of the presented solutions is proposed as a tool or a plugin for secure development. In our work, the search and analysis process is more substantial. Indeed, we present a more important number of solutions, which are intended to be used as IDE plugins.

The closest work to our research is the assessment study proposed by Mitra et al. [14]. It evaluates the effectiveness of vulnerability detection tools for Android applications. The authors reviewed 64 tools and empirically evaluated 14 vulnerability detection tools against the *Ghera* benchmark [9] that implements each vulnerability inside a single Android application. As a result, they found that the evaluated tools for Android applications are very limited in their ability to detect known vulnerabilities. The sample of tools in this study is intended for use by pen-testers after the application release. In addition, the evaluation process is limited to the academic tools. In our work, we are interested in academic and industrial free tools, which are specifically designed as security assisting tools.

We did not find existing research work that studies Android IDE plugins from a security perspective. After analysing the existing benchmarks, we consider that *Ghera* repository is the most useful means for evaluating the analysis tools. Indeed, *Ghera* summarises a non-exhaustive list of well known vulnerabilities related to the development of Android applications. It provides an open source Android application implementing each vulnerability. Therefore, to conduct our study, we used the same benchmark as Mitra et al. [14] to evaluate the list of selected plugins.

IV. Classification Framework and Methodology

The classification framework aims to answer the following questions: (i) **Which** IDE plugins are used to check Android application vulnerabilities?; (ii) **How** the selected tools analyse the checked vulnerabilities? (the adopted analysis approach); (iii) **What** are the vulnerabilities among the presented ones are covered by the selected tools?; and finally (iv) **When** these tools can be used in the development process (specification, design, coding and testing). We present in Figure 1 the followed search methodology to identify relevant security assistance tools.

A. Overview of the search methodology

This phase highlights the tools used by designers and/or developers to prevent security issues in Android applications. Our primary source of information were published academic reviews [11] and public GitHub repositories [15] [16]. For industrial plugins, we consider only free and available ones extracted from the OWASP list[17]. We also included the tools we investigated while we were building the PermDroid[18], a tool to prevent permissions related security issues based on formal methods. On the other hand, some excluding criteria are considered: (i) Tools that do not work during the development process like Anadroid [19] (malware detection), and MassVet [20] (analyses packaged applications in Google-Play store); (ii) Tools that cannot be used within the IDE *e.g.* ComDroid [21] warns pen-testers of exploitable inter applications communication errors related to the released applications (see investigations [22][14]); (iii) Tools that are integrated in the IDE but are not concerned by security vulnerabilities, like PMD [23]. These tools are used for checking coding standards, class design problems, but cannot be used for identifying code smells related to security issues.

B. Shallow analysis

The analysis process here is performed through only reading the available documentation and/or the published corresponding papers. We dug the documentations on many stages. Some vulnerabilities such as **A1.V4** (the over-privilege use of permissions) have been investigated by some of our students and revised by the first author of this paper. The remaining vulnerabilities analysis is realised by the first author and revised by the second author. Other features relevant to our study are also extracted.

C. Deep analysis

In this phase we perform an experimental analysis that completes the preceding one. It consists of performing an empirical evaluation by *running* the selected tools against the defined vulnerabilities according to the evaluation process summarised in Figure 2.

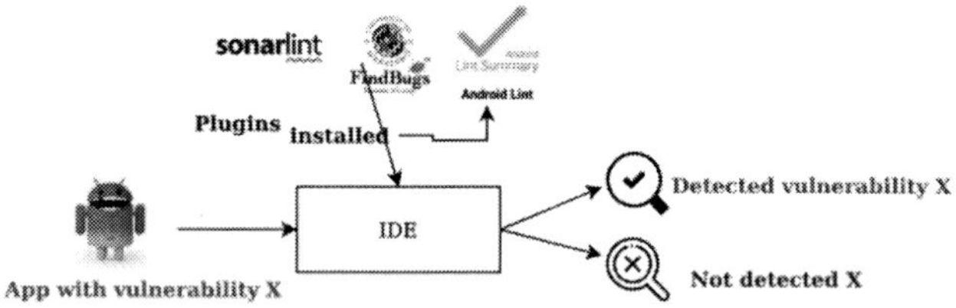

Figure 2. Deep Analysis Process

This evaluation is conducted for only available and free tools such as Sonarlint, Androidlint, FixDroid and FindBugs. We attempted to experiment more tools but this was not possible due to the unavailability of the tools. We contacted the authors of PerHelper, 9Fix and Vandroid but we did not receive an answer yet. Consequently, we decided to perform a second iteration on the documentation analysis for the unavailable tools instead of experimenting them (which was not possible). Finally, as our study is on vulnerabilities that could be found at the code level, our deep analysis could not be applied on tools such as Sema, PoliDroid–As, Page because the inputs of these tools are respectively: GUI Storyboards for Sema, Textual specification for PoliDroid–As and Page of the application, and not the application source code.

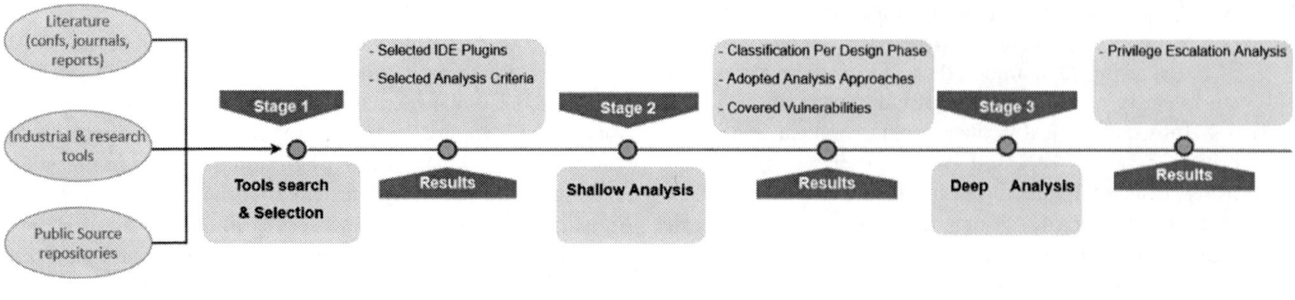

Figure 1. Search Methodology

TABLE I
IDE SECURITY ANALYSIS TOOLS FOR ANDROID APPLICATIONS

Tool Name	Ref.	Year	SD Stage	Focus	Approach	Method	Availability	AV
Curbing	[7]	2011	CR	Permission Over-privilege	Static, Manual	AST	No	2.2
Lintent	[24]	2013	CR	Communication	static	FM	Ye	4.x
PermitMe	[25]	2014	CR	Permission Over-privilege	Static	AST	No	5.0
Page	[26]	2014	Spec	Privacy policies	Static	NL	No	-
Vandroid	[27]	2018	CR	Communication	Static	FM	No	9.0
Androidlint	[28]	2019	CR	Communication	Static	AST	Yes	all
Sema	[29]	2019	Design	General Security Properties	Static	FM	Yes	10
PerHelper	[30]	2019	CR	Permission Over-privilege	Static	AST	No	10
PoliDroid-As	[31]	2017	Spec	Privacy security policies	Static	NLP	No	8
9Fix	[32]	2021	CR	General Code smells	Static	AST	No	12
Sonarlint	[33]	2021	CR	General Code smells	Static	TA	Yes	12
FindBugs	[34]	2016	CR	General Code smells	Static	AST	Yes	7
Cocunut	[35]	2018	Spec	Privacy policies	Static	H	Yes	-
FixDroid	[36]	2017	CR	General Code smells	Static	AST	Yes	7

[1] AST: Abstract Syntax Tree; CR: Code Review; FM: Formal Methods; Spec: Specification;
[2] SD Stage: Software Development Stage; AV: Android Version

V. ANALYSIS AND EVALUATION RESULTS

In this Section, we present analysis results of tools with regards to the classification criteria presented in Section IV.

A. *Shallow analysis*

1) IDE plugins: As a result of the applied selection process. We present 14 plugin for Android vulnerabilities analysis (*cf.* Table I). We reported for each tool the software development stage (SD stage), the type of covered security vulnerabilities (Focus), the analysis approach, the analysis method, its availability and the Android Version (AV), a useful up-to-date information.

2) Analysis approaches: 98% of the analysis approaches are static, mainly AST analysis and formal methods.

- **Static AST Analysis** Most of IDE plugins investigate statically the program AST provided by the IDE such as Sonarlint, FindBugs and AndroidLint. Other tools, such as PerHelper, PermitMe and Curbing also investigate the AST to find the declared permissions in the application and the list of API calls requiring those permissions. The goal is to detect extra declared permissions that are not associated to any API call.
- **Formal Methods**: Lintent analyses the data-flow to formally check flow information with regards to security properties. Lintent uses the Formal Calculus for reasoning on the Android inter-component communication API, and Type and Effect to statically prevent privilege escalation attacks on well typed components. In the same line, Sema uses Formal Verification of security properties in order to generate a secure code.

When comparing our observations with the security analysis methods presented in Section II, we found that only some static ones are adopted by studied plugins. Dynamic and hybrid approaches are not referred despite their advantages. We underline this point in detail in Section VI.

3) Security vulnerabilities: The shallow analysis covers all the vulnerabilities of Appendix [10]. For each category, we observe whether the associated vulnerabilities are covered (or not) by the tools. We consider True Positive [TP] (resp. False Negative [FN]) cases: a vulnerability is present and detected (resp. not detected) by the tool. We identified three main classes:

- Tools that are specialised in a specific and unique security concern were *easy* to investigate. Based on the corresponding published papers for the plugins: Curbing, PermitMe and PerHelper. They are clearly specialised in detecting privilege escalation attacks **(A1)** resulting from the extra use of permissions **(V4)** in the application. For other tools such as 9Fix, the list of covered vulnerabilities was explicitly declared in the related paper. Consequently, it was easy to know that these tools detect **A3.V1** vulnerability. Last but not least, Coconut, FindBug, Page and PoliDroid-As cover other types of vulnerabilities not included in our study.
- Tools specialised in detecting a specific type of attacks but the number of covered vulnerabilities is too large are *less easy* to investigate. As an example, Lintent could theoretically detect a large number of vulnerabilities as it formalises a notion of safety against privilege escalation. Based on the related published paper, it was not easy to decide whether the tool detects the vulnerability or not as the described formal model was too general. Fortunately, we found the list of covered vulnerabilities mentioned in the corresponding git repository [37]. Thus, we found that **A1.V1**, **A1.V4** and **A5.V4** are covered by the tool. For Sema it is explicitly declared that it covers all the vulnerabilities present in *Ghera*. However, we could not experiment the tool as the inputs of Sema are graphical storyboards and not source code.
- Finally, for industrial tools such as Androidlint, Sonarlint, FixDroid, it was hard to investigate the covered vulnerabilities based on the documentation. The scope of these tools is general and the documentation is too large. We found that the following vulnerabilities: **A2.V1, A4.V1, A4.V2, A4.V3** are covered by Sonarlint. For the remaining properties, we did not found any information

indicating whether they are covered by these tools or not.

4) Design Level: It is broadly admitted that security concerns should be handled as early as possible during the development. Secure development lifecycle (SDLC) methodologies have been adopted by many software organisations, e.g., Microsoft through their Microsoft Security Development Lifecycle (SDL) [38], OWASP with their SDLC and Software Assurance Maturity Model (SAMM) processes [39], etc. Table I shows that most tools focus on coding:

- *Specification*: PoliDoid–AS, Page, Cocunut
- *Design*: Sema, Vandroid
- *Coding & Testing*: Curbing, Lintent, PermitMe, Androidlint, Vandroid, 9Fix, PerHelper, Sonarlint, FindBugs, FixDroid.

On the one hand, we found that most of IDE plugins are considered at the *coding* phase of the development life cycle. They act as code review tools notifying developers about their "unconscious" security issues. On the other hand, a few works allowing security checks at *specification*, *design* and *verification* phases have been proposed.

B. Deep analysis results

The objective of this part of our study is to confirm shallow analysis results with an experimental evaluation using Android application benchmarks. We mainly focused on the considered vulnerabilities, especially the A1 (privilege escalation) attacks. Indeed, we found in CVE details [2], that privilege escalation witnessed the most significant increase among the Android security threats in the last couple years. Vulnerabilities related to Privilege escalation also represent 69.9% of attacks against Android applications. The results are published in the *technical report* [10].

We can observe that the deep evaluation confirmed that the following tools: Curbing, PermitMe, and PerHelper are specifically oriented to detect over-privilege vulnerabilities (A1.V4) and not the other vulnerabilities (A1.V1, A1.V2, A1.V3, A1.V5). Our deep evaluation also confirmed that none of the privilege escalation vulnerabilities are covered by Sonarlint, FindBugs, FixDroid and Androidlint. For tools that are not available (Vandroid and 9Fix), an additional careful documentation-based analysis also confirmed that none of the privilege escalation vulnerabilities is covered.

To conclude, none of the studied tools covers all the privilege escalation attacks and we plan to tackle this limitation.

VI. Discussion

Our analysis study raised some lessons:

- Tools outdatedness and availability: Since the creation of the first version of Android in 2008, the system and the framework levels have shown many security improvements to protect users privacy. A new Android version is released every six months. As a consequence, most of the security assisting IDE plugins become outdated, and not able to deal anymore with new types of application components, or new released APIs. Four factors are of interest when considering outdated tools: (i) the date of the last commit, (ii) the supported IDE type, (iii) information leaks, (iv) the integration of the tools within the last IDE versions. Besides observing that the date of the last commit for many tools is old, most tools are still supported by Eclipse only, which is no more used for developing Android applications. Furthermore, among the proposed tools, only a few is available for use in real Android development projects. Hence, among the 14 analysed tools, eight academic tools are not available for use.
- Tools Effectiveness: Tools such as Lintent, PerHelper, PermitMe are based on Felt et al. [40] permission mapping over-privileged applications detection. This permission mapping is outdated and does not consider an accurate permission set. Our study shows that none of the assessed industrial plugin covers over-privilege vulnerabilities.
- Analysis approaches for security: as observed in Section II, most tools use static approaches to extract information that enables to check the validity of security properties patterns. As a first direction of improvement, static analysis performances of IDE plugin could be improved by adopting complementary analysis techniques such as Symbolic Execution, to allow sound results in case of inter-component communication analysis. Other static analysis techniques have started being used by static analysis tools like SonarQube. The latter tool performs Static Taint Analysis to detect vulnerabilities related to fault injection. Finally, we were surprised to observe that none of the investigated tools takes advantage from the integrated IDE Android simulator to perform dynamic analysis. Adopting dynamic analysis approaches could be an interesting direction to improve security IDE plugin analysis results. This enables to analyse API calls performed dynamically. Furthermore, other dynamic analysis techniques could be used such as dynamic code instrumentation to exploit run-time source code, and fuzzing as a software testing technique for automatic input generation.
- Benchmark availability and incompleteness: *Ghera* is an excellent reference to be used to evaluate the security analysis plugins that deal with open source projects, as it implements an open source application with most known vulnerabilities. However, it suffers from the lack of some vulnerabilities, such as service hijack. It also suffers from the lack of a complete description (component hijacking description). Availability of more relevant benchmarks could be a real breakthrough towards more thorough security analysis.

VII. Conclusion and Future Work

In order to secure Android applications development against software vulnerabilities, it is necessary to integrate security in the software development cycle for assisting developers. In this paper, we provided Android developers an overview of existing security analysis plugins capabilities with regards to Android application development. To provide meaningful and exploitable results, we performed two types of analysis: a shallow analysis, then an experimental analysis for evaluating the selected IDE plugins security coverage against the defined vulnerabilities. In the empirical part of our study, we mainly focused our efforts on privilege escalation vulnerabilities as these ones are among the hardest vulnerabilities to mitigate, and are related to a complementary research work within our team. Our study highlighted two main research gaps, which could benefit from future work such as: the need of developing tools that cover the whole life-cycle; and enrich the existing benchmarks by new open source applications implementing other Android related vulnerabilities.

The main perspectives related to our work will consider: 1) Extending the list of analysed vulnerabilities to better cover the presented attacks; 2) adding new attacks related to networking, web and phishing; 3) and completing the empirical analysis step.

REFERENCES

[1] Global market share held by mobile operating systems since 2009. [Online]. Available: https://www.statista.com/statistics/272698/global-market-share-held-by-mobile-operating-systems-since-2009/

[2] Cve details: Android vulnerability statistics. Retrv: 12, 2021. [Online]. Available: https://www.cvedetails.com/product/19997/

[3] R. Balebako, A. Marsh, J. Lin, J. I. Hong, and L. Cranor, "The Privacy and Security Behaviors of Smartphone App Developers," in *USEC Workshop, NDSS 2014*. The Internet Society, 2014.

[4] G. L. Scoccia, A. Peruma, V. Pujols, I. Malavolta, and D. E. Krutz, "Permission issues in open-source android apps: An exploratory study," in *2019 19th International Working Conference on Source Code Analysis and Manipulation (SCAM)*. IEEE, 2019, pp. 238–249.

[5] Z. Ahmed and S. C. Francis, "Integrating security with devsecops: Techniques and challenges," in *2019 International Conference on Digitization (ICD)*. IEEE, 2019, pp. 178–182.

[6] A. K. Jha, S. Lee, and W. J. Lee, "Developer mistakes in writing android manifests: An empirical study of configuration errors," in *2017 IEEE/ACM 14th International Conference on Mining Software Repositories (MSR)*. IEEE, 2017, pp. 25–36.

[7] T. Vidas, N. Christin, and L. Cranor, "Curbing android permission creep," in *Proceedings of the Web 2.0 Security and Privacy 2011 workshop (W2SP 2011)*, 2021.

[8] W. Ahmad, C. Kästner, J. Sunshine, and J. Aldrich, "Inter-app communication in android: Developer challenges," in *2016 IEEE/ACM 13th Working Conference on Mining Software Repositories (MSR)*. IEEE, 2016, pp. 177–188.

[9] Ghera repository. Retrv: 07, 2022. [Online]. Available: https://bitbucket.org/secure-it-i/android-app-vulnerability-benchmarks/

[10] "Ide plugins evaluation against privileges escalation attacks," TR-2022. [Online]. Available: https://uncloud.univ-nantes.fr/index.php/s/mzwoC44xs5xiowN

[11] J. Li, S. Beba, and M. M. Karlsen, "Evaluation of open-source ide plugins for detecting security vulnerabilities," in *Proceedings of the Evaluation and Assessment on Software Engineering*, 2019, pp. 200–209.

[12] A. Z. Baset and T. Denning, "Ide plugins for detecting input-validation vulnerabilities," in *2017 IEEE Security and Privacy Workshops (SPW)*. IEEE, 2017, pp. 143–146.

[13] J. Mejía, P. Maciel, M. Muñoz, and Y. Quiñonez, "Frameworks to develop secure mobile applications: A systematic literature review," in *World Conference on Information Systems and Technologies*. Springer, 2020, pp. 137–146.

[14] V.-P. Ranganath and J. Mitra, "Are free android app security analysis tools effective in detecting known vulnerabilities?" *Empirical Software Engineering*, vol. 25, no. 1, pp. 178–219, 2020.

[15] Android references. Retrv: 03, 2022. [Online]. Available: https://github.com/impillar/AndroidReferences

[16] Android security assessment tools. Retrv: 09, 2021. [Online]. Available: https://bitbucket.org/secure-it-i/android-app-vulnerability-benchmarks/

[17] Owasp - source code analysis tools. Retrv: 03, 2022. [Online]. Available: https://owasp.org/www-community/Source_Code_Analysis_Tools

[18] M. E. A. Tebib, P. André, O.-E.-K. Aktouf, and M. Graa, "Assisting developers in preventing permissions related security issues in android applications," in *European Dependable Computing Conference*. Springer, 2021, pp. 132–143.

[19] S. Liang, A. W. Keep, M. Might, S. Lyde, T. Gilray, P. Aldous, and D. Van Horn, "Sound and precise malware analysis for android via pushdown reachability and entry-point saturation," in *Proceedings of the Third ACM workshop on Security and privacy in smartphones & mobile devices*, 2013, pp. 21–32.

[20] K. Chen, P. Wang, Y. Lee, X. Wang, N. Zhang, H. Huang, W. Zou, and P. Liu, "Finding unknown malice in 10 seconds: Mass vetting for new threats at the {Google-Play} scale," in *24th USENIX Security Symposium (USENIX Security 15)*, 2015, pp. 659–674.

[21] E. Chin, A. P. Felt, K. Greenwood, and D. Wagner, "Analyzing inter-application communication in android," in *Proceedings of the 9th international conference on Mobile systems, applications, and services*, 2011, pp. 239–252.

[22] I. Ul Haq and T. A. Khan, "Penetration frameworks and development issues in secure mobile application development: A systematic literature review," *IEEE Access*, 2021.

[23] Pmd-idea. Retrv: 03, 2022. [Online]. Available: https://plugins.jetbrains.com/plugin/4596-qaplug--pmd

[24] M. Bugliesi, S. Calzavara, and A. Spanò, "Lintent: Towards security type-checking of android applications," in *Formal techniques for distributed systems*. Springer, 2013, pp. 289–304.

[25] E. Bello-Ogunu and M. Shehab, "Permitme: integrating android permissioning support in the ide," in *Proceedings of the 2014 Workshop on Eclipse Technology eXchange*, 2014, pp. 15–20.

[26] M. Rowan and J. Dehlinger, "Encouraging privacy by design concepts with privacy policy auto-generation in eclipse (page)," in *Proceedings of the 2014 Workshop on Eclipse Technology eXchange*, 2014, pp. 9–14.

[27] A. Nirumand, B. Zamani, and B. T. Ladani, "Vandroid: A framework for vulnerability analysis of android applications using a model-driven reverse engineering technique," *Softw. Pract. Exp.*, vol. 49, no. 1, pp. 70–99, 2019. [Online]. Available: https://doi.org/10.1002/spe.2643

[28] Improve your code with lint checks. Retrv: 03, 2022. [Online]. Available: https://developer.android.com/studio/write/lint

[29] J. Mitra, V.-P. Ranganath, T. Amtoft, and M. Higgins, "Sema: Extending and analyzing storyboards to develop secure android apps," *arXiv preprint arXiv:2001.10052*, 2020.

[30] G. Xu, S. Xu, C. Gao, B. Wang, and G. Xu, "Perhelper: Helping developers make better decisions on permission uses in android apps," *Applied Sciences*, vol. 9, no. 18, p. 3699, 2019.

[31] R. Slavin, X. Wang, M. B. Hosseini, J. Hester, R. Krishnan, J. Bhatia, T. D. Breaux, and J. Niu, "Toward a framework for detecting privacy policy violations in android application code," in *Proceedings of the 38th International Conference on Software Engineering*, 2016, pp. 25–36.

[32] A.-D. Tran, M.-Q. Nguyen, G.-H. Phan, and M.-T. Tran, "Security issues in android application development and plug-in for android studio to support secure programming," in *International Conference on Future Data and Security Engineering*. Springer, 2021, pp. 105–122.

[33] Sonarlint ide extension for code security. [Online]. Available: https://www.sonarlint.org/

[34] Findbugs-idea. Retrv: 02, 2022. [Online]. Available: https://plugins.jetbrains.com/plugin/3847-findbugs-idea

[35] T. Li, Y. Agarwal, and J. I. Hong, "Coconut: An ide plugin for developing privacy-friendly apps," *Proceedings of the ACM on Interactive, Mobile, Wearable and Ubiquitous Technologies*, vol. 2, no. 4, pp. 1–35, 2018.

[36] D. C. Nguyen, D. Wermke, Y. Acar, M. Backes, C. Weir, and S. Fahl, "A stitch in time: Supporting android developers in writingsecure code," in *Proceedings of the 2017 ACM SIGSAC Conference on Computer and Communications Security*, 2017, pp. 1065–1077.

[37] Lintent: Towards security type-checking of android applications. Retrv: 03, 2022. [Online]. Available: https://github.com/alvisespano/Lintent

[38] Explore the microsoft security sdl practices. Retrv: 04, 2022. [Online]. Available: https://www.microsoft.com/en-us/securityengineering/sdl

[39] Software assurance maturity model. Retrv: 04, 2022. [Online]. Available: https://owasp.org/www-project-samm/

[40] A. P. Felt, E. Chin, S. Hanna, D. Song, and D. Wagner, "Android permissions demystified," in *Proceedings of the 18th ACM conference on Computer and communications security*, 2011, pp. 627–638.

AC-SIF: ACE Access Control for Standardized Secure IoT Firmware Updates

Joel Höglund, Anum Khurshid, Shahid Raza
RISE Research Institutes of Sweden
Isafjordsgatan 22, 16440 Kista, Stockholm
{joel.hoglund, anum.khurshid, shahid.raza}@ri.se

***Abstract*—Globally identifiable, internet-connected embedded systems can be found throughout critical infrastructures in modern societies. Many of these devices operate unattended for several years at a time, which means a remote software update mechanism should be available in order to patch vulnerabilities. However, this is most often *not* the case, largely due to interoperability issues endemic to the Internet of Things (IoT). Significant progress toward global IoT compatibility has been made in recent years. In this paper, we build upon emerging IoT technologies and recommendations from IETF SUIT working group to design a firmware update architecture which (1) provides end-to-end security between authors and devices, (2) is agnostic to the underlying transport protocols, (3) does not require trust anchor provisioning by the manufacturer and (4) uses standard solutions for crypto and message encodings. This work presents the design of a firmware manifest (i.e., metadata) serialization scheme based on CBOR and COSE, and a profile of CBOR Web Token (CWT) to provide access control and authentication for update authors. We demonstrate that this architecture can be realized whether or not the recipient devices support asymmetric cryptography. We then encode these data structures and find that all required metadata and authorization information for a firmware update can be encoded in less than 600 bytes with this architecture.**

***Index Terms*—ACE; SUIT; COSE; IoT; security.**

I. INTRODUCTION

The need for secure firmware updates in the Internet of Things (IoT) has been apparent for several years. Seen in a longer perspective, the IoT is still in its infancy, and the current situation regarding software updates for IoT is comparable to personal computers in the 1990s [1]. Most embedded systems do not have a system in place for remote software updates, which means device operators must manually download and install them on each device [2]. As a result, many IoT deployments are simply never updated, even after vulnerabilities are found, because the labor cost outweighs the perceived benefit.

The IoT is traditionally characterized by a lack of standards, which incentivizes companies to develop proprietary solutions [3]. For example, Texas Instruments (TI) and Amazon Web Services introduced an update framework specifically for TI devices running Amazon FreeRTOS [4]. This approach leads to *vendor lock-in*, where each manufacturer offers mutually incompatible software ecosystems. This ultimately hurts the industry and consumers: it prevents end users to freely compose networks of devices from different manufacturers, and it creates prohibitively high costs for smaller companies to enter the market and compete, whose only option might be to

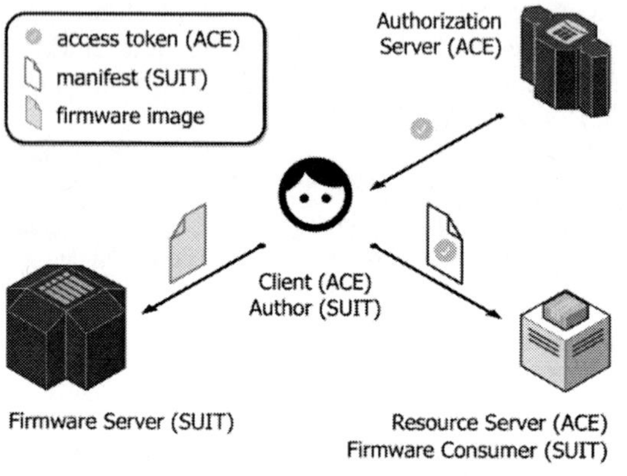

Fig. 1. Our proposed firmware update architecture, combining ACE authorization mechanisms with proposed Software Updates for IoT (SUIT) solutions.

become sub-providers to providers of proprietary ecosystems. Embedded systems come with a wide range of hardware, operating systems, capabilities and constraints, which should not be a reason for incompatibility. New standards, such as 6LoWPAN [5], DTLS [6], CoAP [7] and OSCORE [8], enable secure IPv6 networking on devices with only tens of kilobytes of RAM, resulting in constrained devices being globally addressed with internet protocols. Although the *content* of firmware updates varies between devices, an industry-wide standard for the distribution of these updates enables the desired interoperability, where the same update infrastructure can serve multiple, or heterogeneous, deployments, instead of requiring several custom solutions. The need for common standards in the area and its challenges is identified within the Internet Engineering Task Force (IETF) standard [9] leading to the formation of the Software Updates for IoT (SUIT) working group. To have long term impact, a secure update framework must support existing embedded systems and systems which have yet to be conceived. The working group describes a firmware update solution consisting of three components: a mechanism for transporting updates, a *manifest* containing metadata about the update, and the firmware image [10]. SUIT suggests the following design requirements for the update architecture: (i) agnostic to firmware image distribution, (ii) friendly to broadcast delivery, (iii) built on state-of-the-art security mechanisms, (iv) not vulnerable to rollback attacks,

(v) minimal impact on existing firmware formats, (vi) enables robust permissions controls and (vii) diverse modes of operation.

Among the challenges of specifying and implementing an architecture to meet these requirements are how to solve access control and credential management. Without adequate security, an update mechanism becomes an attack vector in itself, and can be used to install malware or simply brick devices. Hence, IoT devices must be able to verify the origin and integrity of the firmware specified in the manifests, and the permissions of the update author. In this paper, we present a solution to this problem based on the Authentication and Authorization for Constrained Environments (ACE) framework. A high level illustration is shown in Figure 1. The main contributions of this work are presented through the following sections:

- IV A firmware manifest design and update architecture, based on the ACE framework and SUIT recommendations, to provide both authentication and authorisation mechanisms for secure updates.
- V Proposals for the use of CBOR Web Tokens (CWT) for Proof-of-Possession (PoP) in the update architecture.
- VI An implementation and evaluation of the manifest and access tokens described in Sections IV and V.

The rest of the paper is organized as follows. The IoT security standards providing the basis of our update architecture are discussed in Section II. Related work is presented in Section III. In Section VII we discuss the security consideration of the proposed architecture, and conclude the paper in Section VIII.

II. Background and Threat Model

This section presents IoT security standards and protocols which form the basis of our proposed update architecture, followed by the assumed threat model.

We briefly summarize the Constrained Application Protocol (CoAP), Concise Binary Object Representation (CBOR), CBOR Object Signing and Encryption (COSE), Public Key Infrastructure (PKI), Authentication and Authorization for Constrained Environments (ACE) and CBOR Web Tokens (CWT).

A. The Constrained Application Protocol (CoAP)

Typical constrained devices are sensors, actuators or both. Heavy computations are offloaded to more powerful devices, while the nodes receive commands, transmit sensor readings and perform periodic tasks. These types of networks are well-suited to RESTful services, but traditional web protocols like HTTP incur an unacceptable overhead for small devices. This has been alleviated by CoAP, a lightweight version of HTTP using binary message encodings rather than human-readable formats and running on top of UDP instead of TCP.

B. CBOR encoding and COSE

In web applications, where computing resources are plentiful and human readability is advantageous, data representations such as XML and JSON have widespread use. For the IoT, CBOR has become the preferred encoding scheme as it

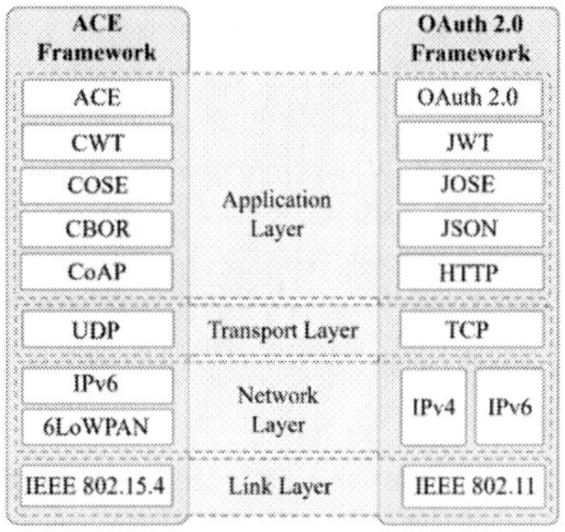

Fig. 2. Network protocols for token-based authentication in the IoT (ACE) along with their web counterparts (OAuth2.0).

is compact, offers lower message overhead and is designed for efficiency [11]. In applications requiring cryptographic operations, COSE is a standard with increasing usage in IoT [12]. COSE provides a standardized format for encryption, signing and Message Authentication Codes (MAC).

C. Public Key Infrastructure (PKI)

PKI provides the basis of authentication and access control in modern networked systems, by managing the distribution and revocation of digital certificates. These certificates rely on asymmetric cryptography, which is computationally demanding for constrained devices. New standards and proposals for lightweight certificate enrollment targeting IoT have provided important PKI building blocks [13][14]. Experimental analyses of these protocols have demonstrated that PKI enrollment is now within the capabilities of constrained devices [15][16]. However, many existing IoT networks still rely on Pre-Shared Keys (PSK), shared with all parties the devices communicate with, or raw public keys (i.e., asymmetric cryptography without attached certificates).

D. The ACE Framework

ACE is an authentication and authorization framework for IoT, built on CBOR, COSE, CoAP and OAuth 2.0 [17]. Clients request access to protected resources from an Authorization Server (AS). If successful, the AS grants the client a token which is bound to a secret key in the client's possession, a specific resource and an expiration date. This token is then used as proof of authorization when accessing the Resource Server (RS). The RS can optionally send an *introspection* request to the AS to confirm the token's validity. A network stack with ACE is shown in Figure 2. In the context of our proposed architecture, the recipient IoT devices act as the RS, as illustrated in Figure 1.

There exists a number of proposals for profiling ACE to be used together with DTLS [18], OSCORE [14] or MQTT [19].

E. CBOR Web Tokens (CWT)

The ACE framework uses CWT instead of their OAuth counterpart, JSON Web Tokens (JWT) [20]. A *token* is essentially a small, serialized object containing *claims* about a *subject*, with some cryptographic guarantees generated by the *issuer* (i.e., the AS). The precise encoding of CWT claims are use-case dependent, but all signatures, MACs and encryption are done following COSE format specifications. *Access tokens* are bound to a key known to the token bearer. These are known as Proof-of-Possession (PoP) keys, and the semantics of binding them to CWTs and requesting them through ACE are described in two separate documents, [21] and [22].

F. Threat Model

Our assumptions on the capabilities of an attacker follow the Dolev-Yao adversarial model [23]. An attacker can eavesdrop and record sent messages, and inject messages into the communication. We assume that the adversary cannot break chryptographic functions, and does not have direct access to tampering with the IoT devices.

III. Related Work

Firmware updates can be grouped into two categories: image-based updates and differential updates. A 2017 survey among embedded software engineers found that almost 60% of respondents had a way of remotely updating their products and all of them used systems developed in-house, with a clear preference for image-based updates [2]. Bootloaders that utilize this approach, such as *MCUboot* [24], partition the device ROM into two sections – one for the old image and one for the new – in a way that a backup exists if the new firmware fails to boot. Differential firmware updates are far more diverse, encompassing module-based approaches [25][26], binary patching [27], binary compression [28], and more. Our work regards the secure distribution of firmware updates, and is agnostic to the firmware content or installation method.

A. Update Distribution Architectures

Software updates on systems with relatively few resource constraints are done via package managers, such as RPM or dpkg, and various commercial app stores. The trust anchors required to verify updates with PKI operations, such as code signing, are pre-installed in the operating system. A 2010 paper argued that because update architectures are an attractive target to attackers, recipients should never rely on a single signature [29]. Instead, the authors advocated for a (t, n) signature threshold scheme, whereby a recipient will not accept an update unless t out of n trusted signers have provided a signature. A profile of this scheme for constrained IoT was later proposed in 2018 [30]. Devices would be provisioned with the Original Equipment Manufacturer (OEM) certificate and trust anchors. The OEM would send signed update metadata to a device owner's *domain controller* server. This server would then sign and forward the message to the end devices; hence the update is $(2, 2)$ in the (t, n) notation.

Code signing by firmware update authors presents a problem for the IoT. In order for devices to verify the signatures, they must be provisioned with a list of authorized authors and their trust anchors. Moreover, update authors (for instance the OEM) are likely to be from outside the device owner's organization, and the device's lifetime may exceed that of the validity period of the update author's certificate which was available when initially deploying the IoT device. Our work solves these problems by incorporating a token-granting Authorization Server, which is capable of handling all certificate-based authentication on behalf of the IoT devices.

B. Software defined IoT

An approach to software updates for IoT is presented in [31], where more powerful devices act as controllers for more constrained IoT devices, building upon earlier work to define software defined networks for IoT [32]. This approach can offer solutions for heterogeneous networks which include both more powerful devices and devices which are themselves too constrained to act as fully independent endpoints, but does not address questions of standardisation.

C. Ongoing Standardisation Work

Key points of providing well specified mechanisms for secure software updates, are to achieve long time support capabilities and limit the risks of reliance on proprietary systems. Hence proposals for solutions need to relate to the ongoing standardisation efforts in the area. The SUIT working group within IETF has produced three core documents: one RFC describing the SUIT architecture [33], one RFC on a firmware manifest information model [34] and one draft specifying a proposal for a manifest format [35]. The proposal describes one instantiation of firmware manifests with CBOR/COSE encoding. It includes a new scripting language and recommendations that a series of commands should be embedded in SUIT manifests for firmware installation. This approach has its drawbacks, most notably the steep increase in parser complexity, which is likely to deter some vendors from adopting the standard. Including scripts in the manifest would also introduce new security vulnerabilities. The proposed scripting format contains instructions to verify firmware digests and check update compatibilities. This generates new issues about error handling, and how the device should proceed if an update author neglects to include critical security checks in the installation script. Our work defines a set of procedures to be followed by all manifest recipients; the manifest itself contains no instructions. The SUIT documents do not, however, describe how manifest encryption keys are to be distributed, nor how recipient devices are meant to verify author permissions. With the exception of scripting support, our manifest design follows the recommendations stated in these documents, and extends it by including lightweight solutions for authorization.

A 2019 paper by Zandberg et al. was the first to provide an implementation and performance analysis of a SUIT firmware manifest [36]. The work focused primarily on the RAM, ROM and CPU overhead incurred based on the choice of signing algorithm used for the manifest. Our work, in contrast, is focused specifically on how a SUIT manifest must be encoded to support token-based access control and key distribution, and considers both PSK and certificate-based use-cases. A recent survey on IoT update solutions shows that the study of SUIT related solutions is so far in its infancy, with only one other work mentioned besides the Zandberg et al. paper [37]. The short paper by Hernández-Ramos et al. discuss update related challenges. They conclude that the SUIT proposals might benefit from being aided by blockchain based mechanisms, which illustrates their complementary approaches [38].

D. Lightweight Machine-to-Machine

The Lightweight Machine-to-Machine (LwM2M) protocol is a device management protocol targeting IoT. The versions of the protocol since 2018 include a firmware update object [39]. This specification is similar to the SUIT model as it supports a *push* or *pull* architecture for firmware metadata, and firmware images can either be packaged with the metadata or retrieved from another server. However, security considerations are explicitly left outside the scope and no threat model is described. Access control, authentication and confidentiality are left entirely to the transport and application layer security mechanisms. This means that LwM2M is not a competitor to the SUIT proposals, but rather a possible framework in which the update solutions could be used. Early attempts in this directions have been reported in [40].

IV. Proposed Firmware Update Architecture

The communication architecture proposed in SUIT is flexible in a way that updates can be triggered either by the devices or the firmware/update authors (i.e., *push* or *pull*). The manifests can be distributed with or without the corresponding firmware images [33]. Our proposed architecture abides by these principles, but deviates in the way authors are authenticated and firmware is verified. SUIT states that a manifest should be directly signed by its author. This requires the provisioning of trust anchors and legitimate author identities. Moreover, the most constrained devices which still rely on symmetric keys (i.e., PSK) lack the ability to verify digital signatures. We approach this as an access control problem and provisioning devices with a list of trusted authors before deployment is insufficient for a number of reasons, such as:

- Author certificates may expire or are revoked.
- Original trusted Update Authors may fail to issue updates (e.g., when devices outlive their warranty).
- Device owners may not want to accept all updates issued by the manufacturer.

Hence we conclude that authentication is not sufficient for authorization. To address these concerns, we propose integrating the SUIT communication model with access control mechanisms provided by the ACE framework. This solution would allow device operators to centrally manage the list of authorized Update Authors (UA), and could be realized entirely using existing standard-based building blocks. Additionally, our proposed architecture can be realized whether or not the recipient IoT devices can verify digital signatures.

Combining SUIT and ACE results in the architecture illustrated in Figure 1. The recipient IoT devices act as *firmware consumers* from the SUIT perspective. Update Authors (UA) in SUIT play the role of the *client* in ACE (i.e., the entity requesting tokens). The client requests access to the firmware/update from the Authorization Server (AS). Finally the firmware updates are stored at, and can be downloaded from, a SUIT *firmware server*.

A. Authorization Tokens

A simple approach to distributing firmware updates with ACE would be to use one of the mentioned proposed profiles of the framework for secure channel establishment (with DTLS, OSCORE or MQTT). With an encrypted and mutually authenticated channel between the Update Author and recipient, manifests and images would not require further signatures or authentication codes. However, to enable a larger range of use-cases, firmware manifests must be standalone verifiable objects [9]. In our proposed update architecture, tokens are issued to the UA simply to authorize the distribution of manifests. The manifests themselves are authenticated and (partially) encrypted, and can be sent over any channel.

An ACE exchange always begins with establishing a security context between the client (i.e., UA) and the Authorization Server (AS). At this time, the AS authenticates the client and verifies their permissions to distribute updates before issuing an *access token*. If a symmetric PoP key is requested, it will be sent to the client over this secure channel. *Access tokens* are not required for the distribution of firmware images. Instead, the manifests contain a secure message digest of the corresponding image. This ensures integrity, and allows devices to retrieve firmware images from another server. The firmware retrieval could take place over an encrypted channel, or a combination of untrusted channels and encryped firmware images, depending on the confidentiality needs. We leave the details of this outside the scope of our architecture.

Our update architecture leverages the ACE framework for the provisioning of CBOR Web Tokens for PoP. There is some flexibility in how these tokens are protected and authenticated with COSE, which is discussed in Section V. The CWT standard defines a set of common claims to include in each token, but leaves the precise meaning of the fields up to the particular use-case. We use four of these and define them as:

`iss` : issuer i.e., the URI of the AS server
`aud` : audience i.e., the recipient device class's UUID
`iat` : issued at i.e, the start of the *access token's* validity
`exp` : expiration i.e., the end of the *access token's* validity

In addition, all tokens contain the confirmation field (`cnf`) which contains the PoP key, following the specification in [21].

B. Manifest Distribution

Our proposed architecture is designed to support both image-based and differential updates with dependencies. In the latter case, recipient devices must parse the dependency list, retrieve corresponding manifests, and parse their dependency lists (illustrated in Figure 3). Installing updates often requires devices to reboot, and potentially lose track of the state in the update process. We propose that devices query a known

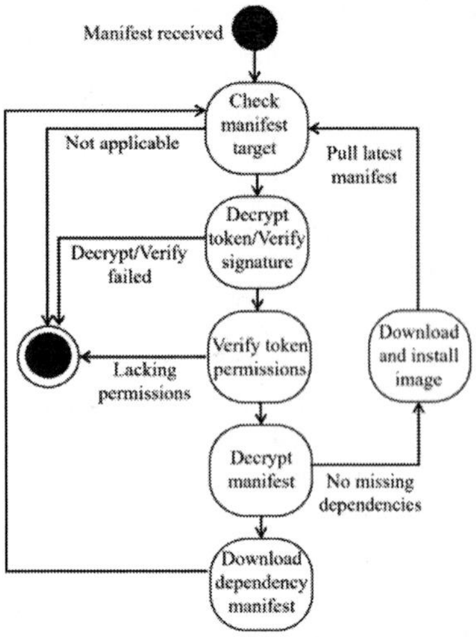

Fig. 3. Procedure followed by recipient devices for manifest dependency tree traversal and firmware update installation.

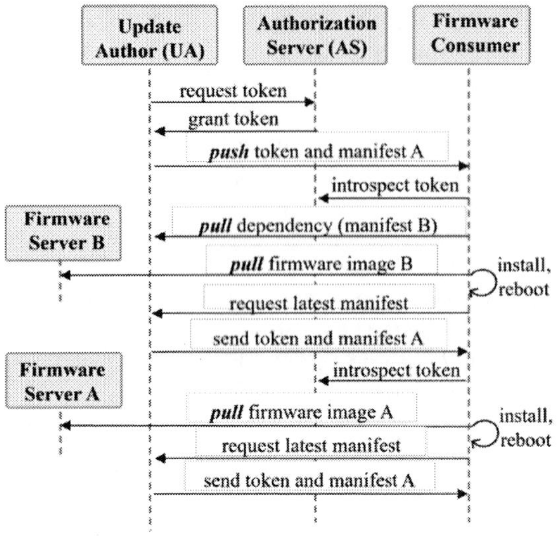

Fig. 4. Update sequence diagram for one possible use-case. The Update Author (UA) establishes a secure channel with the AS before pushing firmware manifest A to a recipient device. Since firmware update A is dependent on firmware update B, the device pulls the dependency list and parses it. Note that token introspection is an optional step.

manifest distributor at startup and request the latest manifest and corresponding access token. The device will know the update is complete when it receives a manifest matching its current firmware.

SUIT describes three categories of update architectures: *server-initiated*, *client-initiated* and *hybrid* updates. The recursive process for dependency installation used in our architecture is categorized as a client-initiated update. Figure 4 depicts interactions between actors for an update with a single dependency. The flow is server-initiated, for the cases where the update author has a known access path to the IoT device, but could easily be turned into client initiated through adding a polling step by the IoT device.

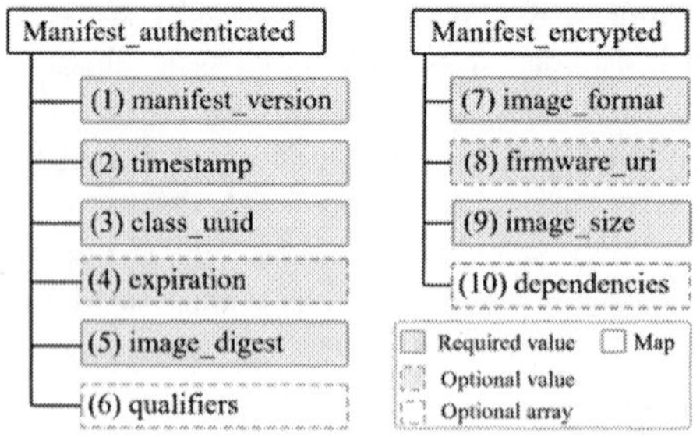

Fig. 5. Our proposed firmware manifest structure. The manifest is encoded as two separate CBOR maps, with the integer key values indicated in parentheses.

C. Manifest Design

We propose encoding firmware manifests as two separate CBOR maps: one containing information about the intended recipient of the update and another containing information about dependencies and image contents. The latter is encrypted, and both are authenticated in a single operation using an Authenticated Encryption with Associated Data (AEAD) algorithm. With this design, it is possible for a UA to broadcast an access token and manifest to a fleet of IoT devices, and any devices to which the update does not apply can quickly ascertain this without performing any cryptographic operations. Hence it is in line with SUIT recommendations to keep the update mechanism broadcast friendly. It is sensible to encrypt information about the image contents, in order to conceal information that is useful to an adversary attempting to gain insights into the software running on devices and its potential vulnerabilities. This includes the dependencies and the exact firmware URI.

In accordance with SUIT's recommendations, device classes representing the target IoT devices are given a 128-bit Universally Unique Identifier (UUID) [41], which is present through the manifest's `class_uuid` field. In our proposed architecture, devices ascertain whether the source of the manifest is authorized to issue updates by comparing this field to the `aud` value in the accompanying *access token*. A timestamp is mandatory in order to prevent rollback attacks, in which an attacker replays an earlier, legitimate firmware manifest with known vulnerabilities. IoT devices must verify that a manifest is issued more recently than their current firmware version. By storing the included timestamp of the current firmware version, a simple ordering check is sufficient to determine the temporal relation between manifests, and does not require access to a well synchronized clock.

The hash of the corresponding firmware image is included in the `image_digest` field. The URI of the firmware server can be specified in the encrypted `firmware_uri` field unless the location is already known to the devices. To handle use-cases where only devices with certain old firmware versions require a patch, the manifests optionally include a `qualifiers` list. This contains a list of firmware digests that a device must already have installed for the update to apply; otherwise it is discarded. The encrypted

TABLE I
CRYPTOGRAPHIC ALGORITHMS EXECUTED BY THE RECIPIENT FOR EACH APPROACH DESCRIBED IN SECTION V.

	AEAD	ECDSA	ECDH	KDF
A	manifest, token			
B	manifest, token	token	manifest	
C	manifest	token	manifest	manifest
D	manifest	token	manifest	

`dependencies` field indicates a list of firmware images which must be installed before installing the present one. This enables differential updates and is handled as per Figure 3.

D. COSE Wrappers

Our proposed manifest is designed for AEAD algorithms, several of which are supported natively by the COSE standard. These algorithms take a Content Encryption Key (CEK), a plaintext and some Additionally Authenticated Data (AAD) as inputs, and produce a ciphertext as output. The unencrypted portion of our manifest design is used as the AAD, and the encrypted portion forms the plaintext. The resulting ciphertext is encapsulated in a `COSE_Encrypt` object. In total, a recipient IoT device will receive three separate CBOR-encoded objects, all of which must be valid in order to accept the update: the token, the AAD, and the COSE-wrapped encrypted manifest data. The `recipients` field in a COSE wrapper is used to encipher the CEK with Key Encryption Keys (KEK) known only to the intended recipients. There are several ways to derive this KEK, which is discussed in further detail in the upcoming sections.

V. AUTHENTICATION OPTIONS

Access control and cryptography in the IoT must be discussed in the context of device capabilities; this ultimately determines the available options. To this end, we group devices into two broad categories: (i) devices that rely entirely on PSK, (ii) devices that possess unique asymmetric key pairs (e.g., digital certificates) and can verify digital signatures. In this section we describe four distinct applications of COSE for protecting firmware manifests and the corresponding access tokens. Only the first option is applicable to devices restricted to only using PSK; the others are applicable wherever asymmetric cryptography is available, where devices are provisioned with certificates via a PKI. The message overhead of each option is analyzed in Section VI.

A. Symmetric PoP Key with PSK

Reliance on PSK for security precludes the use of digital signatures and Diffie-Hellman key exchange algorithms. In addition, since the network's security is based entirely on the secrecy of the PSK, these keys should never be sent to a third party (i.e., an Update Author). We address these constraints by issuing a unique symmetric PoP key with each access token. The key is sent to the author over its secure channel with the AS, and is also included in the `cnf` field of the access token. The token is encapsulated in a `COSE_Encrypt0` object using the network PSK for encryption by the AS, and the manifest is encapsulated in another using the PoP key. It should be noted that this approach is subject to attack vectors not present in the other authentication methods (see Section VII).

B. Symmetric PoP Key

Symmetric PoP keys are an option also where asymmetric cryptography is available. We suggest the following approach, which is not conventional, but well-suited to this particular application. The AS generates the PoP key and encrypts it *with itself* in a `COSE_Encrypt0` object. This is then included in the `cnf` field of the access token, and the token is encapsulated as the payload of a `COSE_Sign1` object signed by the AS. (The following later verification of this signature is what requires asymmetric cryptography capabilities by the receiving IoT device.) The UA distributes the CEK to recipient devices via the `recipients` field in the manifest's COSE wrapper. Recipients can then verify that this CEK is the one contained in the signed token by decrypting the `cnf` field. The motivation for this approach is to avoid including any recipients in the token itself, as this would require the AS to have knowledge of the intended recipients' public keys. The UA must know the recipients' public keys in order to encipher the CEK.

C. Asymmetric PoP Key, Direct Key Agreement

In the case of asymmetric PoP keys, the `cnf` field of the CWT contains the COSE encoding of a public key belonging to the UA. The token is then encapsulated in a `COSE_Sign1` wrapper. The UA now has two options for deriving a CEK for the manifest. The first is through direct key agreement. This type of algorithm applies a key exchange protocol – in this case Elliptic Curve Diffie-Hellman (ECDH) – and a Key Derivation Function (KDF) to generate the CEK directly. The author must use the key pair bound to the token to prove their authorization.

D. Asymmetric PoP Key, Key Wrap

The second asymmetric PoP key approach is to use the key derived through ECDH as a Key Encryption Key (KEK) to encipher a randomly-generated ephemeral CEK. These two approaches have implementation nuances and security considerations which are discussed in Sections VI and VII. Table I summarizes the cryptographic operations that recipient devices much perform in order to process manifests and tokens with each of the four described authentication options.

VI. IMPLEMENTATION

The encoding scheme for each authentication options discussed in the previous section is shown in Table II. In this section, we generate firmware manifests and access tokens for each of the four cases. The purpose of this exercise is both to demonstrate the viability of the proposed architecture, and to evaluate the differences in storage and transmission overhead.

TABLE II
COSE WRAPPERS FOR EACH MANIFEST-TOKEN COMBINATION DESCRIBED IN SECTION V.

	Authentication	Manifest	Token
A	PSK	COSE_Encrypt0	COSE_Encrypt0
B	Symmetric PoP key	COSE_Encrypt	COSE_Sign1
C	Asymmetric PoP key	COSE_Encrypt	COSE_Sign1
D	Asymmetric PoP key	COSE_Encrypt	COSE_Sign1

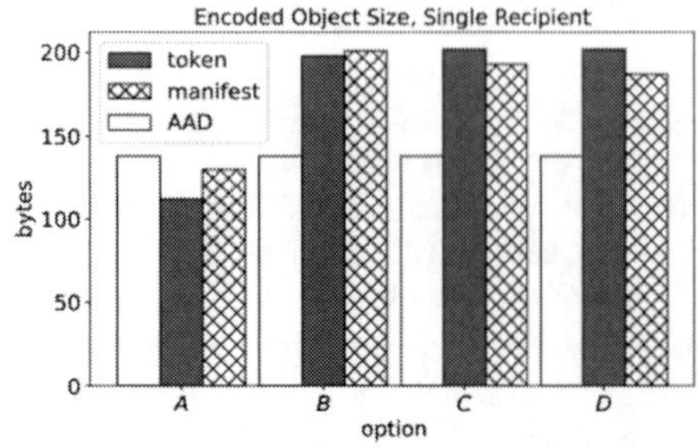

Fig. 6. Encoded sizes of the **manifest**, **token** and **AAD** for each approach in Section V.

A. Profile and Assumptions

For our implementation and analysis, we populate the manifest fields illustrated in Figure 5 with example data. In order to do so we make the following assumptions:

- Images are identified with 32-byte digests.
- Timestamps are represented in relative time.
- The manifest has two qualifiers and two dependencies.
- The firmware server URI is *coaps://example.com*.
- The Authorization Server URI is *coaps://example.com*.

The authenticated and encrypted example manifest components are 138 and 116 bytes, respectively, after CBOR serialization. COSE offers a variety of algorithms with a range of key sizes for each cryptographic operation. For our implementation, we have chosen the following:

- ECDSA signatures with 256-bit keys.
- AES-CCM with 128-bit keys, 64-bit tag and a 13-byte nonce for content encryption.
- AES 128-bit key wrap.
- ECDH Ephemeral-Static (ES).
- HMAC-Based Extract-and-Expand Key Derivation Function (HKDF) with SHA-256.

B. Results and comparison with other SUIT proposals

The update and authentication information is separated into three separate CBOR-encoded objects: the **token**, the encrypted **manifest** data, and the plaintext authenticated manifest data (a.k.a. the additionally authenticated data, or **AAD**). The results are shown in Figure 6. Option A has the smallest total size, with all three CBOR objects totalling 380 bytes. Option C has the largest footprint, totalling 537 bytes. Since the differences are relatively minor, the choice of method should be guided by the offered security properties, as discussed below in VII.

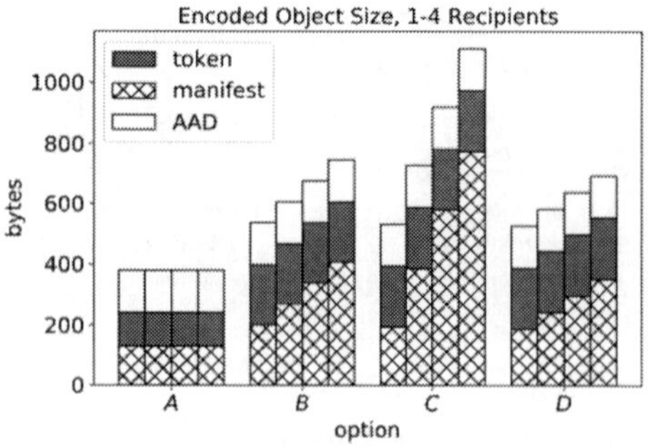

Fig. 7. Encoded sizes of the **manifest**, **AAD** and **token** when the update has multiple recipients.

In the most recent SUIT manifest proposal there are example manifest samples, which allow us to compare our proposals with the draft. In [35] the minimal manifest is only 237 bytes, but for example manifests with content similar to the sample used in our evaluation, the size is between 270 and 400 bytes. The main difference is the addition of our relatively large access tokens, since they are designed to be independent authorization tokens, compliant with ACE requirements. Given this added security functionality we find the added overhead to be clearly acceptable.

In some deployments, it may be preferable for UAs to upload both manifests and firmware images to a dedicated firmware server to be retrieved by devices at a later time. This is feasible within our framework as long as the corresponding access token is stored alongside the manifest. The storage overhead for manifests encoded with multiple recipients is shown in Figure 7. The plot shows the encoded size of the required objects for 1-4 recipients for each authentication method. In Option A, all recipients receive an identical manifest since they possess the same PSK. In Option B and D, the CEK is wrapped, each additional recipient only requires an additional entry in the recipients field of the COSE object. Option C, however, derives a unique CEK for each recipient, which means the manifest must be re-encrypted for every target device, making C the least efficient option for broadcast scenarios.

VII. SECURITY CONSIDERATIONS

The proposals in this paper are founded on well-vetted standards and encryption algorithms. However, there are protocol details that must be fully understood in order to avoid security lapses. A malicious firmware image could permanently disable expensive hardware and compromise an entire network, therefore, great care must be taken to ensure an update distribution mechanism does not become an attack vector in itself.

A. Non-Repudiation

The PSK use-case described in Section V-A precludes any guarantees for the access token. Since the AS uses a symmetric key known to all recipients, an adversary with control over any device would be capable of generating fraudulent tokens and PoP keys. This is problematic, although PSK networks are already subjected to similar risks. Any adversary in possession of a PSK could cause significant damage and disruption, even without the ability to issue firmware updates. If a symmetric PoP key is used and the token is signed by the AS, as in Section V-B, non-repudiation is only guaranteed for the token, but not necessarily the manifest. The UA must encipher the PoP key for each recipient, so if any of the recipients are controlled by an adversary, that adversary would then be in possession of a valid token and the associated PoP key. The use of symmetric PoP keys also breaks end-to-end security between the author and recipients, because the key is known to the AS. The analysis presented in Section VI demonstrated that asymmetric PoP keys with Key Wrap has a similar overhead but without the risks, making that approach clearly preferable.

B. Key Agreement

The manifest exchange between the author and recipients is one-way, i.e., there is no nonce exchange or handshake like in DTLS or EDHOC. The manifest's CEK is either wrapped (Options B and D) or derived directly (Option C), as described in Section V from the author and recipients' key pairs. In COSE, ECDH key derivation comes in two types: Static-Static (SS) or Ephemeral-Static (ES). In the former case, the author of the COSE object declares that the CEK is either wrapped or derived from the key pairs bound to the author and recipient. In the latter case, the author of the COSE object provides an ephemeral key pair generated for a single encryption operation. ECDH-ES is generally safer to use, because even if an adversary obtains the author's private key, it is not usable for decryption of other manifests or impersonation of the author. It is therefore preferable for UAs to request access tokens bound to an ephemeral public key, not the public key found in their certificate.

C. Firmware Image Digests

Firmware manifests are only linked to firmware images via the inclusion of a secure message digest. If a weak algorithm with the possibility of a hash collision is used for this purpose, such as SHA-1, devices may be exposed to fraudulent images referenced by authentic manifests.

VIII. Conclusion

In this work we have presented an architecture based on existing standards, which can address the urgent need for secure firmware updates in the IoT. We have described the challenges and limitations of access control in constrained environments, and why a token-based framework, such as ACE, is a promising candidate solution. In addition, we have proposed encoding schemes for firmware manifests using the CBOR and COSE standards, and detailed how these would work in conjunction with CWT to provide authorized updates. Examples of these objects were encoded and the result totaled no more than 600 bytes for the firmware manifest data, including authentication and authorization.

Acknowledgments

This research is partially funded by the Swedish Foundation for Strategic Research (SSF) Institute PhD grant, the SSF aSSIsT project and by the H2020 CONCORDIA (Grant ID: 830927) project.

References

[1] B. Schneier, "The Internet of Things is Wildly Insecure– And Often Unpatchable," January 2014. [Online]. Available: https://www.wired.com/2014/01/theres-no-good-way-to-patch-the-internet-of-things-and-thats-a-huge-problem/

[2] E. Stenberg. (2017, September) Key Considerations for Software Updates for Embedded Linux and IoT. [Online]. Available: https://www.linuxjournal.com/content/key-considerations-software-updates-embedded-linux-and-iot

[3] J. P. Vasseur and A. Dunkels, *Interconnecting Smart Objects with IP: The Next Internet*. Morgan Kaufmann, 2010.

[4] N. Lethaby, "A more secure and reliable OTA update architecture for IoT devices," Texas Instruments, Tech. Rep., 2018. [Online]. Available: http://www.ti.com/lit/wp/sway021/sway021.pdf

[5] G. Montenegro, J. Hui, D. Culler, and N. Kushalnagar, "Transmission of IPv6 Packets over IEEE 802.15.4 Networks," RFC 4944, Sep. 2007.

[6] "Datagram Transport Layer Security Version 1.2," RFC 6347, Jan. 2012.

[7] Z. Shelby, K. Hartke, and C. Bormann, "The Constrained Application Protocol (CoAP)," RFC 7252, Jun. 2014.

[8] G. Selander, J. Mattsson, F. Palombini, and L. Seitz, "Object Security for Constrained RESTful Environments (OSCORE)," RFC 8613, RFC Editor, Tech. Rep. 8613, Jul. 2019. [Online]. Available: https://rfc-editor.org/rfc/rfc8613.txt

[9] H. Tschofenig and S. Farrell, "Report from the Internet of Things Software Update (IoTSU) Workshop 2016," RFC 8240, RFC Editor, Tech. Rep. 8240, September 2017. [Online]. Available: https://tools.ietf.org/html/rfc8240

[10] B. Moran, M. Meriac, H. Tschofenig, and D. Brown, "A Firmware Update Architecture for Internet of Things Devices," Internet Engineering Task Force, Internet-Draft draft-ietf-suit-architecture-05, Apr. 2019, work in Progress.

[11] C. Bormann and P. Hoffman, "Concise Binary Object Representation (CBOR)," Internet Requests for Comments, RFC Editor, RFC 7049, October 2013.

[12] J. Schaad, "CBOR Object Signing and Encryption (COSE)," RFC 8152, RFC Editor, Tech. Rep. 8152, Jul. 2017. [Online]. Available: https://rfc-editor.org/rfc/rfc8152.txt

[13] P. van der Stok, P. Kampanakis, M. Richardson, and S. Raza, "EST-coaps: Enrollment over Secure Transport with the Secure Constrained Application Protocol," Internet Requests for Comments, RFC Editor, RFC 9148, April 2022.

[14] G. Selander, S. Raza, M. Furuhed, M. Vučinić, and T. Claeys, "Protecting est payloads with oscore," Working Draft, IETF Secretariat, Internet-Draft draft-selander-ace-coap-est-oscore-05, May 2021. [Online]. Available: https://www.ietf.org/archive/id/draft-selander-ace-coap-est-oscore-05.txt

[15] Z. He, M. Furuhed, and S. Raza, "Indraj: Certificate Enrollment for Battery-powered Wireless Devices," in *Proceedings of the 12th ACM Conference on Security and Privacy in Wireless and Mobile Networks*. ACM, 2019.

[16] J. Höglund, S. Lindemer, M. Furuhed, and S. Raza, "PKI4IoT: Towards public key infrastructure for the Internet of Things," *Computers & Security*, vol. 89, 2020.

[17] L. Seitz, G. Selander, E. Wahlstroem, S. Erdtman, and H. Tschofenig, "Authentication and authorization for constrained environments (ace) using the oauth 2.0 framework (ace-oauth)," Working Draft, IETF Secretariat, Internet-Draft draft-ietf-ace-oauth-authz-46, November 2021.

[18] S. Gerdes, O. Bergmann, C. Bormann, G. Selander, and L. Seitz, "Datagram transport layer security (dtls) profile for authentication and authorization for constrained environments (ace)," Working Draft, IETF Secretariat, Internet-Draft draft-ietf-ace-dtls-authorize-18, June 2021. [Online]. Available: https://www.ietf.org/archive/id/draft-ietf-ace-dtls-authorize-18.txt

[19] C. Sengul and A. Kirby, "Message queuing telemetry transport (mqtt)-tls profile of authentication and authorization for constrained environments (ace) framework," Working Draft, IETF Secretariat, Internet-Draft draft-ietf-ace-mqtt-tls-profile-17, March 2022. [Online]. Available: https://www.ietf.org/archive/id/draft-ietf-ace-mqtt-tls-profile-17.txt

[20] M. Jones, E. Wahlstroem, S. Erdtman, and H. Tschofenig, "CBOR Web Token (CWT)," RFC 8392, May 2018.

[21] M. Jones, L. Seitz, G. Selander, S. Erdtman, and H. Tschofenig, "Proof-of-possession key semantics for cbor web tokens (cwts)," Internet Requests for Comments, RFC Editor, RFC 8747, March 2020.

[22] L. Seitz, "Additional oauth parameters for authorization in constrained environments (ace)," Working Draft, IETF Secretariat, Internet-Draft draft-ietf-ace-oauth-params-16, September 2021. [Online]. Available: https://www.ietf.org/archive/id/draft-ietf-ace-oauth-params-16.txt

[23] D. Dolev and A. Yao, "On the security of public key protocols," *IEEE Transactions on Information Theory*, vol. 29, no. 2, pp. 198–208, 1983.

[24] MCUboot contributors, "MCUboot," https://github.com/mcu-tools/mcuboot, 2022.

[25] A. Dunkels, N. Finne, J. Eriksson, and T. Voigt, "Run-time dynamic linking for reprogramming wireless sensor networks," in *Proceedings of the 4th International Conference on Embedded Networked Sensor Systems*, ser. SenSys '06. New York, NY, USA: ACM, 2006, pp. 15–28. [Online]. Available: http://doi.acm.org/10.1145/1182807.1182810

[26] P. Ruckebusch, E. De Poorter, C. Fortuna, and I. Moerman, "Gitar," *Ad Hoc Netw.*, vol. 36, no. P1, pp. 127–151, Jan. 2016. [Online]. Available: https://doi.org/10.1016/j.adhoc.2015.05.017

[27] Jaein Jeong and D. Culler, "Incremental network programming for wireless sensors," in *2004 First Annual IEEE Communications Society Conference on Sensor and Ad Hoc Communications and Networks, 2004. IEEE SECON 2004.*, Oct 2004, pp. 25–33.

[28] M. Stolikj, P. J. L. Cuijpers, and J. J. Lukkien, "Efficient reprogramming of wireless sensor networks using incremental updates," in *2013 IEEE International Conference on Pervasive Computing and Communications Workshops (PERCOM Workshops)*, March 2013, pp. 584–589.

[29] J. Samuel, N. Mathewson, J. Cappos, and R. Dingledine, "Survivable key compromise in software update systems," in *Proceedings of the 17th ACM Conference on Computer and Communications Security*, ser. CCS '10. New York, NY, USA: ACM, 2010, pp. 61–72. [Online]. Available: http://doi.acm.org/10.1145/1866307.1866315

[30] N. Asokan, T. Nyman, N. Rattanavipanon, A. Sadeghi, and G. Tsudik, "Assured: Architecture for secure software update of realistic embedded devices," *IEEE Transactions on Computer-Aided Design of Integrated Circuits and Systems*, vol. 37, no. 11, pp. 2290–2300, Nov 2018.

[31] N. Xue, D. Guo, J. Zhang, J. Xin, Z. Li, and X. Huang, "Openfunction for software defined iot," in *2021 International Symposium on Networks, Computers and Communications (ISNCC)*, 2021, pp. 1–8.

[32] Y. Jararweh, M. Al-Ayyoub, A. Darabseh, E. Benkhelifa, M. Vouk, and A. Rindos, "Sdiot: A software defined based internet of things framework," *Journal of Ambient Intelligence and Humanized Computing*, vol. 1, pp. 453–461, 08 2015.

[33] B. Moran, H. Tschofenig, D. Brown, and M. Meriac, "A firmware update architecture for internet of things," Internet Requests for Comments, RFC Editor, RFC 9019, April 2021.

[34] B. Moran, H. Tschofenig, and H. Birkholz, "A manifest information model for firmware updates in internet of things (iot) devices," Internet Requests for Comments, RFC Editor, RFC 9124, January 2022.

[35] B. Moran, H. Tschofenig, H. Birkholz, and K. Zandberg, "A concise binary object representation (cbor)-based serialization format for the software updates for internet of things (suit) manifest," Working Draft, IETF Secretariat, Internet-Draft draft-ietf-suit-manifest-17, April 2022.

[36] K. Zandberg, K. Schleiser, F. Acosta, H. Tschofenig, and E. Baccelli, "Secure firmware updates for constrained IoT devices using open standards: A reality check," *IEEE Access*, vol. 7, pp. 71 907–71 920, 2019.

[37] S. El Jaouhari and E. Bouvet, "Secure firmware over-the-air updates for iot: Survey, challenges, and discussions," *Internet of Things*, vol. 18, 2022. [Online]. Available: https://www.sciencedirect.com/science/article/pii/S2542660522000142

[38] J. L. Hernández-Ramos, G. Baldini, S. N. Matheu, and A. Skarmeta, "Updating iot devices: challenges and potential approaches," in *2020 Global Internet of Things Summit (GIoTS)*, 2020, pp. 1–5.

[39] "Lightweight Machine to Machine Technical Specification 1.0.2," Open Mobile Alliance, Tech. Rep. OMA-TS-LightweightM2M-V1_0_2-20180209-A, February 2018.

[40] IETF. Ietf hackathon: Software / firmware updates for iot devices. IETF. [Online]. Available: https://datatracker.ietf.org/meeting/111/materials/slides-111-suit-suit-hackathon-report-00

[41] P. J. Leach, R. Salz, and M. H. Mealling, "A Universally Unique IDentifier (UUID) URN Namespace," RFC 4122, Jul. 2005. [Online]. Available: https://rfc-editor.org/rfc/rfc4122.txt

LIST: Lightweight Solutions for Securing IoT Devices against Mirai Malware Attack

1st Pallavi Kaliyar
Department of IIK
NTNU
Gjøvik, Norway
pallavi.kaliyar@ntnu.no

2nd Laszlo Erdodi
Department of IIK
NTNU
Trondheim, Norway
laszlo.erdodi@ntnu.no

3rd Sokratis Katsikas
Department of IIK
NTNU
Gjøvik, Norway
sokratis.katsikas@ntnu.no

***Abstract*—Recently, the number of Internet of Things (IoT) devices has increased significantly, as they have become affordable to most people. This spread has highlighted a critical security threat, namely the increasing number of Distributed Denial of Service (DDoS) attacks. As these resource-constrained IoT devices are built to be cost-efficient, their security measures are limited. Moreover, most users are not aware of the security measures that they must apply. Nowadays, almost every IoT device (e.g., fridge, air conditioner, thermostat, toaster) is able to connect to the internet, and this allows the user to access and control it with its own smartphone application. The lack of security measures in these devices was highlighted in September 2016, when a large-scale DDoS attack was launched using a botnet of compromised IoT devices. This type of attack has been since used in different forms and has been classified as *Mirai DDoS Botnet Attack*. This paper presents a detailed analysis of the Mirai attack and of the source code of the Mirai malware, reports on the implementation of the attack in a controlled environment, and proposes possible solutions that could help in mitigating the attack.**

***Index Terms*—Mirai Attack; Authentication; Internet of Things; malware; security.**

I. Introduction

Since its discovery in 2016, the Mirai's diffusion has been rapid and dramatic at the same time [1]. In August 2016, a new trojan that preyed on Unix Operating System's Executable and Linkable Format (ELF) files was discovered by a "MalwareMustDie" whitehat group [2]. The trojan aimed to send telnet attacks to other systems. During 2016 only, Mirai infected thousands of IoT devices. The power of this malware, which works with BASHLITE to carry out a DDoS attack, was clear to everyone in September 2016, when a huge DDoS attack took down Brian Krebs's [3] website with traffic of 620 Gbits/s. The attack was carried out with a huge number of bots that were located all around the world. In the same month, the French cloud and web hosting company OVH [4] became victim of another DDoS attack with a bigger traffic than the previous attack, i.e., 1 Tb/s. In this case, it was reported that the botnet was composed of 145,607 different devices from 8 different regions around the world, and they mainly were IoT devices like IP cameras and Digital Video Recorders.

In October 2016, the code of the Mirai was released so anyone can retrieve it from the internet [5] for analysis purposes. This inevitably led to a bigger diffusion of the code that other parties modified and improved. Due to this, the number of compromised Internet of Things (IoT) devices in 2016 varied from 213,000 to 493,000. In the same month, Dyn [6], a core ISP was hit by a massive DDoS attack against its DNS (Domain Name Server) infrastructure on the east coast of America, and this brought down some of the websites for which it provided services such as Twitter, Spotify, and Reddit. In November 2016, the Mirai took down almost all of Liberia's [7] websites, as the African state has only one internet cable, which provides a single point of failure for internet access. In the same month, a botnet of 400,000 IoT devices was up for rent on the deep web. The price was $2,000 for 20,000 compromised nodes. Furthermore, in December 2016, the British ISP TalkTalk [8] reported that Mirai had targeted customers using its Dlink DSL-3780 router.

In February 2017, Kaspersky Lab [9] researchers found that a hacker had created a variant of Mirai based on the Windows operating system. The researchers claim that the ability of this malware to spread across different Operating Systems is very limited. However, it was a sign that the Mirai power increased after releasing its source code. Later, in December 2017, two suspects admitted their guilt in developing and deploying the Mirai botnet. Obviously, this is not the end of Mirai's history as the vulnerabilities of the IoT devices that the malware uses are still present. If we cannot address this threat, the Mirai will become more powerful as vulnerable devices increase. Some other variants of Mirai are listed in Table I.

The main goal of this work is to suggest lightweight solutions for securing IoT devices against the Mirai malware attacks. We propose three lightweight solutions that can be used to secure resource-constrained vulnerable IoT devices with negligible overhead on the manufacturing cost. The key contributions of this work are:

- First, we present a detailed analysis of the Mirai source code, which is publicly available on the git repository [5] at GitHub since 2017. This analysis is important as it provides a more detailed description of the Mirai attack source code, i.e., what is the role of each Mirai source file in the execution of the Mirai attack.
- Our second contribution is the implementation of the Mirai code in a controlled environment, to show that although the Mirai attack has been long known, it is

TABLE I
DIFFERENT VARIANTS OF MIRAI

No.	Name	First Appearance	Exploit
1	Mirai original [5]	August 2016	Telnet 23/2323, brute force
2	Satori [10]	December 2017	Telnet 23/2323, Port 37215/52869, 2 exploits CVE-2014-8361 and CVE-2017-17215
3	Hajime [11]	March 2017	Telnet 23/2323, brute force, later closes the open ports
4	IoTroop [12]	October 2017	Vulnerability scanning instead of password brute-force
5	Okiru [13]	January 2018	IoT with RISC architecture, telnet default passwords 4 types of router exploits
6	Masuta, PureMasuta [14]	January 2018	EDB 38722 D-Link exploit
7	Jenx [15]	January 2018	2 exploits, CVE-2014-8361 and CVE-2017–17215
8	OMG [16]	March 2018	Make IoT a proxy server
9	Wicked [17]	June 2018	Port 80,81,8080,84433, new exploits, router exploits, cctv rce, CVE-2016-6277 command injection
10	Satori / 2018 [18]	July 2018	Android Debug Bridge (ADB) commands
11	Torii [19]	September 2018	Rich set of features for exfiltration of (sensitive) information, modular architecture capable of fetching and executing other commands and executables
12	Hakai, Yowai [20]	January 2019	Several hard coded exploits, ThinkPHP
13	Covid Mirai [21]	March 2020	TeamSpeak, Huawei default passwords
14	Satori – 2021 [22]	February 2021	Vantage Velocity field, Python script
15	Matryosh [23]	February 2021	Android Debug Bridge, TOR network is used

still very relevant, as a large number of devices are still vulnerable to it.

- Our third contribution is to propose three lightweight solutions to improve the security of IoT devices against Mirai and Mirai-like attacks. Contrary to previously proposed, state-of-the-art solutions, our solutions are applicable to both new and existing IoT devices, they do not require increased computational power, storage capability, or battery capacity, and they do not add any extra manufacturing cost to the devices.

The rest of the paper is organized as follows: Section II briefly discusses Mirai's evolution and analyzes related works that propose solutions to mitigate it. Section III describes how the Mirai attack works, focusing in particular on the Mirai source code. This is followed by the description of a real-world experiment that we conducted to gain remote access to an IoT device by launching a Mirai attack. The last part of Section III discusses three proposed solutions to limit the damage caused by the lack of security measures in IoT devices. Finally, we conclude our work in Section IV.

II. BACKGROUND AND RELATED WORK

In this section, first we briefly present (in sub-section II-A) different variants of the Mirai malware that have appeared in the last six years. Next, we briefly summarize (in sub-section II-B) security solutions proposed by other researchers.

A. Background: Evolution of the Mirai malware

The first variant of the Mirai that appeared in 2016 had separate loader and scanner modules. First it looked for open *telnet* ports and then used the default username, passwords, and password brute-force on port 23/2323. After this first variant, many other variants of Mirai appeared in the last six years. A list with a few of these key variants is shown in Table I. Below we list some of the changes identified in the working methodology of these different variants.

- The bot is able to do the scanning too, no separate scanning module is needed anymore.
- Several new exploits, such as router *http* interface vulnerabilities, Android Debug Bridge remote code execution, are added, in addition to the *telnet* as default.
- Some variants (e.g., IoTroop [12]) can do vulnerability scanning besides finding predictable credentials.
- In addition to being capable of carrying out DDOS attacks, some variants provide extra functionality, such as providing proxying functionality (using IoTs to forward packets in order to hide the source of the packet origin) [16].
- The number of devices involved has been increased, e.g., RISC processors [13].

B. Related work

The increasing number of botnets created using the Mirai attack has motivated cybersecurity researchers to develop efficient solutions to this problem. The solution used in the past proposes to analyze the Mirai traffic to find specific patterns that will allow the identification of the attack. This is the typical procedure that is used to analyse a malware, and it is done by using a *honeypot*. This strategy has been used in [24] [25]. A honeypot works as an IoT device and accepts all the attacker requests and replies with the intended commands. In particular, the honeypot used in [25] is made of two parts, as shown in Figure 1. The front-end part, which interacts with the Mirai malware, replies with the intended *telnet* commands. The back-end part records all the commands used by the malware to compromise the fake device and all the incoming traffic. The authors discovered that in the initial phase, the Mirai executes many *telnet* commands intended to gain control of the device's shell. The possibility to discover if the Mirai malware is attacking a device is an interesting solution, but it does not offer any protection against this type of attack. It would be very difficult to store information for all different IoT devices and the pattern that identifies the malware on the devices, and instruct them to check each access attempt. This approach is infeasible, as we know that most IoT devices have very low computational power and even lower storage capability and battery capacity.

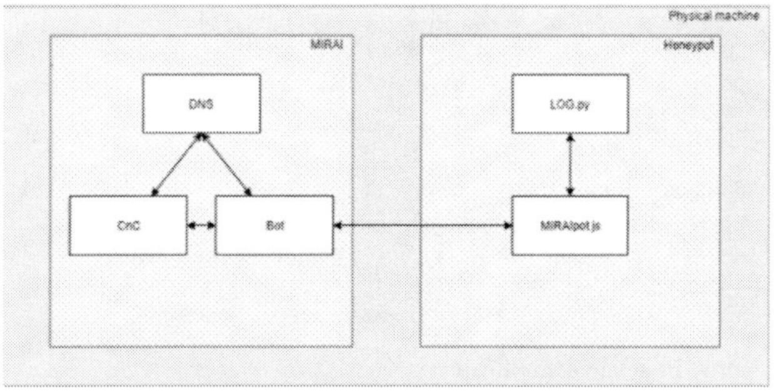

Fig. 1. Multi-component honeypot structure [25]

Another security solution to the Mirai botnet builds a whitelist-based intrusion detection technique for IoT devices [26]. This solution uses a gateway router which acts as a firewall for a set of IoT devices belonging to the local network that the router serves. The proposed mechanism is called *Heimdall*. It uses the gateway router to build a profile for each responsible device. A profile contains mainly a whitelist of the destinations (IP addresses) that a specific device can legitimately reach to perform its functions. Moreover, the profile also stores the typical traffic pattern of that device, including some statistics, e.g., number of TCP, UDP packets of the incoming and outgoing traffic. This is useful to prevent both the device from being attacked by Mirai (incoming traffic) and carrying out the attack (outgoing traffic). The profile is dynamic, so it is continuously updated, increasing the traffic pattern's precision. This approach seems attractive, as it does not require additional resources from the IoT device, because the Heidmall router does all the work. However, the solution faces some serious problems: First, the list of a single device's destinations may change very frequently, as usually the backend services of IoT devices are hosted on some public cloud infrastructure due to the devices' limited capabilities. Accordingly, the IP address of the destination servers may change very often. Secondly, this mechanism can become victim of a DNS poisoning attack. An attacker modifies the IP address from which the traffic is coming into a malicious one, so that the gateway router will reject some legitimate traffic.

After the public release of the Mirai source code, another countermeasure was developed, in the form of a worm called *Hajime* [11] [27]. This piece of "benign" malware works basically as Mirai; it uses the default logins to control IoT devices. It even uses the same username-password dictionary of Mirai. The purpose of Hajime is to gain access to the vulnerable devices to close their open ports, e.g., ports 23, 7547, 5553, and 5358, so that an attacker will not be able to use them. Thus, this code is like an anti-Mirai, as it hacks the devices to secure them. The problem with this approach is that the code is not persistent, as it is loaded on the device's RAM, and therefore it is deleted after each reboot.

Later in [28], the authors employed a static analysis to audit firmware of IoT devices to check its susceptibility against Mirai, which is not a feasible solution considering all scenarios of IoT applications. The authors in [29] propose a model made of a transformer-encode and use a hierarchical structure to extract semantic features from the information and functions to classify the malware. In [30], the authors proposed a Fog Computing-based IoT-DDoS defense framework for contemporary real-time IoT traffic to identify the presence of Mirai malware in the network. The authors in [31] proposed a Machine Learning (ML)-based mechanism for detecting Mirai Botnet attacks in IoT-based networks. The ML-based detection mechanism was detecting the attack using a real traffic dataset of IoT devices.

Having considered all these existing solutions [11], [24]–[31] with their advantages and drawbacks, we propose three new lightweight solutions against the Mirai attack that use an external device to authenticate the user to the IoT device, without the need to increase the capabilities of the device itself.

III. Proposed Approach

In this section, we first analyze the Mirai source code and discuss the Mirai attack on vulnerable, resource-constrained IoT devices. We then propose our solutions for securing the IoT devices against Mirai-like attacks.

A. *Mirai source code analysis*

The main idea behind the Mirai attack (see Figure 3 is to create a botnet made of IoT devices that a BotMaster/attacker can control to carry out a DDoS attack [32]. Initially, the Command and Control (CNC) server starts scanning for IP addresses with port 23 (*telnet*) open to control the bots. When such devices are found, the attacker injects the malware code as it controls the shell, and then the bot's information (IP address, port, and authentication credentials) are stored in a list. Once the malware is installed on the devices, it hides. The device continues its regular activities without knowing that it has been infected.

The Mirai malware source code can be found on the git repository [5] at GitHub. The code is mainly written in two programming languages, namely *Go* and *C*. The *Go* programming language is used to implement the part of the code which is used to control the CNC server [33]. The script named "admin.go" implements the primary administration interface that issues commands from the CNC server. The code script named "clientList.go" keeps track of the data needed to execute an attack, including a map/hashtable of the bots which are charged to carry out a specific attack. This code is also responsible for recording and checking the state of the bots before and after the attack. The attack requests initiated

Username	Password	Username	Password	Username	Password	Username	Password
root	xc3511	admin	meinsm	root	12345	root	7ujMko0vizxv
root	vizxv	guest	12345	user	user	root	7ujMko0admin
root	admin	tech	tech	admin	(none)	root	system
admin	admin	admin1	password	root	pass	root	ikwb
root	88888	administrator	1234	admin	admin1234	root	dreambox
root	xmhdipc	666666	666666	root	1111	root	user
root	default	888888	888888	admin	smcadmin	root	realtek
root	juantech	ubnt	ubnt	admin	1111	root	1010101
root	123456	root	klv1234	root	666666	admin	11111111
root	54321	root	Zte521	root	password	admin	1234
support	support	root	hi3518	root	1234	admin	12345
root	(none)	root	jvbzd	root	klv123	admin	54321
admin	password	root	anko	Administrator	admin	admin	123456
root	root	root	zlxx.	service	service	admin	7ujMko0admin
guest	guest	mother	fucker	supervisor	supervisor	admin	pass

Fig. 2. Default username and passwords in scanner dictionary

by the CNC server are executed by the code script named "attack.go". This part of the code parses and formats the commands received, and sends them to the appropriate bots via code script named "api.go". The code script "attack.go" can also set the attack duration, and the attack command is sent to the individual bot through the code script "api.go".

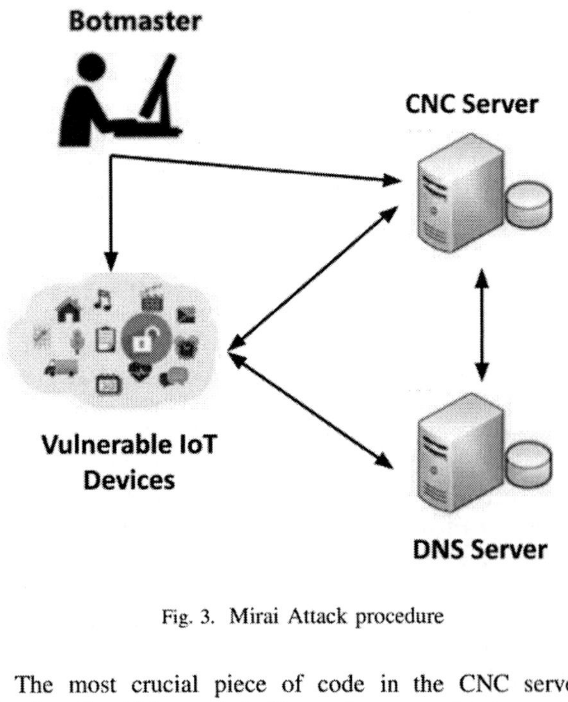

Fig. 3. Mirai Attack procedure

The most crucial piece of code in the CNC server is "main.go", which regularly listens for connections on ports 23 (*telnet*) and 101 (*apibot* responses). If a connection to port 23 is found, the device is acquired and its credentials are stored. In the case of a port 101 connection, the control is handed over to the code script "api.go" which deals with an individual bot.

The code for the bot is written in the C programming language. It includes different functions built explicitly for different types of attack. The script "attack_udp.c" is able to carry out various types of UDP DDoS attacks, such as Generic Routing Encapsulation (GRE), Reflective Denial of Service (bandwidth amplification), DNS Flood via Query of type *A* record (map hostname to IP address), and Flooding of random bytes via plain packets, under specific commands. The code scripts "attack_tcp.c" and "attack_app.c" work similarly and can realize different types of attacks. The code script named "scanner.c" is used by the bots to do a brute force scanning on a range of IP addresses using a port scan (SYN scan) and trying to access vulnerable devices using a dictionary of default usernames and passwords, which is shown in Figure 2. This scanning aims to gain access to other vulnerable IoT devices and add them to the pool of botnets. If accessing a new device is successful, the bot reports to the CNC server information on the victim, i.e., IP address, port number, and authentication credentials. The Mirai also uses the code script "killer.c" which is responsible for killing various processes like *telnet* and *ssh* inside the bot. All the executable of the bot is controlled by the code script "main.c", which establishes the connection to the CNC server, starts the attack, kills processes, and even scans for additional bots to add to the botnet by making use of the other pieces of code as described above.

B. Experimental setup

We performed a real-world experiment to prove how vulnerable are the resource constrained IoT devices which we are using in our daily lives. This experiment (see Figures 4 and 5) was conducted using the Mirai Botnet DDoS attack technique. First, IoT device IP addresses were collected from

```
const DatabaseAddr string   = "127.0.0.1"
const DatabaseUser string   = "root"
const DatabasePass string   = "password"
const DatabaseTable string  = "mirai"

var clientList *ClientList = NewClientList()
var database *Database = NewDatabase(DatabaseAddr, DatabaseUser, DatabasePass, DatabaseTable)

func main() {
    tel, err := net.Listen("tcp", "0.0.0.0:23")
    if err != nil {
        fmt.Println(err)
        return
    }

    api, err := net.Listen("tcp", "0.0.0.0:101")
    if err != nil {
        fmt.Println(err)
        return
```

Fig. 4. Mirai scanning code

```
#define ATK_VEC_UDP        0  /* Straight up UDP flood */
#define ATK_VEC_VSE        1  /* Valve Source Engine query flood */
#define ATK_VEC_DNS        2  /* DNS water torture */
#define ATK_VEC_SYN        3  /* SYN flood with options */
#define ATK_VEC_ACK        4  /* ACK flood */
#define ATK_VEC_STOMP      5  /* ACK flood to bypass mitigation devices */
#define ATK_VEC_GREIP      6  /* GRE IP flood */
#define ATK_VEC_GREETH     7  /* GRE Ethernet flood */
//#define ATK_VEC_PROXY      8  /* Proxy knockback connection */
#define ATK_VEC_UDP_PLAIN  9  /* Plain UDP flood optimized for speed */
#define ATK_VEC_HTTP       10 /* HTTP layer 7 flood */
```

Fig. 5. Mirai DDoS attacks

an open access database. When such a device is found, we look on the website *shodan.io* [34] for the type of device. We used 20 IoT devices with public IP address; 18 of these were found on *shodan.io* database. Based on this, we created an emulated network with all the devices we collected and launched the Mirai Botnet attack. In our emulated network, 20 different devices were placed, with open port 23. For 18 of them, we set up default credentials according to the *shodan.io* database. Since we chose the devices randomly we believe this experiment was a small scale but realistic one. We observed that the botnets were able to carry out the scanning and infection.

C. Lightweight security solutions to mitigate Mirai Attack

In our proposed approach for addressing the Mirai attack, we categorize the different resource-constrained IoT devices in three different levels, which differ with respect to the security features provided by the manufacturer. The details of these levels are as follows:

- Level 0: No Security, i.e., no security measures have been taken or applied to the IoT device.
- Level 1: Medium Security, i.e., few measures have been taken and applied to the IoT device.
- Level 2: Full Security, i.e., continuous security service and monitoring through a service provided by a specialized service provider or by the manufacturer.

We propose lightweight security solutions for the Level 0 (i.e., No security) IoT devices, as these are most commonly used in various real-world applications. The following subsections provide details about our proposed solutions that could help mitigate the different variants of the Mirai attack. Our proposals are based on the assumption that the security solutions must not affect the cost of the devices. This is because the vendors are developing devices that are getting cheaper day by day to make them affordable to many consumers. Hence, our solutions must increase the security of these devices without significantly affecting their cost. Additionally, we provide security not only to the devices that will be built in the future but also to those already in use.

1) Secure Authentication: Despite the solutions which are already presented to mitigate the Mirai attack (refer to Section II-B), we propose to improve the security of IoT devices by protecting them with more secure and hardly guessable login credentials. The malware to control and access these devices is injected only after the device has been compromised due to its weak login credentials. To make the prediction of username & password (authentication process) more complex, an idea is to generate a periodically random username & password for accessing the device. These random values must be built combining more random numbers generated through a pseudo-random number generator (PRNG) such as *Blum Blum Shub* [35].

This approach is somewhat complicated and insufficient because the credentials will be challenging to guess not only by the attacker but even by the owner of the device. Because of this, the random values created periodically must be stored in a different device, such as a smartphone. The idea is to build an Android application that will store only the current values for accessing the device, deleting the older ones, and will keep them secure by using encryption at another layer, e.g., using a password chosen by the user to access the application. Obviously, the communication between the external device and the IoT device for sharing the values must be encrypted so that an attacker cannot sniff the credentials during the data sharing. This leads to the necessity of adding a cryptographic suite to the IoT device. The solution does not significantly affect the manufacturing cost of the device, as the only requirement is to build a PRNG application and cryptographic functions to encrypt the data shared with the android application in the device; these can be implemented in hardware or firmware. Furthermore, the proposed solution is also applicable to existing devices, by means of a firmware update.

2) Biometric Authentication: The second solution aims to reduce the cost of the device even more, as it uses some features that are already present in the externally linked devices, which again can be a smartphone. We propose to utilize the biometric features e.g., digital fingerprint of the user as authentication parameters. Nowadays, it is very common for all smartphones to offer biometric authentication hence we can use these already existing mechanisms for IoT devices. The idea is to link a specific external device to one or more IoT devices so that we do not have direct communication between the IoT device and the database where its credentials are stored. In fact, the external device itself communicates with the Server with its ID, and provides the biometric authentication parameters. If such an external device is authorized for the specific IoT device to which it requires access and the credentials are the same as those stored in the server database, the access is granted. This idea is similar to the OAuth (Open Standard Authorization) concept where the authentication is provided by a third party component and the IoT device is only asking for authorization [36].

To better explain how this process works (see Figure 6), we initially need to define the first part of the authentication phase. When a new IoT device is booted, it must specify which external device will be used for authentication. In order to do this, the IoT device will be provided with some temporary credentials that the user must use to authenticate in a specific android application. Once the access has been completed, the user must create new credentials based on some biometric parameters used for future authentications. During this phase, the server to which the IoT device refers will store the device's serial number from which the application/ios has been used. For some specific devices, the serial number is the Unique Device Identifier (UDID), along with the ID number of the IoT device and the new authentication parameters. So each time a user wants to access an IoT device, it will use the android/ios application that will directly communicate with the server to check the credentials. If everything is correct, it will communicate both with the smartphone to notify the success of the authentication operation and with the IoT device to unlock it.

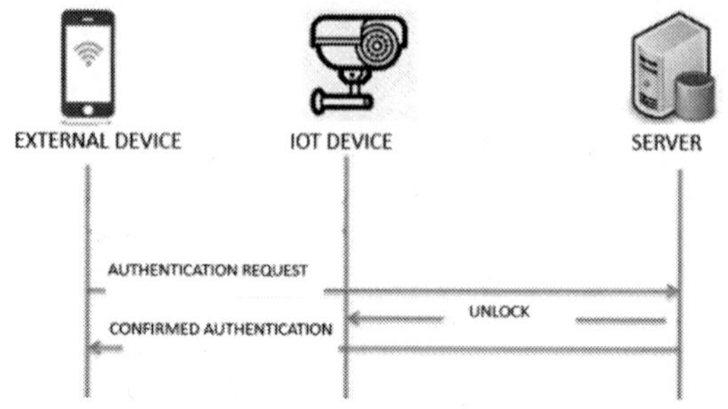

Fig. 6. Authentication process

3) Using One Time Password: The third solution is more convenient and cost-effective than the previous ones, as it does not inflict any additional cost on the IoT device, because the external device does all the computational work. The only weakness in the system is in the first authentication phase, in which the credentials are default credentials and can be easily predicted by an attacker. An initial username and password written in the instruction booklet can be sold with the device to overcome this problem. These can be used only once and only for accessing the application. An even more secure approach is to use a QR code for the first authentication as a One Time Password (OTP). Moreover, the frequency of the OTP based authentications could be optimised to improve the usability of this approach.

IV. CONCLUSION

We discussed how vulnerabilities of IoT devices can be exploited by a class of malware called Mirai, which creates a botnet of IoT devices. We presented a detailed analysis of the Mirai malware source code, and we implemented the Mirai attack using the same code, that is available on the Github. Our conclusion was that the attack is still very relevant and that resource-constrained IoT devices are vulnerable to it. We reviewed existing security solutions, whose take up in practice presents a number of difficulties, and we proposed three new ones, that provide security without increasing the manufacturing cost of the devices. Our future research will focus on validating these solutions by means of extensive experimentation.

REFERENCES

[1] M. A. et. al, "Understanding the mirai botnet," in *26th USENIX Security Symposium (USENIX Security 17)*. Vancouver, BC: USENIX Association, 2017, pp. 1093–1110. [Online]. Available: https://www.usenix.org/conference/usenixsecurity17/technical-sessions/presentation/antonakakis

[2] "Mmd-0052-2016 - overview of "skidddos" elf++ irc botnet," https://blog.malwaremustdie.org/2016/02/mmd-0052-2016-skidddos-elf-distribution.html, February 2016.

[3] "Security man krebs' website ddos was powered by hacked internet of things botnet," https://www.theregister.com/2016/09/26/brian_krebs_site_ddos_was_powered_by_hacked_internet_of_things_botnet/, September 2016.

[4] "Inside the infamous mirai iot botnet: A retrospective analysis," https://blog.cloudflare.com/inside-mirai-the-infamous-iot-botnet-a-retrospective-analysis/, September 2016.

[5] "Mirai-source-code," https://github.com/jgamblin/Mirai-Source-Code, accessed: 2010-02-20.

[6] "Ddos attack that disrupted internet was largest of its kind in history, experts say," https://www.theguardian.com/technology/2016/oct/26/ddos-attack-dyn-mirai-botnet, October 2016.

[7] "Did the mirai botnet really take liberia offline?" https://krebsonsecurity.com/2016/11/did-the-mirai-botnet-really-take-liberia-offline/, November 2016.

[8] "Uk isp talktalk confirm loss of 101,000 subscribers after cyber-attack," https://www.ispreview.co.uk/index.php/2016/02/isp-talktalk-suffers-sharp-fall-in-broadband-users-to-3-9-million.html, December 2016.

[9] "Kaspersky lab research shows ddos devastation on organizations continues to climb," https://usa.kaspersky.com/about/press-releases/2017_kaspersky-lab-research-shows-ddos-devastation-on-organizations-continues-to-climb, February 2017.

[10] "Source code of iot botnet satori publicly released on pastebin," https://www.trendmicro.com/vinfo/it/security/news/internet-of-things/source-code-of-iot-botnet-satori-publicly-released-on-pastebin, January 2017.

[11] "Hajime malware: How does it differ from the mirai worm?" https://www.techtarget.com/searchsecurity/answer/Hajime-malware-How-does-it-differ-from-the-Mirai-worm, March 2017.

[12] "Iotroop botnet: The full investigation," https://research.checkpoint.com/2017/iotroop-botnet-full-investigation/, October 2017.

[13] "Mirai okiru: The first new linux elf malware designed to infect arc cpus," https://securityonline.info/mirai-okiru-the-first-new-linux-elf-malware-designed-to-infect-arc-cpus/, January 2018.

[14] "Mirai-based masuta botnet weaponizes old router vulnerability," https://www.securityweek.com/mirai-based-masuta-botnet-weaponizes-old-router-vulnerability, January 2018.

[15] "Jenx: A new botnet threatening all," https://www.radware.com/security/ddos-threats-attacks/threat-advisories-attack-reports/jenx/, January 2018.

[16] "Omg - mirai minions are wicked," https://www.netscout.com/blog/asert/omg-mirai-minions-are-wicked, January 2018.

[17] "Wicked botnet uses passel of exploits to target iot," https://threatpost.com/wicked-botnet-uses-passel-of-exploits-to-target-iot/132125/, June 2018.

[18] "Open adb ports used to spread possible satori variant," https://www.trendmicro.com/en_gb/research/18/g/open-adb-ports-being-exploited-to-spread-possible-satori-variant-in-android-devices.html, July 2018.

[19] "Torii botnet, probably the most sophisticated iot botnet of ever," https://securityaffairs.co/wordpress/76659/malware/torii-iot-botnet.html, September 2018.

[20] "Thinkphp vulnerability abused by botnets hakai and yowai," https://malware.news/t/thinkphp-vulnerability-abused-by-botnets-hakai-and-yowai/26724, January 2019.

[21] "Mirai "covid" variant disregards stay-at-home orders," https://www.f5.com/labs/articles/threat-intelligence/mirai-covid-variant-disregards-stay-at-home-orders, March 2020.

[22] "Satori: Mirai botnet variant targeting vantage velocity field unit rce vulnerability," https://unit42.paloaltonetworks.com/satori-mirai-botnet-variant-targeting-vantage-velocity-field-unit-rce-vulnerability/, March 2021.

[23] "Satori: Mirai botnet variant targeting vantage velocity field unit rce vulnerability," https://unit42.paloaltonetworks.com/satori-mirai-botnet-variant-targeting-vantage-velocity-field-unit-rce-vulnerability/, February 2021.

[24] Y. M. P. P. et. al, "Iotpot: Analysing the rise of iot compromises," in *9th USENIX Workshop on Offensive Technologies (WOOT 15)*. Washington, D.C.: USENIX Association, 2015. [Online]. Available: https://www.usenix.org/conference/woot15/workshop-program/presentation/pa

[25] H. Šemić and S. Mrdovic, "Iot honeypot: A multi-component solution for handling manual and mirai-based attacks," in *2017 25th Telecommunication Forum (TELFOR)*, Nov 2017, pp. 1–4.

[26] J. Habibi, D. Midi, A. Mudgerikar, and E. Bertino, "Heimdall: Mitigating the internet of insecure things," *IEEE Internet of Things Journal*, vol. 4, no. 4, pp. 968–978, Aug 2017.

[27] H. Tanaka, S. Yamaguchi, and M. Mikami, "Quantitative evaluation of hajime with secondary infectivity in response to mirai's infection situation," in *2019 IEEE 8th Global Conference on Consumer Electronics (GCCE)*, 2019, pp. 961–964.

[28] Z. Ahmed, I. Nadir, H. Mahmood, A. Hammad Akbar, and G. Asadullah Shah, "Identifying mirai-exploitable vulnerabilities in iot firmware through static analysis," in *2020 International Conference on Cyber Warfare and Security (ICCWS)*, 2020, pp. 1–5.

[29] X. Hu, R. Sun, K. Xu, Y. Zhang, and P. Chang, "Exploit internal structural information for iot malware detection based on hierarchical transformer model," in *2020 IEEE 19th International Conference on Trust, Security and Privacy in Computing and Communications (TrustCom)*, 2020, pp. 927–934.

[30] M. Snehi and A. Bhandari, "Apprehending mirai botnet philosophy and smart learning models for iot-ddos detection," in *2021 8th International Conference on Computing for Sustainable Global Development (INDIACom)*, 2021, pp. 501–505.

[31] A. R. S. Araujo Cruz, R. L. Gomes, and M. P. Fernandez, "An intelligent mechanism to detect cyberattacks of mirai botnet in iot networks," in *2021 17th International Conference on Distributed Computing in Sensor Systems (DCOSS)*, 2021, pp. 236–243.

[32] J. A. Jerkins, "Motivating a market or regulatory solution to iot insecurity with the mirai botnet code," in *2017 IEEE 7th Annual Computing and Communication Workshop and Conference (CCWC)*, Jan 2017, pp. 1–5.

[33] "Mirai (ddos) source code review," https://medium.com/@cjbarker/mirai-ddos-source-code-review-57269c4a68f, February 2016.

[34] "Shodan," https://www.shodan.io/, accessed: 2010-02-20.

[35] D. Boneh, *Blum–Blum–Shub Pseudorandom Bit Generator*. Boston, MA: Springer US, 2005, pp. 50–51. [Online]. Available: https://doi.org/10.1007/0-387-23483-7_37

[36] "Oauth 2.0," https://nordicapis.com/why-oauth-2-0-is-vital-to-iot-security/, March 2017.

BlockFW - Towards Blockchain-based Rule-Sharing Firewall

Wei-Yang Chiu and Weizhi Meng
SPTAGE Lab, Department of Applied Mathematics and Computer Science,
Technical University of Denmark, Denmark
Email: {weich, weme}@dtu.dk

***Abstract*—Central-managed security mechanisms are often utilized in many organizations, but such server is also a security breaking point. This is because the server has the authority for all nodes that share the security protection. Hence if the attackers successfully tamper the server, the organization will be in trouble. Also, the settings and policies saved on the server are usually not cryptographically secured and ensured with hash. Thus, changing the settings from alternative way is feasible, without causing the security solution to raise any alarms. To mitigate these issues, in this work, we develop BlockFW – a blockchain-based rule sharing firewall to create a managed security mechanism, which provides validation and monitoring from multiple nodes. For BlockFW, all occurred transactions are cryptographically protected to ensure its integrity, making tampering attempts in utmost challenging for attackers. In the evaluation, we explore the performance of BlockFW under several adversarial conditions and demonstrate its effectiveness.**

***Index Terms*—Network security, Firewall, Blockchain technology, Intrusion detection, Consensus algorithm**

I. Introduction

It is difficult to overlook security policies over large networks for network administrators. When attacks occurred from either internal or external network, it can be quite challenging for them to quickly take measures and deploy new policies [3], [16]. For example, performing penetration test toward multiple servers in a network can be quite simple [18], such as setting up scripts for automating the attack. However, it is quite an opposite situation for network administrators, since collecting information and deploying security solutions need to be done one-by-one. This is very time-consuming and labor-costly compared to performing an attack. To overcome this unfair situation, commercialized central-managed security solutions are provided by many security providers. These products give administrators a dashboard or a cockpit, making it easier to overview situations in the network. That is, information can be collected, and policies can be deployed at one-stop.

However, what these solutions are offering can also become a security breaking point of the system [12]. All endpoints, by default, must trust the decision and command coming from the central server of the security solution. If the management server is compromised, it can become a huge loophole of the security status in an organization [20]. For example, attackers can command all security solutions deactivated in order to reveal further exploits of the internal network.

Fig. 1 shows an example of a central-managed security solution with its settings stored in a mutable database. We

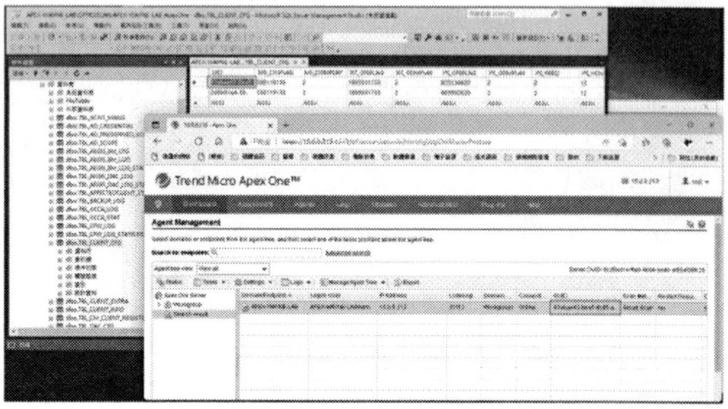

Fig. 1. A Centralized Security Solution with Database in Mutable Storage

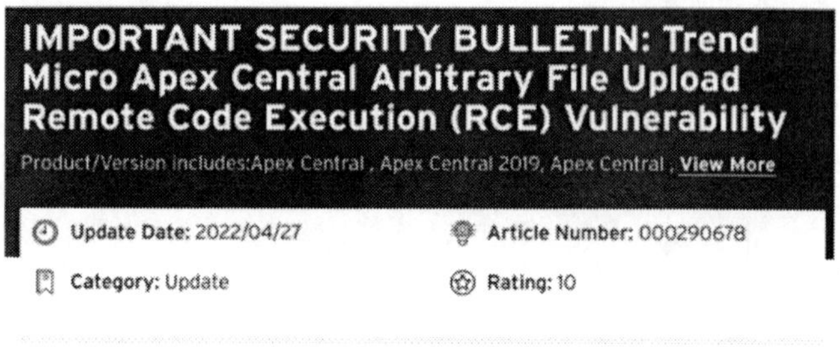

Fig. 2. Security Solution Vulnerability

can perform some value changes, not through the security solution's management console, but through the database console. Then we notice the existence of toolkit that can directly access the offline database file, without any restrictions from the configured database management system. Although the attackers could not obtain the management console's access credential, they have a good chance to change the security solution's settings through several alternative methods, which can be considered as unauthorized changes for the security solution. In this case, although attackers may not be able to find the exploit to the security solution itself, they can still affect the security policies via different vulnerabilities on the server that holds the centralized management of the security solutions, as shown in Fig. 2.

The above potential threat creates the need of having a second pair of eyes to closely monitor the management server itself, making organizations with centralized security solutions more insecure. However, as we closely inspect the example case we are studying, we can see that the issue itself is more related to the underlying database. In other words, changes of a security policy can be made through alternative routes that are outside the designed workflow, which requires the validation and the monitoring from others in the environment.

Motivation. As blockchain becomes a constantly discussed topic recently, several of its characters can tackle the issues of central-managed security solutions [9], [13]. They are the immutability of occurred events, and evidence of transaction events is cryptographically strengthened so that data integrity will become extremely challenging to compromise, and the underlying consensus algorithm will be able to follow one version of the data with their recognition. Further, blockchain requires its participants to hold a partial or full copy of the network transaction log, called *ledger*. Transactions are collected and validated by network maintainers, such characters or equivalent may have different names in different platforms, before being cryptographically sealed into a basic storage unit, named *block*. Generated block contains the cryptographical proof (e.g., hashes) of the previous blocks. This creates a strengthened chain-like storage structure, which is challenging to break [6], [7]. For attackers that would like to alter the previously existed records, it will be extremely time-taking, making such operation infeasible.

If attackers deliberately change the database records by editing it forcefully, it will result in either the node being ditched out of the network due to tremendous differences, or the tampered database records will be restored from other nodes [17]. Both situations are not favorable to the attackers.

Contributions. In this paper, our main goal is to deploy a proof-of-concept of centralized security management on top of blockchain, in order to showcase the feasibility and resilience of such system under cyber-attacks. In particular, we develop BlockFW – a blockchain-based rule-sharing firewall, and investigate its performance under adversarial conditions. The results indicate its capability of lowering the cost of operating a security solution.

The rest of this paper is organized as follows. Section II introduces the background and related work. Section III details the design of BlockFW including the requirements and major components. Section IV presents the performance evaluation under some adversarial scenarios. Section V concludes the work with future work..

II. Background and Related Work

This section introduces the background on blockchain and consensus algorithm, and discusses the related studies.

A. Blockchain

Blockchain, by its design and practice, is considered as a kind of decentralized ledger technology (DLT) [7], [9]. A block is the basic storing unit in the blockchain, which can be formed in a periodic way including the collected transactions within a time period. A consensus algorithm is applied in the network to allow everyone validating the blocks and to reach an agreement on the block version. Basically, consensus algorithm will select a sealer to seal the latest formed block with strong cryptography. The block is then distributed to all network participants for updating their local copies.

To ensure the unification of the decentralized database is the primary designing goal of a consensus algorithm. Below are two typical algorithms.

a) Proof-of-Work (PoW): A PoW-based system will generate a challenging computational problem, in which a difficulty control mechanism is involved. The level of difficulty can be adjusted according to the system's requirements. The participant who first solves the problem will win the turn.

Being the first consensus algorithm in Bitcoin [23] with the easy-to-understand design philosophy, PoW indeed dominates the market of cryptocurrencies. However, with the network participants increasing, many new challenges can be caused, i.e., the tremendous waste of computational power on completing transactions. Profitable mining activities may encourage the forming of mining pools. The concentration of computing power leads to the threat of 51% attack [22]. That is, when a particular group owns 51% or more computational power of the whole network, it has unsurpassed domination on manipulating future records [21].

b) Proof-of-Stake (PoS): As a possible solution to complement PoW consensus algorithm, PoS chooses sealers by rounds of selection rather than computing competitions. More specifically, PoS asks participants to take some of their assets (or coins) to join the election. The system chooses the preferable stake by conditions. The selected stake's owner wins the turn [15]. The criteria of how the system decides the preferable stake is crucial. For example, setting the criteria as preferring a larger stake may cause monopoly. For this issue, *coin-age* that measures a coin's stagnation in an account is considered as a promising solution [4].

PoS provides a more power-efficient method of reaching consensus and providing more fairness of sealer selection toward the participant with less computational power. However, it does not prevent the 51% attack. Though PoS does not suffer from the monopoly of computational power, it may suffer from the monopoly of wealth. As opposite to 51% of computational power, 51% of the wealth can provide unsurpassed advantages on winning the stake [5].

B. Related Work

The application of blockchain technology in developing a firewall is not new. In the literature, Steichen *et al.* [19] introduced ChainGuard, which could use SDN functionalities to filter network traffic for blockchain-based applications. Their system required that all traffic to the blockchain nodes has to be forwarded by at least one of the switches controlled by ChainGuard. Li *et al.* [11] then developed a blockchain-based filtration mechanism (similar to firewall) with collaborative intrusion detection to help protect the security of IoT networks by refining unexpected events. It is found that though some ideas have been proposed on blockchain-based firewall, they have not been widely implemented. This motivates our work to implement a prototype of blockchain-based firewall and examine its performance in a practical setup.

Many research studies are focusing on the combination of blockchain technology with intrusion detection. For instance, Meng *et al.* [14] designed a blockchain-based approach to help enhance the robustness of challenge-based intrusion detection against advanced insider attacks, where a trusted node may suddenly become malicious. Li *et al.* [9] introduced BlockCS-DN, a framework of blockchain-based collaborative intrusion detection for Software Defined Networking (SDN). A similar scheme was also proposed by Meng *et al.* [13], which used blockchain to enhance the robustness of trust management. Some more relevant studies can refer to surveys [2], [9], [10].

III. BlockFW - A Blockchain-based Rule-Sharing Firewall

This section introduces how our proposed blockchain-based rule-sharing firewall works. At first, we briefly describe how to choose and decide a blockchain platform for our case. Then we present the high-level architecture of our system including the major software components.

A. The Requirement for underlying Blockchain Platform

Although different blockchain platforms share similar concepts, the underlying implementation differences provide the platforms with various advantages separately. Not all platforms can become the data storage of our system. For our purposes and goals, we consider a suitable platform that should have the following characteristics:

- `Semi-Dynamic Network`: Servers may be added or removed according to the changes or expands in services. In the trend of X-as-a-Service, cloud, and virtualization, the action of adding or removing service entities can be dynamic. Though being dynamic, there are differences from the public network: authentication is mandatory. Nodes in the network cannot join or leave the network autonomously, authorization entity or authorized personnel must get involved and approve the operation. This specific characteristic creates a semi-dynamic all-known-nodes network. Furthermore, since all network nodes are responsible toward different tasks and may potentially be vulnerable in different ways, we have to assume that part of the network may become malicious. Hence the network we are trying to deploy must be Byzantine-resistible.
- `Stable Connection`: Since servers are regarded as critical infrastructure in IT-enabled businesses, they are usually either connected through the internal network, or the connections can be ensured by telecom SLA with the company. Compared with the wide area network, it has less flickering or instability issues. We consider that it can accept having a blockchain-platform with higher counts of exchanged messages during communication.
- `Timing-Sensitive`: When attacks occurred, we definitely expect that the traffic can be blocked as soon as possible when being a network administrator. However, even deploying security policies through many centralized security solutions may take a while to reach every client. Although it is unreasonable to have everything responded at instant, the actions have been taken will reach and execute by clients eventually. While the time consumption should be in a reasonable length from the command being given to the action being taken. Thus a blockchain system that completes transactions in an estimable time is important.

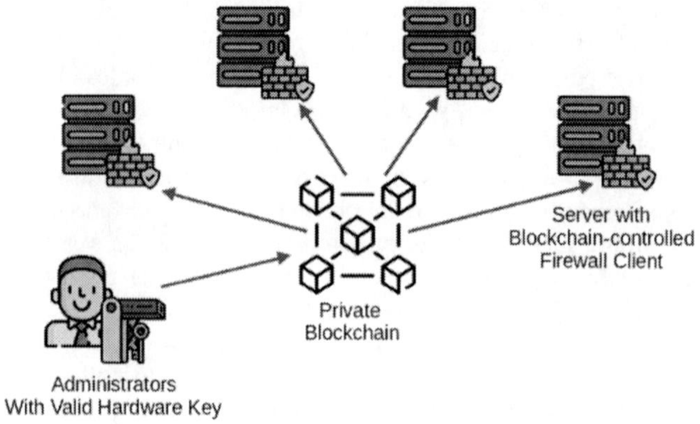

Fig. 3. The Overview Structure of BlockFW

Based on the above characteristics, we figure out that our BlockFW platform needs to be Byzantine tolerable with stable transaction speed, in which these requirements are usually satisfied in a private blockchain.

In this work, we decide to implement the system based upon the DevLeChain platform [25] – a blockchain development environment, which can be used to quickly and easily set up a desired environment [8]. In addition, it supports multiple different blockchain platforms. Hence, we can easily switch between platforms to observe the differences.

B. The System Overview

As shown in Fig. 3, BlockFW features a simple and straightforward system structure, which consists of two major roles and three major pieces of software.

The two roles are:

- `Administrators`: They have the permission to set and alter firewall rules to the system. Each administrator will be given a hardware key that has been registered into the system. Existing administrators can set other keys as administrators. The hardware key is regarded as the wallet file of the administrator when interacting with the blockchain.
- `Clients`: These are endpoints that listen and monitor the given rules on the blockchain. They are installed with firewall software, which can act according to the rules on the blockchain.

The three major software components are:

- `Management Console`: The console is a command-line interface for administrators to add new firewall rules or manage existing firewall rules, as depicted in Fig. 4.

```
Welcome to BlockFW Interactive Console
Firewall Rules is configured at : 0xc2fcb155aee59030ba74..
#> help
    port <port number> <block | unblock | unmonitor>
    list
    exit
#> list
    Port : 22       unblocked
    Port : 23       blocked
    Port : 80       blocked
    Port : 30303   unblocked
#>
```

Fig. 4. The BlockFW Management Console

```
Refresh
    Port 22 remains the same
    Port 23 blocked
    Port 80 blocked
    Port 30303 new monitored

Refresh
    Port 22 remains the same
    Port 23 remains the same
    Port 80 remains the same
    Port 30303 remains the same
```

Fig. 5. The BlockFW Management Console

It requires the administrator's hardware key to function correctly. If a non-registered hardware key is provided, any command given to the management console will fail. This is because the system's backend smart contract is enforced with Access Control List, which contains the public-key-derived wallet addresses. Any non-registered key will result in transactions that are unacceptable to the smart contract, as it cannot be validated.

- `Firewall-Commander`: The firewall-commander is the middleware between the blockchain and the system. It monitors the blockchain for any changes periodically. If the current firewall state is different from what the blockchain has stated, it will synchronize the rules in local system firewall, as shown in Fig. 5.
- `Blockchain`: The blockchain is acted as the decentralized database among clients and administrators.

IV. Performance Evaluation

In this section, we present the environmental setup and evaluate the system under different adversarial scenarios.

A. System Configuration

To test how effective the proposed system is, we configured **three nodes** with client installed, **one administrator node** with hardware key, and **one attacking node** toward the network. Each node is given and configured with the information listed in Table I.

TABLE I
Environmental Platfrom

VM Reousrces		Software	
Item	Config.	Item	Version
CPU	Intel Xeon W-2133 @ 3.6GHz x2	Hypervisor	vmware ESXi 7.0 U3d
Memory	4GB ECC DDR4-2666	Guest OS	mxLinux 21
Storage	48GB HDD	Blockchain Platform	Ethereum 1.10.18
Network	vmware vSwitch 1G	Contract Platform	EVM

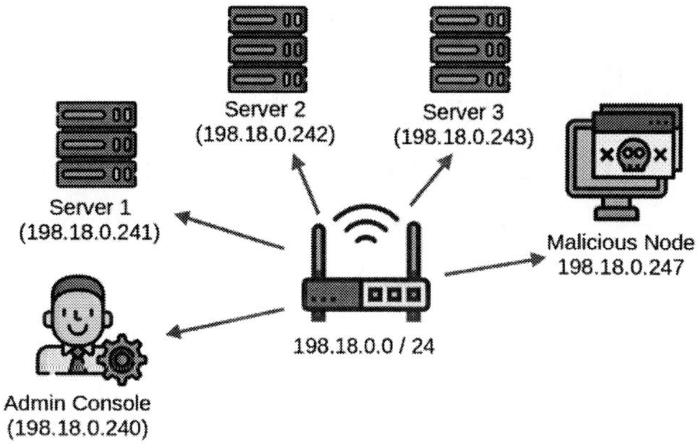

Fig. 6. The network configuration for the testing environment

For concise and clear demonstration, we set up all entities under the same network, as illustrated in Fig. 6. Servers are running three common services: the SSH (Port 22), the Telnet (Port 23), and the HTTP (Port 80).

B. Experiment-1: Attacking toward a Group of Servers

In this test, we assume that malicious node can brute-force the SSH and Telnet, while sending invalid HTTP packet to the web server. If any centralized security solution has not been implemented, then administrators have to do it one by one. In the comparison, our blockchain-based solution can complete this task more quickly. For example, the administrators can use the following commands via the management console, as demonstrated in Fig. 7.

In particular, we configured the Firewall-Commander to refresh the rules every 5 seconds, as Clique consensus algo-

```
#> port 22 block
Port 22 blocked
#> port 23 block
Port 23 blocked
#>
```

Fig. 7. Blocking Port 22 and Port 23 through the Console

```
Refresh
    Port 22 blocked
    Port 23 blocked
```

Fig. 8. Client updating firewall rules

rithm can finish packaging and generate blocks very quickly, as shown in Fig. 8. It is guaranteed that the Firewall-Commander can reach the updated rules within the refreshing period.

After updating the firewall rules, the attack could be instantly stopped as shown in Figure 9. The attacker cannot performs either SSH or Telnet to the protected servers.

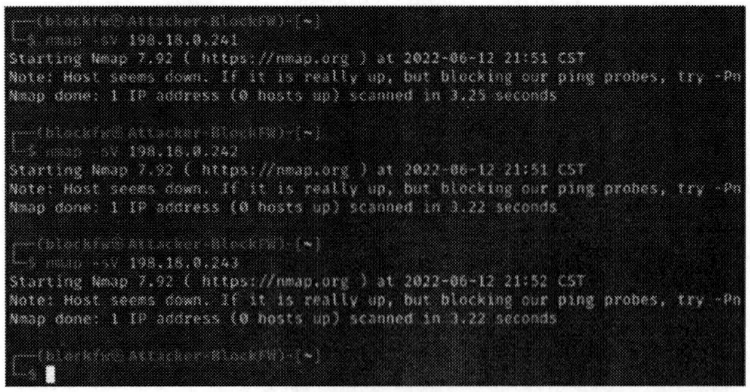

Fig. 9. The NMAP scanning result of the server

C. Experiment-2: When the Network is under Stressed

Many centralized security solutions can be often affected under the Denial-of-Service (DoS) attack. If the traffic flow was stressed out the centralized management server, it becomes difficult for clients to send or receive heartbeat toward and from the server. Hence, the deployment of security rules may become challenging.

Although blockchain is, theoretically, not affected much from DoS attacks toward single node, we still have to know how much it may affect the system. Consensus algorithms, especially those for private chains, have intensive message-exchange protocols. In this case, if the message could not be effectively exchanged, it will affect the rule deployment.

However, it is difficult to perform the experiment by really stressing the nodes with loads, as they are all on the same machine, and even the network switch is emulated. However, it does not mean that we could not emulate the environment through different ways. In this experiment, we deliberately configured the vSwitch [24] to emulate an unreliable network environment, as shown in Fig. 10. We configured the network with the following parameters:

- `Bandwidth`: 128 kbps Full-Duplex

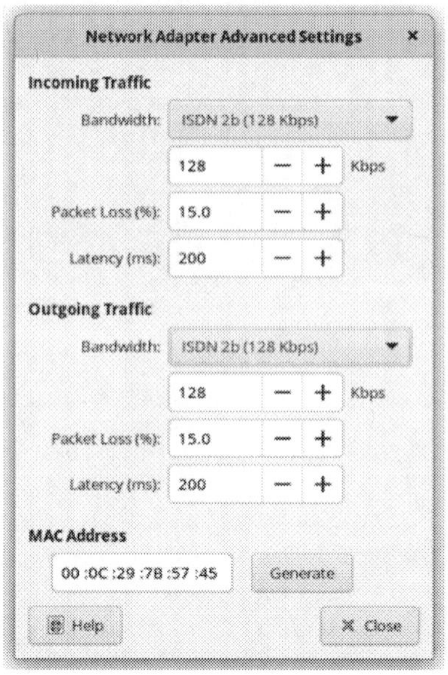

Fig. 10. Creating an unreliable network

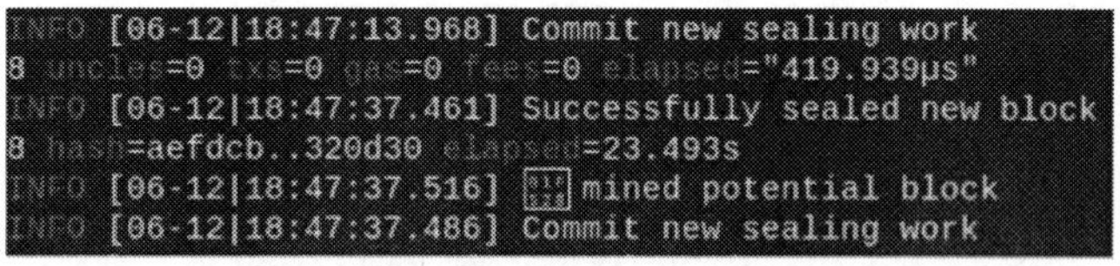

Fig. 11. The mining output from the console

- `Packet Loss`: 15.0%
- `Latency`: 200 ms

As shown in Fig. 11, the time of generating a new block instantly bumped up to around 23 seconds. Other nodes that do not join the mining took another 2-3 seconds to receive the new block. On the Firewall-Commander console, it took around 30 seconds on average to complete the deployment of new firewall rules.

Overall, it is found that our BlockFW system can still work under a stressed network, while the speed of making a policy may slow down. On the positive side, though it is becoming slower, the policy is still reachable to the endpoint.

D. Experiment-3: When a Server is Tampered

As long as the administrator's hardware key is removed from the system, the smart contract on the blockchain cannot be altered. However, we still tried to deliberately corrupt the ledger copy in one of the servers, in order to investigate how the system will react under this condition.

More specifically, we deliberately blank out one of the blockchain database files, and see how the system reacts. As shown in Fig. 12, it is found that the blockchain client detected these anomalies in the local ledger, and immediately started to sync with other nodes.

In conclusion, although an attacker can deliberately tamper a local ledger copy, the blockchain client will instantly notice the anomalies, start downloading chain data from other nodes and

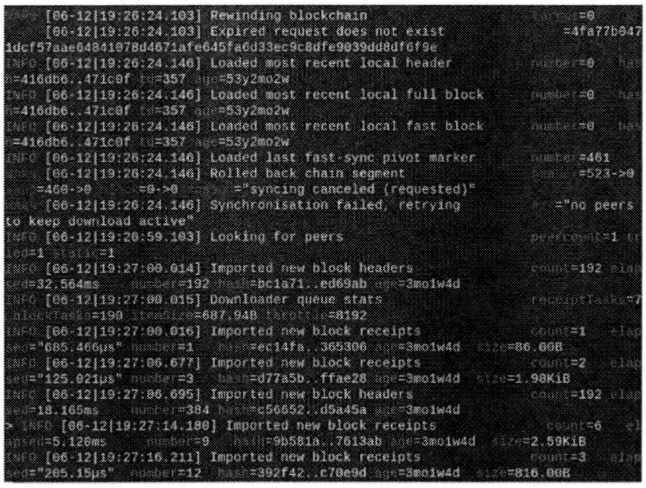

Fig. 12. Blockchain Synchronization Triggered

replacing the corrupted local copy. In this case, our BlockFW can be more robust than a centralized security solution, if the server is under attack.

V. Conclusion and Future Work

In this paper, we developed a blockchain-based rule-sharing firewall (called BlockFW) that can offer validation and monitoring among multiple nodes. In the evaluation, we tested BlockFW in several harsh network conditions and investigated whether it can perform better than a traditional central-managed security solution. Based on the results, it is found that our blockchain-based solution can continue to serve correctly under a stressful network condition. Also, as no central server exists in our system, there is no use for attackers to stress out one of the servers to crash the system. We further demonstrated the adversarial scenario when attackers tried to modify the policies by directly editing the blockchain storage file on one node, and identified that our system could recover itself from other reachable nodes, making the attacker's tampering trial unsuccessful. These provide a good evidence that making blockchain as the underlying database for the security solution is viable with particular advantages.

However, the BlockFW system we are developing requires some further improvements. On functionality phase, the implementation is less than a traditional firewall has, in which we are actively developing a new version to overcome this issue. Another important topic that we have not discussed is whether BlockFW can handle a large network the same as the current central-managed security solutions. This is because permission-based blockchain has to utilize voting-based consensus algorithms that require to exchange many messages to reach consensus compared with a traditional lottery-based consensus algorithm (e.g., PoW / PoS). Too many nodes may result in slowdown and a waste of network resources. Thus, the scalability issues are always important when developing a blockchain-based solution.

Acknowledgment

This work was funded by the European Union H2020 DataVaults project with GA Number 871755. The source code of BlockFW is available at SPTAGE Lab: https://nopkirouter1.compute.dtu.dk/project/blockfw.zip.

References

[1] N. Atzei, "A survey of attacks on ehtereum smart contracts (sok)," *Proc. POST*, pp. 164-186, 2017.
[2] O. Al-Kadi, N. Moustafa, and B.P. Turnbull, "A Review of Intrusion Detection and Blockchain Applications in the Cloud: Approaches, Challenges and Solutions," *IEEE Access* 8, pp. 104893-104917, 2020.
[3] A.A. Almutairi, S. Mishra, and M. Alshehri, "Web Security: Emerging Threats and Defense," *Comput. Syst. Sci. Eng.* 40(3), pp. 1233-1248, 2022.
[4] F. Baldimtsi, V. Madathil, A. Scafuro, and L. Zhou, "Anonymous Lottery In The Proof-of-Stake Setting," *Proc. CSF*, pp. 318-333, 2020.
[5] W.Y. Chiu and W. Meng, "Mind the Scraps: Attacking Blockchain based on Selfdestruct," *Proc. the 26th ACISP*, pp. 451-469, 2021.
[6] W.Y. Chiu and W. Meng, "EdgeTC - A PBFT Blockchain-based ETC Scheme for Smart Cities," *Peer-to-Peer Networking and Applications*, vol. 14, pp. 2874-2886, 2021.
[7] W.Y. Chiu, W. Meng, and C.D. Jensen, "My Data, My Control: A Secure Data Sharing and Access Scheme over Blockchain," *Journal of Information Security and Applications*, vo. 63, 103020, 2021.
[8] W.Y. Chiu and W. Meng, "DevLeChain - an Open Blockchain Development Platform for Decentralized Applications," *Proc. The 5th IEEE International Conference on Blockchain*, pp. 167-176, 2022.
[9] W. Li, Y. Wang, W. Meng, J. Li, and C. Su, "BlockCSDN: Towards Blockchain-based Collaborative Intrusion Detection in Software Defined Networking," *IEICE Transactions on Information and Systems*, vol. E105.D, no. 2, pp. 272-279, 2022.
[10] W. Li, W. Meng, and L.F. Kwok, "Surveying Trust-based Collaborative Intrusion Detection: State-of-the-Art, Challenges and Future Directions," *IEEE Commun. Surv. Tutorials*, vol. 24, no. 1, pp. 280-305, 2022.
[11] W. Li, Y. Wang, and J. Li, "Enhancing blockchain-based filtration mechanism via IPFS for collaborative intrusion detection in IoT networks," *J. Syst. Archit.* 127, 102510, 2022.
[12] W. Meng, W. Li, and L.F. Kwok, "EFM: Enhancing the Performance of Signature-based Network Intrusion Detection Systems Using Enhanced Filter Mechanism," *Computers & Security*, vol. 43, pp. 189-204, 2014.
[13] W. Meng, W. Li, and J. Zhou, "Enhancing the Security of Blockchain-based Software Defined Networking through Trust-based Traffic Fusion and Filtration," *Information Fusion*, vol. 70, pp. 60-71, 2021.
[14] W. Meng, W. Li, L.T. Yang, and P. Li, "Enhancing challenge-based collaborative intrusion detection networks against insider attacks using blockchain," *Int. J. Inf. Sec.* 19(3), pp. 279-290, 2020.
[15] W. Meng, E.W. Tischhauser, Q. Wang, Y. Wang, and J. Han, "When Intrusion Detection Meets Blockchain Technology: A Review," *IEEE Access*, vol. 6, no. 1, pp. 10179-10188, 2018.
[16] Y. Meng and L.F. Kwok, "A Framework for Protocol Vulnerability Condition Detection," *Proc. SECURWARE*, pp. 91-96, 2011.
[17] R. Mukta, H.Y. Paik, Q. Lu, and S.S. Kanhere, "A survey of data minimisation techniques in blockchain-based healthcare," *Comput. Networks* 205, 108766, 2022.
[18] M. Rak, G. Salzillo, and D. Granata, "ESSecA: An automated expert system for threat modelling and penetration testing for IoT ecosystems," *Comput. Electr. Eng.* 99, 107721, 2022.
[19] M. Steichen, S. Hommes, and R. State, "ChainGuard - A firewall for blockchain applications using SDN with OpenFlow," *Proc. IPTComm*, pp. 1-8, 2017.
[20] R.L. Trope and E.K. Ressler, "Mettle Fatigue: VW's Single-Point-of-Failure Ethics," *IEEE Secur. Priv.* 14(1), pp. 12-30, 2016.
[21] 51% Attack (accessed on 15 June 2022) https://dci.mit.edu/51-attacks
[22] Frankenfield, J., "51% Attack Definition," (accessed on 15 June 2022) https://www.investopedia.com/terms/1/51-attack.asp
[23] Nakamoto, S., "Bitcoin: A Peer-to-Peer Electronic Cash System," (accessed on 15 June 2022) https://bitcoin.org/bitcoin.pdf
[24] Open vSwitch (accessed on 15 June 2022) https://www.openvswitch.org/
[25] DevLeChain Platform (accessed on 15 June 2022) https://devlechain.compute.dtu.dk/

Authentic Batteries: A Concept for a Battery Pass Based on PUF-enabled Certificates

Julian Blümke
C-ECOS
Technische Hochschule Ingolstadt
Ingolstadt, Germany
e-mail: julian.bluemke@carissma.eu

Hans-Joachim Hof
C-ECOS
Technische Hochschule Ingolstadt
Ingolstadt, Germany
e-mail: hof@thi.de

***Abstract*—The European Union's Green Deal and other similar regulations advocate to reuse batteries of electrical vehicles ("second life") to reduce greenhouse gases. To ease the assessment of the best fitting second life applications for a distinctly used battery, product life cycle data plays an important role. A digital battery pass will be mandatory for future batteries and will contain such data collected throughout the product's life cycle. Having trustworthy data is one key element of the battery pass in order to provide authentic batteries. This paper presents a concept to securely bind the pass to the battery itself by using physical unclonable functions for creating a unique identifier per battery. The approach is based on certificates and makes use of Certificate Transparency to foster trust in the issued certificates. Attacks on product life cycle data or certificates and counterfeiting batteries can be detected.**

***Index Terms*—physical unclonable function; Certificate Transparency; electric vehicle battery; battery identity; battery pass.**

I. Introduction

The European Union's (EU) Green Deal aims to reduce greenhouse gases towards net-zero emissions by 2050 [1]. One of the measures is to lower the use of fossil energies in the transportation sector. Electrically driven vehicles foster this goal and are expected to achieve high sales numbers in the upcoming years: The Faraday Institute forecasts a worldwide demand of more than 5,900 GWh in the year 2040 (2020: 110 GWh) [2]. The rise of Electrical Vehicles (EV) is accompanied by an increasing need for high voltage batteries. However, batteries degrade during usage and charging. They can only be used in an EV until their capacity degraded to 80% [3] [4]. This will result in a large number of dismounted and unusable EV-batteries having a negative economical, ecological and social impact [5]–[7]. However, these batteries may be still fine for other use cases. To support recycling and reusing of products and materials the EU introduced the Circular Economy Action Plan containing the reuse of batteries as one pillar [8]. Its goal is to set up applications for a battery's second life either as complete product in a different environment or dismantled in new products.

The new mass market for EV batteries will also encourage the production of counterfeit batteries. Non-certified or non-qualified batteries can introduce safety risks due to deviations from specifications of genuine products and especially due to cost-savings in risk reducing controls and management systems [9]. Reduced capacity and lifetime, overheating, and self-ignition, as well as social aspects like underpaid workers and bad working conditions during manufacturing are examples for likely effects when using counterfeit EV-batteries.

Circular economy and the fight against counterfeiting emphasize a need for authentic batteries: Trust in the battery's quality, evidence in the correct implementation of the specification, and traceability of the product life cycle enhance the opportunities for second life applications and lower the risk of introducing low quality and dangerous products into the market.

Both, the readiness for circular economy and the circulation of only high-quality batteries, shall be regulated within the new and as of today drafted EU-regulation about the treatment of (old) batteries [10]. The proposal presents a digital battery pass as a record of manufacturer, materials, and specifications of every single battery. This paper presents an approach to inherently bind the digital pass to the physical battery by using certificates based on Physical Unclonable Functions (PUF).

Physical Unclonable Function: A PUF uses physical deviations that occur during production to create a unique and unclonable identifier [11]. It is described as a challenge-response-pair (CRP) where a device to be authenticated needs to prove the ownership of the PUF-identifier. There are two different types: weak PUFs always provide the same identifier, strong PUFs can create multiple identifier. An example for a weak PUF is the SRAM-PUF which takes advantage of the cells' random behavior after powering whereas an optical PUF where randomly distributed particles on a surface are illuminated from different directions creating unique shadows is an example for a strong PUF [12]. PUFs are used as an computational and financial inexpensive alternative of storing cryptographic keys or identifier in non-volatile memory [11].

Certificate Transparency: Certificate Transparency (CT) was originally developed by Google and is about transparent and trust-worthy issuing of certificates used in the Web PKI [13]. It is summarized in the experimental RFC 6962 [14] and deals with the difficulties of trusting Certificate Authorities (CA) in general: private keys associated with a certificate may be stolen or created in a wrongful way such that encryption itself would not be damaged but an attacker might be able to decrypt the communication without knowledge of the the necessary key. A common way to check the trustworthiness of CAs is to examine audits. However, audits often check for formal aspects only than for a correct implementation of technical processes.

The idea of CT is about storing certificates in publicly available append-only logs that can be validated by everyone. Figure 1 shows the steps needed to implement CT: The owner of the domain requests a certificate by the CA which creates a pre-certificate and sends it to the log. The latter is managed as a Merkle Tree [15]. A Signed Certificate Timestamp (SCT) ensuring that the certificate is added to the log is send to the CA. The certificate is extended with the SCT and transferred the domain owner. From this time on, the domain owner can use it as normal certificate, e.g., for hosting websites. At the end user's site, the certificate is checked for the existence of SCTs, e.g., during TLS handshake. Some internet browser require that the certificate is signed with at least two SCTs. The certificate logs are checked periodically by external monitors. The domain owner is informed if there are new and especially odd activities with certificates of its domain.

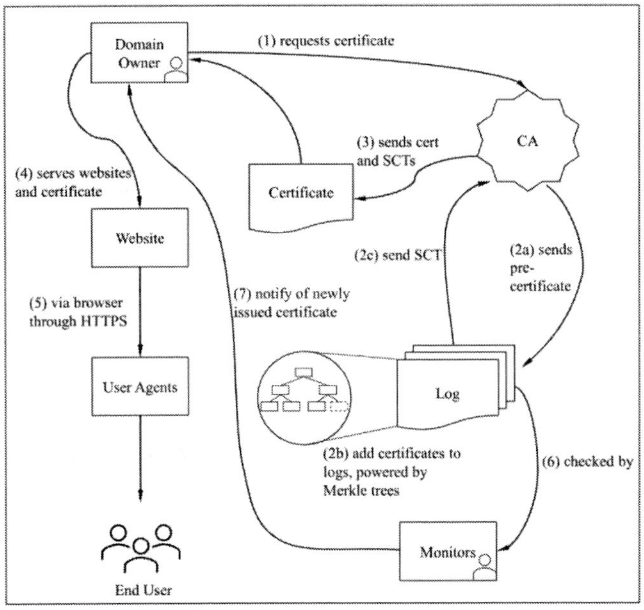

Fig. 1. Implementation of certification transparency (illustration based on [13]).

Furthermore, there are other methods for detecting counterfeit products, e.g., by statistical measures [16], physical inspection, or electrical examination [17]. However, the presented concept is triggered by the EU regulation concerning the battery pass and therefore, the concept of logging and auditing is reasonable.

The remaining paper is structured as followed: Section II describes related work as a basis for a concept for authentic batteries which is introduced in Section III. Current and future activities are summarized in Section IV.

II. Related Work

To the best of our knowledge, the idea of a digital product pass for single products is unique to batteries. Other applications do have static product records or they are only implemented for a group of products and not for single devices, e.g., like the International Material Data System (IMDS) [18], the Building Information Modeling (BIM) based Material Passport [19], or the Cradle-to-Cradle (C2C) Passport [20]. Additionally, the battery pass will be the first pass that is required by law. The following related research results introduce only comparable parts of the presented concept.

A. PUFs based on batteries

In [21], Bosch describes the calculation of PUF identifiers out of a set of different parameters: pressure drop between two sides of the battery, the batteries natural frequency, the temperature pattern, the open circuit voltage (OCV) or the air leak rate [21]. The created PUF identifier is saved as a physical tag on top of the battery or in the battery management system's memory. However, the identifier can only be calculated in a dismounted state. This method shows the possibility of a battery PUF creation in general.

[22] presented a method to authenticate an outstation in a distributed energy storage network. This work takes advantage of the fact that the cells' voltages differ at the same state of charge (SoC). Both, the outstation and the master station, sanitize a challenge-reply-table with continuously updated measurements presenting a model of every cell. The authentication challenge is formed out of a selection of cells. The SoC and the voltages are measured and sent back to the master station. If the actual measurements match with the values in the challenge-reply-table the outstation is accepted as authentic.

Both works demonstrate that it is feasible to use PUFs on batteries. However, existing works use the PUF as a mechanism to create an identity. We want to extend this to use the PUF as a derivation for cryptographic keys.

B. Blockchain with PUFs

A common mechanism to implement digital product passes is the use of blockchain [23] [24]. Casino et al. described a blockchain as "distributed append-only timestamped data structure" [25] where no central and trusted authority is involved. Exchanging assets, digital or physical, between two blockchain participants is achieved and recorded with transactions. They have to be validated by other participating nodes using a consensus algorithm in order to prevent corruption or forgery of branches. Blockchains in the sector of supply chain management can increase trust, traceability, transparency and accountability. They are installed for better visibility and enhanced optimization of a supply chain. [25]

PUFChain is a method that combines blockchain with PUFs within the Internet-of-Everything (IoE) domain where trusted nodes authenticate IoE-data collected from client nodes [26]. The process is divided in three phases: During the enrollment, the client's PUF-CRP are calculated and stored in a secure database. The phases of transactions consist of data collection, PUF response generation, and hashing of both. The data and the hash is added to the blockchain and needs to be authenticated by trusted nodes. These nodes recalculate the hash by using the client data and the pre-calculated PUF response retrieved from the database and validate the block if both hashes match. An application of PUFChain in the Internet-of-Energy can be found in [27].

An approach to enable trust in supply chain by tracing was presented in [28]. Newly manufactured devices need to be registered in a blockchain with a unique ID, e.g., a PUF. Device transfers are recorded in the blockchain. The contractual ownership alters only after a transfer confirmation which is done by calculating the unique device ID of the received device and comparing it with the ID mentioned in the transaction payload. End users can check the device's authenticity by matching the computed ID with the blockchain content.

Whereas blockchain is a popular method for storing tamper-proofed data, we decided to use a different approach. In our opinion, the system consists for trusted partners. Therefore, a decentralized distribution of data is not necessary. A database can be hosted, e.g., by the EU enforcing the battery regulations. Another aspect is that in this specific application consensus algorithms are useful only to a limit extent as it will just provide a proof of formal attributes of transaction but not on the transaction content itself: For example a blockchain party validating a new block cannot check the correctness of, e.g., a new temperature maximum or a degradation of capacity as it does not have access to the battery itself.

III. CONCEPT FOR AUTHENTIC BATTERIES

A. Introduction

The general aim of our method is to have one single source of truth containing information about the battery's life cycle including the manufacturing process, product acceptance tests (PAT), measures of quality control, and the usage history. Tracing materials and processes foster consumer's trust in the battery and enables an easier assessment of the batteries' status for recycling or reusing.
The data of the life cycle record is stored in a database that can be permissioned in order to control and restrict read and write access of supply chain parties involved. Access control also protects the parties' intellectual property (IP). It is mandatory to have a secure binding between the life cycle record and the battery itself ensuring the correspondence between both. The secure binding is established by the use of certificates in combination with PUFs that provide unique identifiers for each battery.

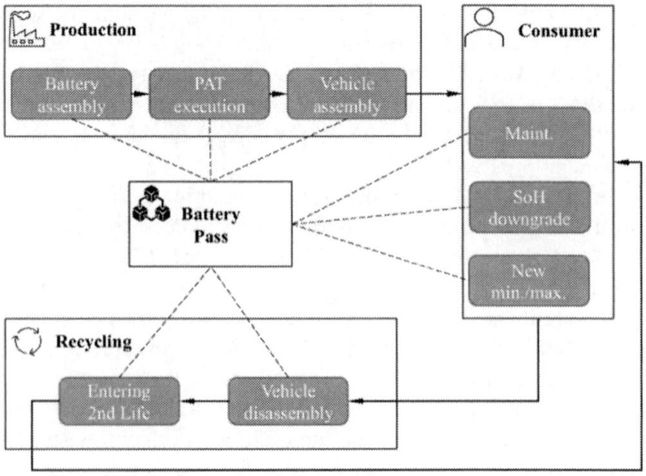

Fig. 2. Battery pass as life cycle record.

B. Data for battery pass's records

Data is added to the battery pass during manufacturing, product testing, and quality controlling. At end user level, the data is needed to emphasize a remarkable downgrade of, e.g., the state of health (SoH) or capacity and to record minimum and maximum temperatures, voltages and currents. The latter are important to assess the batteries health for a second life application. The data acquisition building the life cycle record is split into three phases (see Figure 2).
Assembly and initial product testing takes place during the production stage at the battery OEM (original equipment manufacturer). Information about manufacturer, working conditions, date of production, and results of acceptance tests are stored in the battery pass. Afterwards, the battery is transferred to the vehicle's OEM to be built into the intended vehicle. Again, information about the vehicle manufacturer, working conditions, and the vehicle including the vehicle identification number (VIN) are stored in the record.
We are assuming the car to be delivered to the consumer directly after production. At this stage the battery will be used in its intended environment. Significant changes of the battery's quality will be logged to the life cycle record. These changes include temperature, voltage and current maxima and minima and SoH and capacity downgrade. This information will ease the battery's assessment before entering the second life.
The preparation of the second life is divided into two steps: First, the battery is dismounted from the vehicle and the date and the implementing company are stored in the life cycle record. The activity of entering the second life contains events like firmware updates, quality tests and maintenance activities. Again, the battery will be transferred to a consumer. We assume an environment in which the life cycle record can be sanitized. Therefore, the stage of the second life equals the consumer stage.

The format of the battery pass's data is not defined inhere.

However, the JSON data format may be reasonable as it is widely used and easy to read and process.

C. Security Considerations

With the presented concept the following security related aspects shall be considered: The battery pass and its records shall be bound to the battery in order to state out that these records are only valid for this specific battery. Manipulation of the battery pass has to be detectable as well as the circulation of counterfeit batteries having no or stolen battery passes. Updates of the records shall only be possible from the battery itself or from a system that has access to the battery. This ensures the validity of the data without the possibility of data added by a third-party not involved in the process. Trust and transparency shall be treated to foster the battery pass's acceptance by the user and in general a successful assessment of second life applications.

D. Security Architecture

The technical implementation of our method is based on signed battery data whereas the keys are derived from the battery's PUF. Figure 3 shows the overall process of adding data and verifying the battery's identity. We are assuming the private and public key derived from the PUF already exist. As elaborated in the related work section (Section II), this is a reasonable assumption.

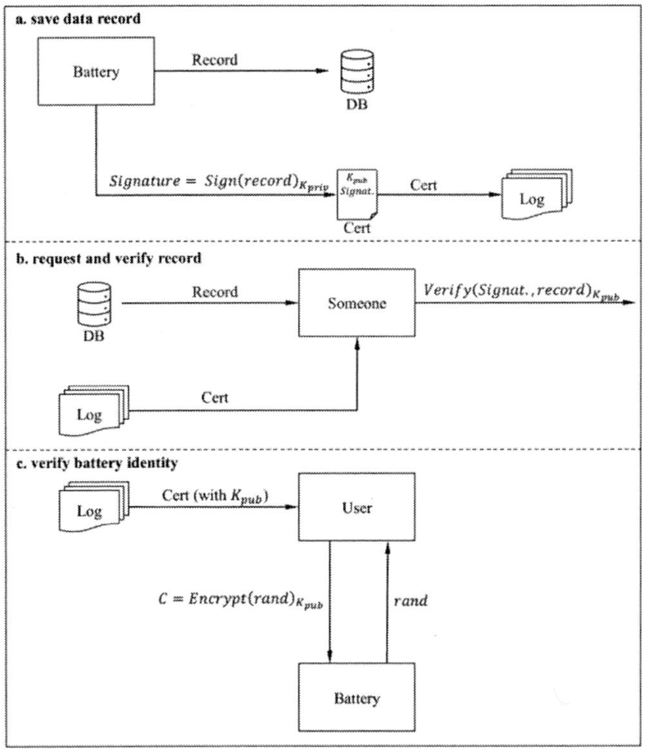

Fig. 3. Implementation of digital pass with certificates. **a.** Update of battery records **b.** Verify that certificate belongs to records **c.** Verify that battery belongs to certificate.

Three phases are applicable:
The most functional part of the method is adding and updating data of the battery as it is described in Sec. III-B. If new data is generated it will be sent to a central database containing historic and current data of each battery (Figure 3a). In the battery the data is signed with its private key. Only the signature is added to a battery specific certificate also containing the public key. If a certificate already exists for the battery a reissuing is needed and the old one has to be revoked. The certificate itself is attached to an append-only log. We are relying on Certificate Transparency which is a commonly used method developed by Google to store and handle identity certificates in a trusted and verifiable way. Whereas the log itself does not fulfill any functional requirement, it provides additional trust and transparency into the certificate as it can be validated from external and public parties.
One could argue to add the battery data to the certificate introducing the advantage of having one single document containing all relevant information about the battery. However, having this, the battery's data is publicly available and therefore, IP may be revealed as well as the opportunity for malicious analysis about production statistics and performance of a battery OEM. A dedicated database can be restricted to a reduced number of users.

In order to check the validity of the data in accordance with the corresponding certificate, access to the data and the certificate is needed. Using the public key stored in the certificate the signatures can be verified (Figure 3b). In this context, another opportunity to avoid disclosure of IP may be possible by letting the signatures be checked by the database itself and letting it deliver a summary of data not revealing IP.

In the third phase, it is checked that the certificate belongs to the battery as described in Figure 3c. Therefore, a challenge-response-mechanism is used where the user sends a challenge consisting of random number encrypted with the public key to the battery. The challenge is decrypted using the battery's private key and the response is sent back to the user. If the response equals the original random number it is verified that the certificate belongs to the battery as the private key is directly derived from the battery's PUF.

To reduce the risk of stolen or reproduced keys by an attacker the derived key may be stored in a Hardware Security Module (HSM), e.g., placed on the Battery Management System (BMS). However, the cost-efficiency of HSMs in the context of industrial applications with large quantities having high pressure on costs has to be evaluated [29].

E. Challenges

The main challenge of the presented method is the derivation of keys from the battery's PUF. It is required that the keys do not change over time. However, due to aging of cells and the battery pack the PUF and therefore, the keys may change. The validation steps mentioned above cannot be executed anymore resulting in a failure of the complete method. The same applies

for genuine repairs or maintenance activities of the battery. Single cells will not be exchanged probably, but battery packs. This would result in a new PUF and so in invalid existing private and public keys.
To overcome both, two approaches might be appropriate: First, using a model forecasting the cell and battery aging in order to create static cryptographic keys. And second, if an imminent change is foreseeable having a mechanism to modify the existing keys, e.g., with pre-calculated challenges and a hash chain for tracking expired keys.
Instead of using the battery's cells to create unique identifier one could also use the surrounding electrical components as origin for physical unclonable functions. The entropy might be enough to create cryptographic keys as there are many components built in one battery pack. These components do not age in the same way as cells do.

Challenges also arise in the general use of the battery pass. Standardization across companies is mandatory to enable comparability of batteries. This also applies for the update procedure of the battery pass. Questions concerning the frequency and the resolution of record updates have to be answered.

F. Security Analysis

In the following section it is analyzed if the presented concept complies with the requirements stated in Section III-C.

Attack Model: We assume that the attacker has read and write access to the database. As the certificates are stored publicly following the methods of Certificate Transparency the adversary can read certificates. However, the attacker cannot read or re-create the battery's private key as we assume that the physical access to the battery and its related components is restricted.

Binding battery pass and battery: The battery pass and the physical battery are bound using the cryptographic keys created from the battery's PUF.

Detection of manipulated battery pass: A manipulation of data in the database will be recognized when the data's signature is verified. The verification of the signatures should be a mandatory step when working with these batteries, e.g., for an assessment of the second life applications.

However, manipulation or deletion of data can result in financial and ecological damage as it is the basis for further use of the battery. If the data is deleted, assumptions based on statistical measures have to be consulted which may result in a worse assessment of the state of health.

Circulation of counterfeit batteries: If an attacker duplicates the certificate in order to sell a counterfeit battery with a pseudo-valid certificate, the attack may not be recognized until the link between the certificate and the battery is verified. Whereas signature for the data is valid, the challenge-response will fail: The public key of the certificate does not match to the private key of the battery. Therefore, the decryption of the response will fail.

Update of battery pass only with access to battery: Records can be added to the database without having access to the battery. However, the battery pass, i.e., the certificate can only be reissued with the record's signature which is created with the cryptographic keys derived from the PUF. Therefore, a valid update of the battery pass is only possible with physical access to the battery.

Generating trust and transparency: Trust and transparency for user's acceptance and for trustworthy assessment of second life applications is created with the use of cryptographic keys on the one hand and on the other hand with the use of Certificate Transparency where certificates can be validated by external parties.

Several attack scenarios have been described. None of them can be executed on its own as there need to be attacks on multiple system parts to be successful. However, it also showed that a verification of the different links between certificate, data and battery is mandatory to ensure the system's security.

Nevertheless, a complete and in-depth security analysis will be executed in the future to strengthen the given statements.

G. Efficiency of Data Transfer and Verification

In the current EU project MARBEL (Manufacturing and assembly of modular and reusable Electric Vehicle battery for environment-friendly and lightweight mobility) the efficiency of data transfer with a state-of-the-art BMS has been analyzed in a Proof-of-Concept. Tests have been made with a frequency of data transfer ranging from 5 Hz to 200 Hz sending single MQTT (Message Queuing Telemetry Transport protocol) messages. Authentication and encryption was established using the Transport Layer Security (TLS) protocol adding a security related overhead to every message. The average message size summed up to 90 bytes which corresponded to a measured maximum data rate of 144 kBits/s. The findings from these tests appear to support the assumption of an efficient data transfer. However, a continuous stream of battery data might not be required as the degradation of the battery's state of health is a slow process. Data may be also buffered over a defined time and sent in blocks.
Data will be verified on servers which can be highly optimized. Therefore, it is expected that the verification can be carried out efficiently as well.

IV. Conclusion and Future Work

Circular economy and the fight against product counterfeiting increase the need for authentic products. The digital battery pass is one example for achieving trust and traceability of a product. The paper presented a concept to manage a battery's life cycle record by using certificates. The correspondence between the batteries identity and the battery pass is achieved with PUFs constructed of the battery's physical deviations. Using the PUF-enabled certificates, it is possible to detect counterfeit as well as low-quality batteries. Challenges occur in the consistency of PUFs due to aging and maintenance issues of the product pass.

Future work includes the implementation of a Proof-of-Concept followed by a performance analysis and an in-depth formal security analysis in order to evaluate the functionality in general and the security measures of the concept. Other mechanisms for detecting counterfeit electronic products will be analyzed and might enhance the presented concept. The consistency of PUFs in the context of batteries will be part of further extensive investigations.

ACKNOWLEDGMENT

This project has received funding from the European Union's Horizon 2020 research and innovation programme under grant agreement No 963540.

I want to thank my research colleagues for supporting me during the concept creation. I also want to acknowledge the research group of Prof. Dr. rer. nat. Hans-Georg Schweiger for discussions about the topic of PUFs for batteries.

REFERENCES

[1] European Commission, "Regulation (eu) 2021/1119 of the european parliament and of the council of 30 june 2021 establishing the framework for achieving climate neutrality and amending regulations (ec) no 401/2009 and (eu) 2018/1999 ('european climate law'): European climate law," 2021. [Online]. Available: http://data.europa.eu/eli/reg/2021/1119/oj

[2] "Lithium, cobalt and nickel: The gold rush of the 21st century." [Online]. Available: https://faraday.ac.uk/get/insight-6/

[3] E. Wood, M. Alexander, and T. H. Bradley, "Investigation of battery end-of-life conditions for plug-in hybrid electric vehicles," *Journal of Power Sources*, vol. 196, no. 11, pp. 5147–5154, 2011.

[4] E. Hossain, D. Murtaugh, J. Mody, H. M. R. Faruque, M. S. Haque Sunny, and N. Mohammad, "A comprehensive review on second-life batteries: Current state, manufacturing considerations, applications, impacts, barriers & potential solutions, business strategies, and policies," *IEEE Access*, vol. 7, pp. 73 215–73 252, 2019.

[5] L. A.-W. Ellingsen, G. Majeau-Bettez, B. Singh, A. K. Srivastava, L. O. Valøen, and A. H. Strømman, "Life cycle assessment of a lithium-ion battery vehicle pack," *Journal of Industrial Ecology*, vol. 18, no. 1, pp. 113–124, 2014.

[6] J. F. Peters, M. Baumann, B. Zimmermann, J. Braun, and M. Weil, "The environmental impact of li-ion batteries and the role of key parameters – a review," *Renewable and Sustainable Energy Reviews*, vol. 67, pp. 491–506, 2017.

[7] C. Thies, K. Kieckhäfer, T. S. Spengler, and M. S. Sodhi, "Assessment of social sustainability hotspots in the supply chain of lithium-ion batteries," *Procedia CIRP*, vol. 80, pp. 292–297, 2019.

[8] European Commission and Directorate-General for Communication, *Circular economy action plan: for a cleaner and more competitive Europe*. Publications Office, 2020.

[9] A. B. Lopez, K. Vatanparvar, A. P. Deb Nath, S. Yang, S. Bhunia, and M. A. Al Faruque, "A security perspective on battery systems of the internet of things," *Journal of Hardware and Systems Security*, vol. 1, no. 2, pp. 188–199, 2017.

[10] European Commission, "Proposal for a regulation of the european parliament and of the council concerning batteries and waste batteries, repealing directive 2006/66/ec and amending regulation (eu) no 2019/1020," 17.03.2022. [Online]. Available: http://data.consilium.europa.eu/doc/document/ST-7317-2022-INIT/X/pdf

[11] G. E. Suh and S. Devadas, "Physical unclonable functions for device authentication and secret key generation," in *Proceedings of the 44th annual Design Automation Conference*, ser. ACM Conferences, S. P. Levitan, Ed. New York, NY: ACM, 2007, p. 9.

[12] T. McGrath, I. E. Bagci, Z. M. Wang, U. Roedig, and R. J. Young, "A puf taxonomy," *Applied Physics Reviews*, vol. 6, no. 1, p. 011303, 2019.

[13] Google, "Certificate transparency: How ct works," 2022. [Online]. Available: https://certificate.transparency.dev/howctworks/

[14] B. Laurie, A. Langley, and E. Kasper, "Certificate transparency," 2013. [Online]. Available: https://www.rfc-editor.org/info/rfc6962

[15] R. C. Merkle, "A digital signature based on a conventional encryption function," in *Advances in Cryptology — CRYPTO '87*, C. Pomerance, Ed. Berlin, Heidelberg: Springer Berlin Heidelberg, 1988, pp. 369–378.

[16] K. Huang, Y. Liu, N. Korolija, J. M. Carulli, and Y. Makris, "Recycled ic detection based on statistical methods," *IEEE Transactions on Computer-Aided Design of Integrated Circuits and Systems*, vol. 34, no. 6, pp. 947–960, 2015.

[17] U. Guin, K. Huang, D. Dimase, J. M. Carulli, M. Tehranipoor, and Y. Makris, "Counterfeit integrated circuits: A rising threat in the global semiconductor supply chain," *Proceedings of the IEEE*, vol. 102, no. 8, pp. 1207–1228, 2014.

[18] F. B. de Oliveira, A. Nordelöf, B. A. Sandén, A. Widerberg, and A.-M. Tillman, "Exploring automotive supplier data in life cycle assessment – precision versus workload," *Transportation Research Part D: Transport and Environment*, vol. 105, p. 103247, 2022.

[19] M. Honic, I. Kovacic, P. Aschenbrenner, and A. Ragossnig, "Material passports for the end-of-life stage of buildings: Challenges and potentials," *Journal of Cleaner Production*, vol. 319, p. 128702, 2021.

[20] T. Adisorn, L. Tholen, and T. Götz, "Towards a digital product passport fit for contributing to a circular economy," *Energies*, vol. 14, no. 8, p. 2289, 2021.

[21] K. Vittilapuram Subramanian and A. Madhukar Lele, "A system and method for generation and validation of puf identifier of a battery pack," Patent WO2 022 023 280A2, 2022.

[22] I. Zografopoulos and C. Konstantinou, "Derauth: A battery-based authentication scheme for distributed energy resources," in *2020 IEEE Computer Society Annual Symposium on VLSI (ISVLSI)*. IEEE, 2020, pp. 560–567.

[23] M. Kouhizadeh, J. Sarkis, and Q. Zhu, "At the nexus of blockchain technology, the circular economy, and product deletion," *Applied Sciences*, vol. 9, no. 8, p. 1712, 2019.

[24] T. K. Agrawal, V. Kumar, R. Pal, L. Wang, and Y. Chen, "Blockchain-based framework for supply chain traceability: A case example of textile and clothing industry," *Computers & Industrial Engineering*, vol. 154, p. 107130, 2021.

[25] F. Casino, T. K. Dasaklis, and C. Patsakis, "A systematic literature review of blockchain-based applications: Current status, classification and open issues," *Telematics and Informatics*, vol. 36, pp. 55–81, 2019.

[26] S. P. Mohanty, V. P. Yanambaka, E. Kougianos, and D. Puthal, "Pufchain: A hardware-assisted blockchain for sustainable simultaneous device and data security in the internet of everything (ioe)," *IEEE Consumer Electronics Magazine*, vol. 9, no. 2, pp. 8–16, 2020.

[27] R. Asif, K. Ghanem, and J. Irvine, "Proof-of-puf enabled blockchain: Concurrent data and device security for internet-of-energy," *Sensors (Basel, Switzerland)*, vol. 21, no. 1, 2020.

[28] P. Cui, J. Dixon, U. Guin, and D. Dimase, "A blockchain-based framework for supply chain provenance," *IEEE Access*, vol. 7, pp. 157 113–157 125, 2019.

[29] Y. Xie, Y. Guo, S. Yang, J. Zhou, and X. Chen, "Security-related hardware cost optimization for can fd-based automotive cyber-physical systems," *Sensors (Basel, Switzerland)*, vol. 21, no. 20, 2021.

Digital Forensics Investigation of the Tesla Autopilot File System

Kevin Gomez Buquerin
Technische Hochschule Ingolstadt and
Friedrich Alexander University Erlangen Nürnberg
CARISSMA Institute of Electric, Connected, and
Secure Mobility (C-ECOS)
Germany
email: extern.kevinklaus.gomezbuquerin@thi.de

Hans-Joachim Hof
Technische Hochschule Ingolstadt
CARISSMA Institute of Electric, Connected, and
Secure Mobility (C-ECOS)
Germany
email: hans-joachim.hof@thi.de

***Abstract*—Tesla vehicles offer a wide range of services, including an autopilot. As a central vehicle component, the autopilot has been the focus of much media and research attention. Several articles have highlighted flaws in the autopilot service. These flaws make the autopilot service relevant for Automotive Digital Forensics (ADF) investigations since vehicle automation is likely to cause accidents. This paper presents an ADF investigation of the file system of a Tesla autopilot hardware version 2.0. We identified metadata characteristics, including general information (such as Linux user accounts, extensions, and timestamps) and vehicle-specific characteristics (including surveillance and safety-related information that is of great use in investigations of modern vehicles). The paper evaluates the forensic reliability of memory acquisition and the usability of the identified features.**

***Index Terms*—automotive, vehicle, digital forensics, automotive digital forensics, tesla, autopilot, metadata, vehicle forensics**

I. INTRODUCTION

The total number of Tesla deliveries has steadily increased in recent years. In the first quarter of 2021, Tesla delivered 184,800 vehicles [21], in the second quarter of 2021, 201,250 [22], in the third quarter, 241,300 [23] and in the fourth quarter of 2021, 308,840 [24]. These figures show an increase of 66,99% in one year. The company's electric vehicles offer various services, including the autopilot. According to an investigation by Isidore and Valdes-Dapena [25], bugs regularly appear in Tesla's autopilot. As a result, its vehicles and autopilot are likely to be part of ADF investigations. Understanding the Tesla car and its features, including the autopilot and file system, is key to a successful ADF investigation. Buchholz and Spafford show that the file system is essential in Digital Forensics (DF) and ADF investigations [26]. This leads to the following research question, "*What are DF- and ADF-specific characteristics that can be captured in the file system of a modern vehicle?*" with the hypothesis "*The file system of the Tesla autopilot contains metadata relevant to answer forensic questions in ADF investigations.*" Our contributions are:

- Identification of metadata characteristics of a Tesla autopilot hardware version 2.0.
- Identification of general DF characteristics of a vehicle-specific file system.
- Identification of vehicle-specific characteristics from a Tesla autopilot snapshot.
- Evaluation of the forensic soundness of the data acquisition method from the Tesla autopilot Electronic Control Unit (ECU).

This paper is structured as follows – Section II highlights related work in Tesla analysis and ADF investigations. The research question is further analyzed in Section III by considering the characteristics and metadata of the Tesla autopilot and their relevance to ADF. The implementation of a forensic analysis of the Tesla autopilot is presented in Section IV. Section V summarizes the results of the investigation. The evaluation in terms of forensic soundness, usability, limitations, and assumptions is presented in Section VI. Section VII concludes the paper and gives an outlook on future work.

II. RELATED WORK

We are not the first to look at Tesla vehicles. In this Section, we highlight different research focusing on security analysis of Tesla vehicles, its components, and services. Such investigations hold valuable information that can be used in DF investigations. Furthermore, we highlight ADF investigations on Tesla vehicles in existing research and how our approach and research goals differ.

In [17], Tencent's Keen Security Labs present a security analysis of a Tesla vehicle. They reverse-engineered the in-vehicle Controller Area Network (CAN) bus and show problems that lead to wireless exploitation of such vehicles. A similar problem was presented in [16], where the authors remotely compromised the gateway of the Body Control Module (BCM) of Tesla vehicles. ADF investigations can benefit from such security analysis. Such information helps determine where logs and other valuable information are stored to answer forensic questions.

Tristan Rice published a multi-part blog post about a security analysis of a Tesla Model 3, starting with [20]. The author reverse-engineered various services (e.g., the autopilot and software update system), the internal structure, security configurations (e.g., firewalls and iptables), and the internal API. Such descriptions enable forensic scientists to identify locations with characteristics relevant to DF investigations. This knowledge is valuable for security analysis and benefits ADF investigations.

In [19], Gomez et al. focus on the architecture, communication data, and snapshot capabilities of a Tesla autopilot hardware version 2.0, and the authors evaluate how these features affect the handling of personal data. Our work analyzes the same autopilot version but focuses on the relevance of the file system for ADF investigations.

Ebbers et al. published an article analyzing several IOS and Android apps for different vehicles [18]. They sent Subject Access Requests (SARs) to Original Equipment Manufacturers (OEMs) to get all the information OEMs have about each user. The authors found that data for smartphone apps may be encrypted or stored in plain text on smartphones. Some OEMs - such as Tesla - can transmit various vehicle data that could be relevant to DF investigations. Others OEMs - such as Ford and Mercedes [18] - are pretty limited in data availability.

The highlighted articles focus on security issues and data handling in Tesla vehicles. To the best of our knowledge, no article has been published on the Tesla autopilot file system and its relevance of DF investigations.

III. Investigation of the characteristics of the Tesla autopilot

Carrier defines digital investigations as "*a process by which we develop and test hypotheses that answer questions about digital events*" [15]. Thus, DF investigators need to reconstruct digital events based on the data they collect and analyze. As highlighted by Gomez et al. in [14], this is also true for ADF, but with a focus on automotive systems. In addition, the authors mention the importance of forensic questions of interest. The questions are in focus throughout this article and are:

- *Who* performed or is responsible for a digital event?
- *What* digital event was performed?
- *When* did the digital event take place?
- *Where* did the digital event take place?
- *How* did the digital event take place?
- *Why* did the digital event take place?

A. Tesla's autopilot from the perspective of digital forensics

The Tesla autopilot is an advanced driver assistance system. It supports the driver with various services such as cruise control, lane assistant, navigation, and automatic distance assistant. Tesla introduced autopilot in hardware version 1 in 2014, followed by hardware version 2.0 and 2.5 in 2016 [12]. The latest version is 3, which was introduced in 2019 and installed in all new Tesla vehicles since then [11]. We will focus on hardware version 2.0 due to its availability in the investigated vehicle. In addition, snapshots of the Tesla autopilot in hardware version 3 are usually encrypted. Based on a study by MIT, hardware version 2.0 is still installed in Tesla vehicles on the road [1] [2].

As mentioned by Rice in [20], the autopilot introduces several services and features. Examples include the service itself and the *Hermes* service, enabling communication between the OEM backend and Tesla vehicles. Hermes is also used to provide updates to features and components in the vehicle. Tesla vehicles store the files of the autopilot in encrypted form [10]. This causes problems with extracting the autopilot from in-vehicle systems during ADF investigations. Older versions of the autopilot were not encrypted, as described in an article by Keen Security Labs [9]. During the ADF investigation, the analyst must decrypt any encrypted autopilot. To do so, the analyst needs either the corresponding decryption key or an exploit for the autopilot.

B. Metadata in digital forensic investigations of file systems

Buchholz and Spafford define characteristics related to metadata based on the forensic questions *who*, *where*, *when*, *what*, *why*, and *how* [26]. They emphasize the importance of metadata in file systems to answer these forensic questions. As described by Carrier in [15], metadata is directly linked to the describing object. Thus, its metadata also changes when the object is modified, deleted, or otherwise changed. This fact makes metadata an important consideration in DF studies. Compared to deleting files (e.g., log files) or modifying text files, manipulating metadata is more challenging for an attacker.

As a result, DF investigators must validate the *trustworthiness* of the collected information to trust the metadata. In DF, trustworthiness is referred to as *forensic soundness* [8], which corresponds to the degree of the following attributes, as shown by [7]:

- Correctness: information that was actually stored in memory when the snapshot was taken.
- Atomicity: There should be no signs of concurrent system activity.
- Integrity: Captured memory areas will not be modified after the capture timestamp t.

The goal of DF investigations is to achieve a high level of forensic soundness to ensure the trustworthiness of the captured metadata.

IV. Digital forensic features of a Tesla autopilot hardware version 2.0

This paper focuses on the Tesla autopilot, i.e., hardware version 2.0. We analyzed the collected data using two approaches to enable comparability and minimize analysis errors by forensic tools: (1) developing a Python tool for analysis and (2) using Magnet AXIOM, a sophisticated DF tool. This approach also allows us to determine general characteristics of the Tesla autopilot relevant to future studies.

We conducted the ADF investigation following the process model proposed by [14]. The authors highlight four steps:

1) Forensic readiness: Determine if relevant data sources and tools are available to conduct an investigation.
2) Data collection: Obtain necessary information.
3) Data analysis: Analyze the data collected.
4) Documentation: Prepare a report presenting the results.

Forensic readiness is given for Tesla autopilot analyses. Snapshots can be created using various methods, e.g., chip-off or live acquisition. Tools for analysis are available with a custom Python tool and Magnet AXIOM. We discuss data acquisition and analysis in the following. This paper is the documentation of the results of the ADF investigation.

A. Acquisition of the Tesla autopilot

We acquired a Tesla autopilot (hardware version 2.0) from a 2017 Tesla Model S. We performed a chip-off of the installed memory device on the autopilot ECU. Chip-offs are a DF technique that has proven successful in ADF investigations, as [6] demonstrated in the analysis of a Volkswagen infotainment system.

Data on the extracted chip was acquired using a memory adapter that translates the pin-out to Universal Serial Bus (USB). Using a write blocker, we could ensure the data's integrity during the acquisition process. Write blockers are used in investigations to prevent changes to the data on the target evidence.

The result of the acquisition process was a snapshot of the Tesla autopilot. We created a duplicate and continued working on the duplicate only.

B. Python tool for Tesla autopilot analysis

The next step is to analyze the collected data. As suggested by [14], the data should be initially reviewed. We expected the snapshot to be encrypted. However, we were able to read the contents of the snapshot. In addition, we found that the snapshot was stored as *SquashFS* (a common read-only file system for Linux). This confirmed the security analysis results presented in [9].

We mounted the file system and identified several folders, all related to the classic Linux file system structure. Examples include *bin*, *etc*, *home*, and *lib*. We have also identified vehicle-specific folders such as the *opt* folder. It contains binaries for the autopilot and the *Hermes* service used for communication between the Tesla backend and Tesla vehicles. Another interesting folder for ADF investigations is the *lib* folder that stores all libraries used. Those can be valuable during penetration testing and identification of vulnerable libraries.

To automate the analysis process, we implemented a custom Python tool - in form of a Jupyter Notebook - to collect various metadata from the mounted file system. The tool uses "*os.walk()*" to recursively collect all directories and files. In addition, the implementation determines the timestamp of the last modification and the extension of each file. Finally, we create graphs to present the results.

The tool collected 4216 unique files and 447 directories from the mounted file system. We used the framework *python-magic* [5] to determine the file type. For 291 files (6.91%), the framework was unable to determine the type. We assume that the reason are corrupted magic bytes of the files (e.g., from custom file-types) and dot files from Linux. However, we were not able to confirm our assumption. The same is true for timestamps. The timestamp for 275 files and folders (6.52%) could not be determined for the same reasons.

As shown in Figure 1 and Table I, the most commonly used extension is *.so*, followed by *.0* (linked file on a Linux system), *.crt*, *.pem* and *.conf*. The extensions with numbers (e.g., *.1* or *.2*) are user-defined extensions probably used to arrange files within a directory.

TABLE I
NUMBER OF FILE EXTENSIONS WITHIN A TESLA AUTOPILOT

Extension	Count	Extension	Count
.so	356	.4	19
.0	221	.rules	18
.crt	140	.56	15
.pem	133	.hwdb	14
.conf	103	.6	14
.mo	100	.5	11
.sl	46	.10	9
.1	41	.wav	9
.2	33	.pdf	8
.img	32	.3	7
.sh	28	.profile	7
.txt	26	.00	7
.map	26	.13	6
.hlp	25	.16	6
.bin	24		

We created the line graph shown in Figure 2 from the collected timestamps. Several peaks in the timestamps are clearly visible. Table II lists the ten most frequently timestamps.

TABLE II
THE TIMESTAMP RESULTS WERE USED TO CREATE A LINE GRAPH.

Timestamp	Occurrences
Fri Jul 19 05:16:47 2019	1234
Fri Jul 19 05:51:13 2019	587
Fri Jul 19 05:51:12 2019	332
Fri Jul 19 05:28:04 2019	208
Fri Jul 19 05:28:03 2019	192
Fri Jul 19 05:51:06 2019	158
Fri Jul 19 05:23:04 2019	112
Fri Jul 19 05:51:18 2019	108
Fri Jul 19 05:29:59 2019	105
Fri Jul 19 04:22:50 2019	74

C. Analysis of the Tesla autopilot using Magnet AXIOM

To validate our results from Section IV-B and compare the findings of another tool, we analyzed SquashFS using Magnet AXIOM. The forensics tool identifies various indicators and presents them in a final report. Magnet AXIOM identified so-called *people*. In the case of a Tesla autopilot, these relate to Linux user accounts. Magnet AXIM identified a total of 103 accounts that contain usernames and IDs. These include common user accounts such as *root*, *daemon*, and *bin*. In addition, automotive and autopilot-specific usernames were also identified, including *temperature_monitor*, *visualizer*, *legacyvehicle*, *drivermonitor*, *gps*, and *hermes*.

The autopilot contains various media files. In particular, these are audio files used in the infotainment system. Examples

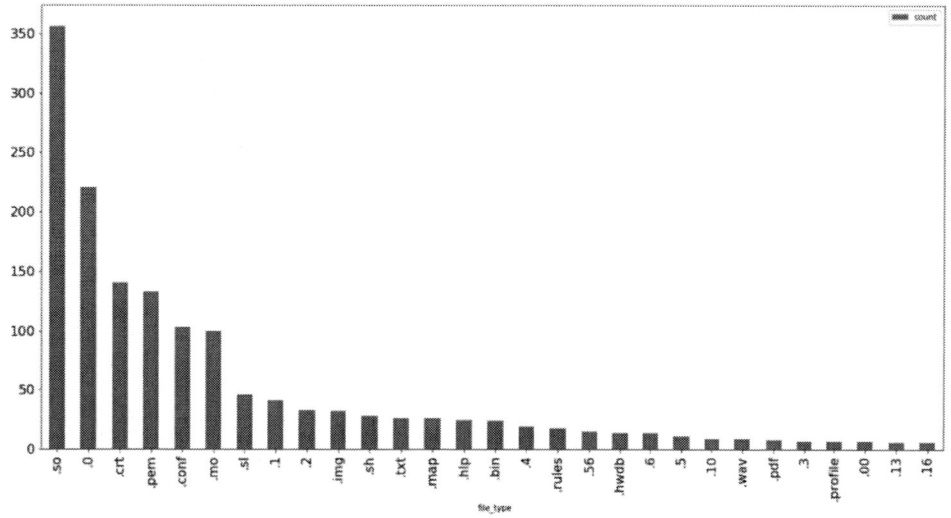

Figure 1. File types in the Tesla autopilot

are *.wav* files for steering wheel warnings or forward collision warnings.

Another category highlighted by Magnet AXIOM is *documents*. For the autopilot, these include a *.csv* sample file, 8 *.pdf* user manuals, and 26 *.txt* files, i.e., READMEs.

Magnet AXIOM has identified 32 *.img* files. These files are the firmware images of the various services implemented in the Tesla autopilot hardware version 2.0. All the *.img* files contain the string "*HW2*", indicating that these files refer to hardware version 2.0.

For the operating system information, Magnet AXIOM correctly detected the use of buildroot. The operating system version is specified as "*2016.05-g977a322*". This is the string that is included in the buildroot configuration.

V. Results of the Forensic Analysis

We implemented an ADF investigation on the Tesla autopilot file system and performed two analyses using a custom Python tool and Magnet AXIOM.

A. *Answering forensic questions using the collected metadata*

The metadata found is able to answer most of the forensic questions highlighted in Section III. Table III summarizes the results related to the forensic questions. The questions about "*Who performed or is responsible for a digital event?*" can be traced to the user accounts highlighted by Magnet AXIOM. In addition, "*who*" can be answered cron-jobs too. The next question relates to "*Where did the digital event take place?*" and is to be answered with the file and folder structure within the file system. "*When did the digital event take place?*" uses the timestamp collected by the custom Python tool as well as logs located in different location within the file-system. Some log files are located in the *etc* folder. However, these are general system logs and not application logs. Together with the configuration files (i.e., the *.conf* and *.profile* extensions), we can partially answer the question "*How did a digital event take place?*". The collected metadata cannot answer the question "*Why did a digital event take place?*".

If different log-files or other event management systems store information such as the user accounts, cron-jobs, and time-stamps, such data can be correlated with the results we highlighted. Hence, this information can be used to prove who or what is responsible for a digital event.

TABLE III
RESULTS OF THE ANALYSIS IN RELATION TO THE FORENSIC QUESTIONS

Forensic questions	Corresponding identified metadata
Who	User accounts and cron-jobs
Where	Files and folders structure
When	Timestamps of the files and log-files
What	Log files within the *etc* folder
How	Configuration files (*.conf* and *.profile* extension
Why	Can not be answered using the collected metadata

B. *Specific characteristics of digital forensics for the automotive sector*

In Section IV, several general metadata characteristics were identified. Some of which are specific to the automotive sector. These were also listed but not elaborated on.

The analysis revealed several metadata features that are specific to ADF. One example is the distribution of timestamps. Vehicles, unlike smartphones or personal computers, are cyber-physical systems. Therefore, they interact with the physical outside world. This leads to safety requirements and regulations. Consequently, updates must undergo in-depths testing

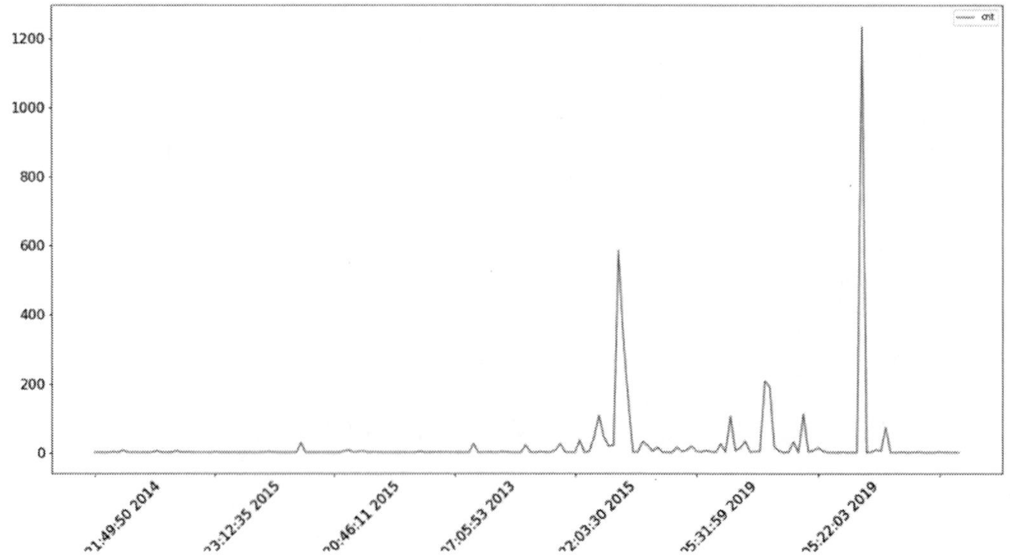

Figure 2. Timestamp of the files within the Tesla autopilot

and certification prior to roll-out. An update must ensure that it does not affect safety-critical systems such as brakes and airbags. This could be a reason for the distribution of timestamps. Tesla could update its autopilot in larger releases compared to small update cycles as known from common IT systems. This allows the manufacturer to verify and certify the update for use in vehicles in the field. Unfortunately, we cannot verify this assumption based on the available information.

As can be seen in Table I, *.so* is the most common extension. Thus, the Tesla autopilot uses a lot of shared libraries. With the use of shared libraries, the behavior of different services becomes comparable. Shared libraries store similar logs and perform related digital events. Hence, using shared libraries is a valuable autopilot feature for DF and penetration testing. In penetration testing, a vulnerability in a shared library can be used to exploit multiple services that use the *.so* file.

Magnet AXIOM identified several user accounts. Most are common to Linux Operating System (OS). However, some are specific to automotive. Two user accounts are named *cantx* and *canrx*. Both refer to the onboard CAN bus protocol. In addition, several user accounts in the file system snapshot refer to cyber-physical systems, e.g., *temperature_monitor*, *roadestimator*, *drivermonitor*, and *rainlightsensing*. Monitoring and safety-related user accounts are also part of the autopilot. The *dash_cam*, *camera*, *backup_camera*, *vision*, and *gps* are examples. Further research on these services for ADF-specific data classes [4] could be valuable.

As a result, several vehicle-specific DF features could be identified within the metadata of the file system of a Tesla autopilot snapshot. Therefore, we can confirm our hypothesis that the file system of the Tesla autopilot contains metadata relevant to answering forensic questions in ADF investigations.

VI. EVALUATION

This Section discusses the forensic soundness of the data acquisition, the usability of the identified characteristics, as well as limits and assumptions of the investigation.

A. Forensic soundness

Forensic soundness is the degree of correctness, atomicity, and integrity in memory acquisitions [7]. The definitions of these three attributes were revised by Ottmann et al. in [8] to allow for literal usability. Snapshots that satisfy integrity also satisfy atomicity and correctness [8]. SquashFS is a read-only file system, and we used a write blocker during collection. Since we performed a chip-off, the memory is *frozen* at time t when we removed the chip from the ECU. Thus, the integrity of the acquired snapshot is guaranteed.

B. Usability in automotive digital forensic investigations

We have published our custom Python tool on GitHub [3]. Therefore, the results can be replicated on other Tesla autopilot snapshots. The identified metadata characteristics are valuable for future research. This is especially true for the vehicle-specific characteristics mentioned in Section V-B. Future studies and research can use the information obtained in this article.

C. Limits and assumptions

We assume that the timestamps were not tampered while the autopilot was running. Furthermore, we assume that the system clock is correct. Otherwise, the timestamp analysis could not be conducted in the presented way [26]. The highlighted ADF-specific characteristics are specific to the analyzed Tesla autopilot. However, due to the reuse of hardware and software in modern vehicles, those characteristics will be helpful in future investigations.

VII. Conclusion and Future Work

In this article, we investigated the properties of metadata in modern vehicles. We focused on a Tesla autopilot hardware version 2.0 ADF investigation included the collection of data within the autopilot ECU using a chip-off. Analysis of the collected data was performed using two approaches. First, with a self-written Python tool. Second, with Magnet AXIOM, a sophisticated DF tool.

The analysis captured files and directories, file extensions, timestamps, user accounts, media data (e.g., audio), documents in the form of *.cvs*, *.txt*, and *.pdf* files, image files, and general file system information, e.g., that the image was created with buildroot. The most popular extensions were *.so*, *.0*, and *.crt*. We found that the most commonly used timestamp was July 19, 2019.

Vehicle-specific metadata was also identified during the investigation. This includes cyber-physical system-specific user accounts such as *temperature_monitor*, *visualizer*, *legacyvehicle*, *drivermonitor*, *gps*, and *hermes*. In addition, security-related user accounts were captured. Examples include *dash_cam*, *camera*, *backup_camera*, *vision*, and *gps*.

The investigation revealed several DF features that allow answering forensic questions in ADF: *who*, *where*, *when*, *what*, and *how*. Questions regarding "*why*" cannot be answered with the collected metadata.

The results highlighted in this paper are valuable for future studies of the Tesla autopilot ECU and modern vehicles in general. Future work will focus on the file system of other components of the vehicle ecosystem and on refining the analysis methods. In addition, future work will focus on newer hardware versions of the Tesla autopilot.

References

[1] Massachusetts Institute of Technology, "*Advanced Vehicle Technology (AVT) Consortium*", online, https://agelab.mit.edu/avt, (accessed: 20.09.2022)

[2] L. Fridman, "*Tesla Vehicle Deliveries and Autopilot Mileage Statistics*," online, https://lexfridman.com/tesla-autopilot-miles-and-vehicles/, (accessed: 20.09.2022)

[3] K. Gomez Buquerin, "*Tesla autopilot Jupyter Notebook GitHub repository*," online https://github.com/k-gomez/telsa-ap-analysis, (accessed: 20.09.2022)

[4] K. Gomez Buquerin, C. Corbett, and H.-J. Hof, "*Structured methodology and survey to evaluate data completeness in automotive digital forensics*," 19th escar Europe : The World's Leading Automotive Cyber Security Conference (Conferencepublication), pp. 52-67, 2021

[5] A. Hupp, "*Python-magic GitHub repository*," online, https://github.com/ahupp/python-magic, (accessed: 20.09.2022)

[6] D. Jacobs, K.-K. Raymond Choo, M.-T. Kechadi, and N.-A. Le-Khac, "*Volkswagen Car Entertainment System Forensics*," 2017 IEEE Trustcom/BigDataSE/ICESS, pp. 699-705, 2017

[7] S. Vömel and F. Freiling, "*Correctness, atomicity, and integrity: Defining criteria for forensically-sound memory acquisition*," Digital Investigation, Vol. 9, No. 2, Elsevier BV, pp. 125-137, 2012

[8] J. Ottmann, F. Breitinger, and F. Freiling, "*Defining Atomicity (and Integrity) for Snapshots of Storage in ForensicComputing*," Proceedings of the Digital Forensics Research Conference Europe (DFRWS EU), 2022

[9] Keen Security Labs, "*Experimental Security Research of Tesla Autopilot*," online, https://keenlab.tencent.com/en/whitepapers/Experimental_Security_Research_of_Tesla_Autopilot.pdf, (accessed: 20.09.2022)

[10] S. Dent, "*The Dutch government claims it can decrypt Tesla's hidden driving data*," engadget, online, https://www.engadget.com/a-dutch-government-lab-has-decoded-teslas-driving-data-for-the-first-time-085709633.html, (accessed: 20.09.2022)

[11] T. Simonite, "*Tesla's New Chip Holds the Key to 'Full Self-Driving'*," Wired, online, https://www.wired.com/story/teslas-new-chip-holds-key-full-self-driving/, (accessed: 20.09.2022)

[12] V. Tabora, "*Tesla Enhanced Autopilot Overview — L2 Self Driving HW2*," Medium, online, https://medium.com/self-driving-cars/tesla-enhanced-autopilot-overview-l2-self-driving-hw2-54f09fed11f1, (accessed: 20.09.2022)

[13] B. Erwin, "*The Ultimate Guide to Tesla Autopilot*," Current Automotive, online, https://www.currentautomotive.com/the-ultimate-guide-to-tesla-autopilot/, (accessed: 20.09.2022)

[14] K. Gomez Buquerin, C. Corbett, and H.-J. Hof, "*A generalized approach to automotive forensics*," Forensic Science International: Digital Investigation, Vol. 36, p. 301111, 2021

[15] B. D. Carrier, "*File System Forensic Analysis*," Addison-Wesley, 2005

[16] Keen Security Labs, "*Over-the-air: How we remotely compromised the Gateway, BCM, and Autopilot ECUs of Tesla Cars*," Black Hat Security Conference, 2018

[17] Keen Security Labs, "*Free-fall: Hacking Tesla from Wireless to CAN Bus*," Black Hat Security Conference, 2017

[18] S. Ebbers, F. Ising, C. Saatjohann, and S. Schinzel, "*Grand Theft App: Digital Forensics of Vehicle Assistant Apps*," CoRR, 2021

[19] K. Gomez Buquerin, D. Bayerl, and H.-J. Hof, "*Überwachung in modernen Fahrzeugen*," Datenschutz und Datensicherheit - DuD , Vol. 45, No. 6, Springer Science and Business Media LLC, pp. 399-403, 2021

[20] T. Rice, "*Hacking my Tesla Model 3 - Security Overview*," online, https://fn.lc/post/tesla-model-3/, (accessed: 20.09.2022)

[21] Tesla, "*Tesla Q1 2021 Vehicle Production & Deliveries*," online, https://ir.tesla.com/press-release/tesla-q1-2021-vehicle-production-deliveries, (accessed: 20.09.2022)

[22] Tesla, "*Tesla Q2 2021 Vehicle Production & Deliveries*," online, https://ir.tesla.com/press-release/tesla-q2-2021-vehicle-production-deliveries, (accessed: 20.09.2022)

[23] Tesla, "*Tesla Q3 2021 Vehicle Production & Deliveries*," online, https://ir.tesla.com/press-release/tesla-q3-2021-vehicle-production-deliveries, (accessed: 20.09.2022)

[24] Tesla, "*Tesla Q4 2021 Vehicle Production & Deliveries*," online, https://ir.tesla.com/press-release/tesla-q4-2021-vehicle-production-deliveries, (accessed: 20.09.2022)

[25] C. Isidore and P. Valdes-Dapena, "*Tesla is under investigation because its cars keep hitting emergency vehicles*," online, https://edition.cnn.com/2021/08/16/business/tesla-autopilot-federal-safety-probe/index.html, (accessed: 20.09.2022)

[26] F. Buchholz and E. Spafford, "*On the role of file system metadata in digital forensics*," Digital Investigation, Vol. 1, No. 4, Elsevier BV, pp. 298-309, 2004

Do Cognitive Biases and Dark Patterns Affect the Legality of Consent Under the GDPR?

Joanna Taneva
Utrecht University
Amatas
Sofia, Bulgaria
e-mail: joanna.taneva@amatas.com

Abstract—**Cognitive biases are ever-present in the data subject's decision-making in relation to consent to online tracking. However, the exploitation of cognitive biases via dark patterns can render the obtained consent illegal. This paper aims to combine a variety of legal sources in order to evaluate the legality of consent attained through consent banners. It further provides recommendations on how to resolve this issue in the form of: abolishing the presumption of rationality in data subjects; illustrating the need for more research into the extent to which cognitive biases affect the usability of consent; and normative recommendations for data protection authorities. The results from this study can aid web developers to strive towards designing compliant consent banners.**

Keywords- cognitive bias; consent; consent banners; GDPR; data protection.

I. INTRODUCTION

Currently, most websites collect personal data in order to profit from selling these data to third parties. The ePrivacy Directive (ePD), under Art.5(3), requires the data subject's consent for any storage of tracking technologies on their device [1]. In addition, the General Data Protection Regulation (GDPR) imposes legal requirements for valid consent [2]. Unfortunately, there are no formal requirements as to how consent should be obtained by websites. Recital 17 ePD stipulates that consent can be given by any appropriate method as long as it is "*a freely given, specific and informed indication of the user's wishes*". Consent banners have quickly become the norm where personal data are being processed by websites. They are an inseparable part of the data subject's daily web browsing activities. Research shows it would take the average data subject 244 hours per year to read every privacy policy they encounter on each website they visit [3]. It is argued that data subjects have developed coping mechanisms to deal with the burden of consent banners [4]. Data subjects are prone to deviations from rationality in their decision-making [5, p.1]. This opens the possibility for exploitation of data subjects' decisions via unfair practices such as dark patterns.

The existing literature on cognitive biases and dark patterns shows their potentiality to affect online users' decision-making. However, no assessment of the extent to which exploitation of cognitive biases via dark patterns can affect the legality of consent obtained through consent banners has been made. This paper aims to provide such an assessment.

Section II provides the legal background regarding consent to tracking technologies. Section III provides definitions of cognitive biases and dark patterns. Section IV introduces the immediate gratification bias, maps it to dark patterns and to the GDPR valid consent requirements. Section V follows the same approach in relation to the information overload bias. Section VI provides concluding remarks and recommendations.

II. LEGAL BACKGROUND

Since the right to the protection of personal data is a fundamental right governed by Art. 8 of the European Charter of Fundamental Rights and Art. 8 of the European Convention of Human Rights, any online personal data processing must comply with the existing privacy legislation to safeguard this right [6][7]. Therefore, in the European Union, any use of tracking technologies that process personal data must be compliant with the ePD and the GDPR [8, p.96]. Under Art.5(3) ePD, the use of tracking technologies is only permitted when the user *"has given his or her consent"*. The validity of consent is always assessed under the GDPR according to Art. 2(f) ePD. This is because the GDPR acts as *lex generalis*. It lays down the general rules regarding consent to tracking technologies, while the ePD acts as *lex specialis* – it particularises the general rules of the GDPR in relation to tracking technologies [9, p.13].

Art. 4(11) GDPR defines "consent" as *"any freely given, specific, informed and unambiguous indication of the data subject's wishes by which he or she, by a statement or by a clear affirmative action, signifies agreement to the processing of personal data relating to him or her"*.

Research by Santos et al. [8] provides a comprehensive analysis of the consent requirements by grouping them into several high- and low-level requirements. The legal consent requirements classification from Santos et al. [8] will be used in this paper because it provides an in-depth analysis which does not merely consult the GDPR legal provisions and EU case law but also secondary sources such as Data Protection Authorities' (DPA) decisions and guidelines. Santos et al. [8] derive an additional "readable and accessible" consent requirement from Art. 7(2) GDPR, which states that consent requests must be *"clearly distinguishable from the other matters, in an intelligible and easily accessible form, using clear and plain language."* Additionally, consent must always be revocable under Art. 7(3) GDPR [8].

III. Cognitive Biases and Dark Patterns

To cope with the vast amount of information presented to them daily, data subjects deploy cognitive heuristics to aid their decision-making [10, para 33]. Cognitive heuristics do not require an assessment of a situation in its full intricacy but rather help the data subject arrive at a quick decision with minimum effort by ignoring part of the information presented [5, p.4][11, p.451]. According to Kahnemann's dual-process theory, the mind has two modes: a fast, heuristics-based system and a slow, rational system. The fast system leads to automatic decisions, such as when asking a person what 2+2 equals, people are likely to give an automatic answer. The slow system requires consideration of many factors. An example is *"checking the validity of a complex, logical argument"*. A key element here is that tasks performed through the slow system need attention and cannot be performed if attention is diverted [12].

Cognitive heuristics are generally beneficial because they save people time and mental capacity [13, p.140]. However, cognitive heuristics sometimes lead to cognitive biases. This is because the appropriate decisions are sometimes incorrectly weighted against the consequences [14, p.2]. Cognitive biases have been defined as a *"systematic (...) deviation from rationality in judgment or decision-making"* [5, p.1]. There are many types of cognitive biases, but this paper merely discusses two cognitive biases – the immediate gratification and information overload bias, which according to previous work affect data subjects' tendency to consent to online personal data processing [15, p.105][16, p.16-19][10, para 34].

Existing literature shows that cognitive biases such as the immediate gratification bias affect data subjects' decision-making by making them underestimate the future consequences of personal data disclosure [17, p.25]. Moreover, research shows that rational privacy decision-making is improbable in an economic sense [17, p.22]. Cognitive biases make rational decision-making more challenging due to design manipulation via dark patterns that often nudge data subjects into taking unintended actions [3, p.105]. Therefore, cognitive biases can be exploited via dark patterns [18]. Previously, legal research has been conducted on the legality of dark patterns in consent banners [19]. However, none of the existing literature examines the legality of the exploitation of cognitive biases through their inevitable interaction with dark patterns.

Recently, the European Data Protection Board (EDPB) issued Guidelines on dark patterns in social media interfaces. Dark patterns are defined there as *"interfaces and user experiences implemented on social media platforms that lead users into making unintended, unwilling and potentially harmful decisions in regards of their personal data"* [20, para 3]. Unfortunately, the EDPB's Guidelines do not apply outside of social media interfaces. The recently adopted Digital Services Act also addresses dark patterns in Art. 23a, however, its application is limited to *"providers of online platforms"* [21]. The Digital Services Act does not provide a classification of the different types of dark patterns. The EDPB Guidelines group the different dark patterns into categories with a definition per each one.

Existing literature shows that dark patterns are not only present in social media but also in manipulative practices regarding consent to online personal data collection [4][19]. Most importantly, the use of dark patterns can lead to the invalidation of consent if any of the valid consent requirements under the GDPR are not met [16, p.15][20].

For the purposes of the ensuing legal analysis, the EDPB Guidelines' classification will be used, as if it applies to all intermediary services, in order to map the cognitive biases to their corresponding dark patterns and to establish whether there are any GDPR valid consent violations.

IV. Immediate Gratification Bias

This section introduces the relationship between the immediate gratification bias and dark patterns in consent banners. It further conducts a brief legal analysis on the legality of the exploitation of immediate gratification.

A. Definition

The immediate gratification bias has been defined as the human propensity to disregard future risks or benefits in favor of immediate gratification. It often comes into play when data subjects browse the web and a consent banner interrupts their browsing activity by asking them to consent to all data processing or tailor their privacy preferences.

Research confirms that cognitive biases, such as the immediate gratification bias, can lead to systematic errors in privacy-related decisions [17, p.24]. As data subjects are prone to underestimating the long-term risks associated with personal data disclosure [10, para 47], they often choose the immediate gratification of accepting all processing purposes as opposed to taking the effort to configure their privacy settings [15, p.105][17, p.25].

B. Mapping to dark patterns

The EDPB's dark pattern named Hindering, with a subcategory called Longer Than Necessary is defined as *"When users try to activate a control related to data protection, the user experience is made in a way that requires more steps from users, than the number of steps necessary for the activation of data invasive options. This is likely to discourage them from activating such control."* [20, p.62].

The exploitation of the *immediate gratification bias* by websites comes into play when only the option to "accept" tracking (or "accept all") exists and no "reject all" option is present in the consent banner interface. Often, data subjects are faced with a consent banner that does not give them the option to reject all trackers but only an option to manually configure their privacy settings on a second or third layer of the banner. An example is Figure 1 below.

The absence of a "reject all" option is a clear example of the interactive superiority of the "accept all" button because data subjects can consent to tracking with one click but can refuse tracking by having to click at least once more. Additionally, the empirical study by Nouwens et al. found that eliminating the "reject all" button from the initial page of a consent banner increased the likelihood of consent by 22-23% [22, p.8].

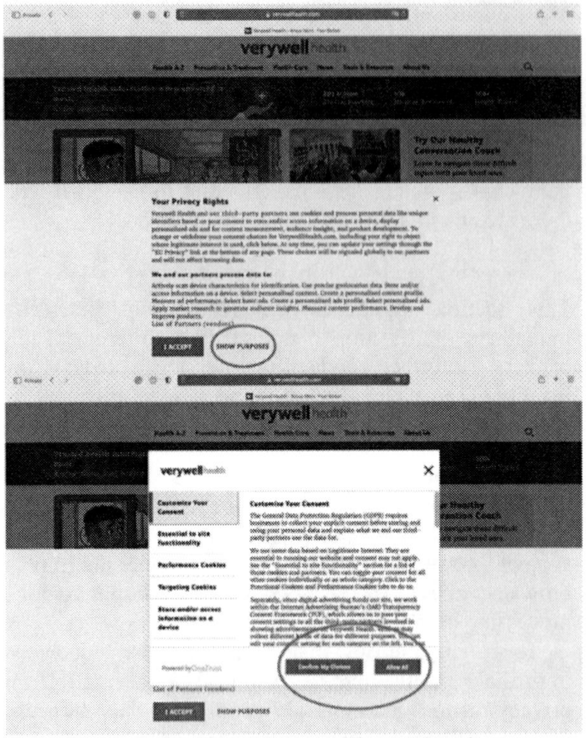

Figure 1. Example of the immediate gratification bias in a consent banner on www.verywellhealth.com accessed on 5 May 2022.

As a result, data subjects prefer to accept privacy-invasive tracking in exchange for immediate access to a webpage [17, p.21].

C. *Mapping to GDPR consent requirements*

According to Art. 4(11) GDPR, as mentioned above, consent must be unambiguous. Santos et al. provide two low-level unambiguous consent requirements called *configurable banner* and *balanced choice* [8]. I argue these low-level requirements are violated when the immediate gratification bias is exploited due to the absence of a "reject all" button.

1) Configurable banner

For consent to be unambiguous, there needs to be a clear "yes/no" option according to Article 29 Working Party (A29WP) and several DPAs [8, p.116]. A29WP has phrased this as *"The user should have an opportunity to freely choose between the option to accept some or all cookies or to decline all or some cookies and to retain the possibility to change the cookie settings in the future."* [23, p. 5]. Therefore, this suggests that a requirement for a "reject all" option can be read from Art. 7(3) GDPR, which states that withdrawing consent should be as easy as providing it. Additionally, Recital 66 ePD states that *"The methods of providing information and offering the right to refuse should be as user-friendly as possible."* The EDPB further identifies that when the *Longer Than Necessary* dark pattern is in effect, this leads to a violation of Art. 7(3) GDPR [20, p.62].

Also, if consent can be collected only through one mouse click, data subjects should be able to refuse data processing just as easily [23, p.2]. This view is further shared by the Italian DPA, which states that the mechanism for refusing consent should be *"as user-friendly and accessible as the one in place for giving one's consent."* [24]. Moreover, the French DPA issued a decision against Facebook because it did not provide a "reject all" option. It was ruled that the method for refusing consent must have *"the same degree of simplicity as the method envisaged for accepting".* Moreover, *"the mere presence of a "Settings" button in addition to the "Accept all" button tends, in practice, to deter refusal and therefore does not allow compliance with the requirements laid down by the GDPR"* [25, paras 90&44].

2) Balanced choice

Balanced choice was interpreted from Art. 7(3) GDPR, which states that withdrawing consent must be as easy as giving it [8, p.117]. Therefore, the choice to accept or refuse tracking must be equivalent. In his Opinion on *Planet49*, AG Szpunar suggests (while referring to accepting and refusing cookies) that *"Both actions must, optically in particular, be presented on an equal footing."* [26, para 66]. While this specifically refers to the visual superiority of the "accept all" option over the "reject all" option, it can be argued that it refers to its interactive superiority as well. In other words, the "accept all" and "reject all" options must be interactively equivalent. This view is shared by the Greek DPA, which states that *"The user must be able, with the same number of actions ("click") and from the same level, to either accept the use of trackers (those for which consent is required) or to reject it..."* [27].

Consequently, if no "reject all" button is provided and data subjects must click more than once to reject data processing, this means that manipulation via Hindering: Longer Than Necessary is taking place. This is further evidenced by the fact that user experience research has shown that users spend no more than a minute on websites and that 93.1% of users faced with consent banners stop at the first layer of the interface [28][22, p.8]. Therefore, the absence of a balanced choice violates the requirement for unambiguous consent.

3) Freely given

Placing the mechanism to refuse consent at the second layer of a consent interface amounts to a subversion of the data subject's will because it obstructs the exercise of their free will by making the mechanism for accepting consent more user-friendly.

The EDPB specifies that *"free" implies real choice and control for data subjects"* in its discussion of freely given consent [29, para 13]. The French DPA confirms this by stating that *"By applying this requirement of freedom of consent to cookies, it considers that making the optout mechanism more complex than the method allowing them to accept cookies, for example, by relegating to a second window the button allowing them to refuse cookies, amounts in actual fact, in general terms, in the context of browsing on the Internet, to altering users' freedom of choice by encouraging them to favour acceptance of these cookies rather than their refusal."* [25, para 97]. The use of dark patterns strips data subjects of their agency because it interferes with their ability to exercise control of their decisions. This is done in various ways, but it mostly relates to a nudge towards the use of their heuristics-based system via an exploitation of the online choice architecture of consent banners. This includes exploiting both the visual design and the language used in consent banners. Accordingly, this exploitation clashes with the notion of freely given consent [30, p.10]. The EDPB refers to the Norwegian Consumer Council and it states that *"Dark patterns aim to influence users' behaviours and can hinder their ability "to effectively protect their personal data and make conscious choices", for example by making them unable "to give an informed and freely given consent"* [20, p.7].

V. INFORMATION OVERLOAD BIAS

This section introduces the relationship between the information overload bias and dark patterns in consent banners. It further conducts a brief legal analysis on the legality of the exploitation of information overload.

A. Definition

When humans are faced with substantial amounts of information that they must read to reach a certain decision, information overload may occur. This means they are more likely to dismiss the presented information entirely as opposed to filtering out the important parts [16, p.16]. The information overload bias comes into play when a data subject is flooded with information regarding the processing of their personal data in a consent banner, which renders selecting the privacy-friendly settings even more difficult [10, para 34]. Literature shows that consent is highly dependent on the "cognitive load" imposed on data subjects, and if they are overburdened with information, it increases the likelihood of them giving consent to personal data processing [10, para 34].

B. Mapping to dark patterns

The use of the information overload bias by websites in consent banners can be correlated with the dark pattern the EDPB has classified as Overloading. The relevant subcategory of this dark pattern is called Too many options and is defined as *"Providing users with (too) many options to choose from. The amount of choices leaves users unable to make any choice or make them overlook some settings, especially if information is not available. It can lead them to finally give up or miss the settings of their data protection preferences or rights."* [20, pp.60-61].

An example of the information overload bias in practice is shown in Figure 2 below. In the example we can see 8 adjustable toggles to enable data collection. When the question mark button is clicked a brief explanation for each purpose is displayed. The consent banner, when visited through the website, contains more than 20 adjustable toggles. As previously mentioned, data subjects do not spend more than a minute on a webpage [28]. It is apparent how presenting the data subject with this many options leads to information overload.

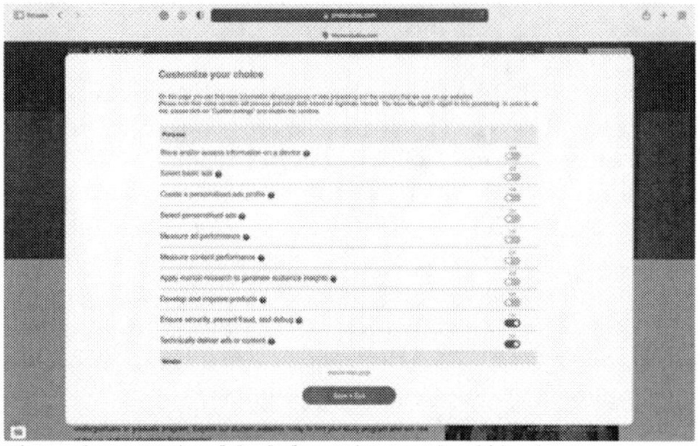

Figure 2. Example of the information overload bias in a consent banner from www.phdstudies.com accessed on 5 May 2022.

C. Mapping to GDPR consent requirements

1) Informed

AG Szpunar ruled informed consent implies that the data subject understands the consequences of the processing [31, para 47]. The CJEU further ruled in *Planet49* that the information provided must be *"clearly comprehensible and sufficiently detailed so as to enable the user to comprehend the functioning of the cookies employed"* [32, para 74].

If data subjects cannot make an informed decision, as previously evidenced by behavioral research findings, due to being overloaded with information [33, p.76], and due to their inability to read all the processing information available in consent banners and privacy policies [34, p.68][15, p.104][33, p.75], then consent cannot possibly be informed under Art. 4(11) GDPR. This leads to the invalidity of consent as a legal basis and to unlawful data processing.

Data subjects must understand what will happen to their data and what the outcome of using their data will be. For example, data subjects need to understand that consenting to targeting cookies may lead to them being exposed to personalized advertisements. The Belgian DPA has ruled that when the user had to follow the policies of 449 vendors, providing informed consent was *"illusory and impracticable"* [35, p.7].

Overloading data subjects with information nudges them into using their fast, heuristics-based system. The large amount of time they would have to spend informing themselves about the different processing purposes and their consequences imposes a high transaction cost. Data controllers provide data subjects with information regarding personal data processing, and the time data subjects spend reading this information is considered the transaction cost. High transaction costs obstruct data subjects from making a rational decision, which is why they are likely to disregard informing themselves about the data processing and are more likely to click consent [36, p. 31].

2) Readable and accessible

Pursuant to Recital 32 GDPR, a consent request must be *"clear, concise and not unnecessarily disruptive to the use of the service for which it is provided"*.

"Clear and concise"

Art. 13 GDPR imposes informational requirements on data controllers when personal data are being collected from data subjects. Art. 12 GDPR imposes requirements on the modalities through which that information is provided to data subjects. Art. 12(1) GDPR provides *"The controller shall take appropriate measures to provide any information referred to in Articles 13 [...] relating to processing to the data subject in a concise, transparent, intelligible and easily accessible form…"*. In a discussion of Art. 12(1) GDPR and its requirement for *"concise"* information, A29WP has recommended that *"data controllers should present the information/ communication efficiently and succinctly in order to avoid information fatigue."* [37, para 8]. Information fatigue is also known as information overload. It was first presented by the sociologist Georg Simmel, who introduced the theory that the overload of sensations in the urban setting made people indifferent and prevented them from logical reactions [38]. Presenting data subjects with too much information is a violation of the requirement for *"concise"* consent requests because it leads to information fatigue. As previously discussed, data subjects do not spend more than a minute on a webpage [28]. This makes it even more apparent how information fatigue is very likely to occur because of the amount of time an average person spends on a webpage and the amount of information they have to process in that minute.

VI. Conclusion and Future Work

The current data protection legal framework needs to be amended and supported with best practices to sufficiently protect data subjects against the exploitation of their vulnerabilities. While it gives data subjects control over their personal data (i.e., the right to decide whether to consent to tracking), it does not protect them against exploitation of the mechanisms used to obtain consent [18, p.48]. Therefore, the following recommendations are provided so that the validity of consent can be improved.

The presumption of rationality in data subjects is wrong. The GDPR imposes on data subjects a presumption of rationality [39]. However, rational decisions are practically impossible given the cognitive load imposed on the data subject. In fact, research has proven that rational privacy decision-making is improbable [17, p.22]. Therefore, the assumption of rationality should be abolished and more emphasis should be placed on cognitive biases and their exploitation via dark patterns in consent banners. Future work from behavioral psychology and behavioral economics research could conduct real-world surveys to examine to what extent cognitive biases affect data subjects' decision-making in relation to accepting tracking via consent banners.

The exploitation of cognitive biases via dark patterns negatively affects the usability of consent. The illegality of the obtained consent leads to an inefficient data protection legal system. A way efficiency could be improved is through increasing the usability of consent banners. There is a need for a contextual interpretation of manipulation via dark patterns that takes into account the human propensity to exhibit cognitive biases. Arguably, this can be achieved through a contextual approach to usability, which considers user needs and limitations, i.e., cognitive biases. More research is needed on the extent to which cognitive biases affect the usability of consent banners. Moreover, research is needed on whether the development of usability tools and usability evaluation methods can improve the usability of consent banners. Future research could also examine whether cognitive biases affect other matters not related to data protection and online consent, such as, for example, users' ability to apply cybersecurity practices, tools and policies.

It is recommended that DPAs issue guidelines on cognitive biases and dark patterns in consent banners, as well as guidance for data controllers on how to achieve valid consent without exploitation. A classification of dark patterns and cognitive biases related to consent will contribute to companies' abilities to recognize and avoid them. Additionally, DPAs could create a set of design principles applicable to consent banners that could standardize their design in order to minimize the possibilities for exploitation of cognitive biases. Furthermore, a way in which it can be ensured that consent banners are not exploiting cognitive biases is conducting usability assessments. Usability assessments can provide scientifically supported evaluations of the extent to which consent banners are compliant with the GDPR consent requirements [40, p.4]. Usability assessments can also aid with the identification of usability problems in the consent banner interface which will further prompt web developers to strive toward GDPR-compliant consent banner design and prevent the exploitation of cognitive biases.

Acknowledgment

The author would like to thank dr. Cristiana Teixeira Santos, Assistant Professor in data protection and privacy law at Utrecht University for her continued support during and after completion of the author's studies. The author would also like to thank her mother, Antonia Prodanova, for her unconditional love and support.

REFERENCES

[1] Directive 2009/136/EC of the European Parliament and of the Council (of 25 November 2009) amending Directive 2002/22/EC on universal service and users' rights relating to electronic communications networks and services, Directive 2002/58/EC concerning the processing of personal data and the protection of privacy in the electronic communications sector and Regulation (EC) No 2006/2004 on cooperation between national authorities responsible for the enforcement of consumer protection laws.

[2] Regulation (EU) 2016/679 Of The European Parliament and of The Council of 27 April 2016 on the protection of natural persons with regard to the processing of personal data and on the free movement of such data, and repealing Directive 95/46/EC ("General Data Protection Regulation") OJ 2 119/1.

[3] A. E. Waldman, "Cognitive biases, dark patterns, and the 'privacy paradox,'" Current Opinion in Psychology, vol. 31, pp. 105–109, 2020.

[4] H. Habib, M. Li, E. Young, and L. Cranor, "'Okay, whatever': An Evaluation of Cookie Consent Interfaces," presented at the CHI Conference on Human Factors in Computing Systems, pp. 1-27, 2022.

[5] F. Blanco, Cognitive Bias. Encyclopedia of Animal Cognition and Behaviour. 2017.

[6] European Parliament., & Office for Official Publications of the European Communities, Charter of fundamental rights of the European Union. 2000.

[7] Council of Europe, The European Convention on Human Rights. 1952.

[8] C. Santos, N. Biielova, and C. Matte, "Are cookie banners indeed compliant with the law?," Technology and Regulation, pp. 91–135, 2020.

[9] European Data Protection Board, "Opinion 5/2019 on the interplay between the ePrivacy Directive and the GDPR, in particular regarding the competence, tasks and powers of data protection authorities.," 2019.

[10] Y. Hermstrüwer, "Contracting Around Privacy: The (Behavioral) Law and Economics of Consent and Big Data," JIPITEC, pp. 9–26, 2017.

[11] G. Gigerenzer and W. Gaissmaier, "Heuristic Decision Making," Annual Review of Psychology, vol. 62, no. 1, pp. 451–482, 2011.

[12] D. Kahneman, Thinking Fast and Slow, 1st ed. Farrar, Straus and Giroux, 2013.

[13] J. van der Lee et al., "Ethical design: persuasion, not deception.," Journal of Digital & Social Media Marketing, vol. 9, no. 2, pp. 135–148, 2021.

[14] J. E. Korteling, A.-M. Brouwer, and A. Toet, "A Neural Network Framework for Cognitive Bias," Front. Psychol., vol. 9, Art. 1561, pp.1-12, Sep. 2018, doi: 10.3389/fpsyg.2018.01561.

[15] F. Z. Borgesius, "Informed Consent: We Can Do Better to Defend Privacy," IEEE Secur. Priv., vol. 13, no. 2, pp. 103–107, Mar. 2015, doi: 10.1109/MSP.2015.34.

[16] CNIL, "IP Report: Shaping Choices in the Digital World, From dark patterns to data protection: the influence of UX/UI design on user empowerment (No. 6)," Commission Nationale de l'Informatique et des Libertés, 2019.

[17] A. Acquisti, "Privacy In Electronic Commerce And The Economics Of Immediate Gratification", EC'04: Proceedings of the 5th ACM conference on Electronic commerce, pp. 21–29, 2004.

[18] L. Jarovsky, "Dark Patterns in Personal Data Collection: Definition, Taxonomy and Lawfulness," SSRN Electron. J., pp.1-50, 2022, doi: 10.2139/ssrn.4048582.

[19] C. M. Gray, C. Santos, N. Bielova, M. Toth, and D. Clifford, "Dark Patterns and the Legal Requirements of Consent Banners: An Interaction Criticism Perspective," in Proceedings of the 2021 CHI Conference on Human Factors in Computing Systems, Yokohama Japan, May 2021, pp. 1–18. doi: 10.1145/3411764.3445779.

[20] European Data Protection Board, "Guidelines 03/2022 on Dark patterns in social media platform interfaces: How to recognise and avoid them," 2022.

[21] European Parliament, Position of the European Parliament adopted at first reading on 5 July 2022 with a view to the adoption of Regulation (EU) 2022/... of the European Parliament and of the Council on a Single Market For Digital Services (Digital Services Act) and amending Directive 2000/31/EC. European Parliament. 2022.

[22] M. Nouwens, I. Liccardi, M. Veale, D. Karger, and L. Kagal, "Dark Patterns after the GDPR: Scraping Consent Pop-ups and Demonstrating their Influence," in Proceedings of the 2020 CHI Conference on Human Factors in Computing Systems, Honolulu HI USA, Apr. 2020, pp. 1–13. doi: 10.1145/3313831.3376321.

[23] Article 29 Data Protection Working Party, "Working Document 02/2013 providing guidance on obtaining consent for cookies," 2013.

[24] Italian DPA, "Guidelines on the use of cookies and other tracking tools – 10 June 2021", Official Journal of the Italian Republic No 163 of 9 July 2021, Garante per la protezione dei dati personali, "Linee guida cookie e altri strumenti di tracciamento - 10 giugno 2021 [9677876]," 2021. Accessed: Sep. 28, 2022. [Online]. Available: https://www.garanteprivacy.it/home/docweb/-/docweb-display/docweb/9677876#english

[25] CNIL, Deliberation of the restricted committee No. SAN-2021-024 of 31 December 2021 concerning FACEBOOK IRELAND LIMITED. 2021.

[26] Opinion of Advocate General Szpunar in Case C 673/17 Planet49 GmbH v Bundesverband der Verbraucherzentralen und Verbraucherverbände – Verbraucherzentrale Bundesverband e.V.

[27] Greek Data Protection Authority, "Guidelines on Cookies and Trackers," 2020. Accessed: Sep. 28, 2022. [Online]. Available: https://iapp.org/news/a/greek-dpa-issues-guidelines-on-cookies-and-trackers/#:~:text=In%20February%202020%2C%20the%20Hellenic,EU%20General%20Data%20Protection%20Regulation

[28] J. Nielsen and D. Norman, "The Definition of User Experience (UX)." https://www.nngroup.com/articles/definition-user-experience/ (accessed Aug. 26, 2022).

[29] European Data Protection Board, "Guidelines 05/2020 on consent under Regulation 2016/679," 2020.

[30] Norwegian Consumer Council, "Deceived by Design: How tech companies use dark patterns to discourage us from exercising our rights to privacy," 2018. Accessed: Sep. 28, 2022. [Online]. Available: https://www.forbrukerradet.no/undersokelse/no-undersokelsekategori/deceived-by-design/

[31] Opinion of Advocate General Szpunar in Case C 61/19 Orange România SA v Autoritatea Naţională de Supraveghere a Prelucrării Datelor cu Caracter Personal (ANSPDCP).

[32] Case C-673/17 Bundesverband der Verbraucherzentralen und Verbraucherverbände - Verbraucherzentrale Bundesverband e.V. v Planet49 GmbH. 2019.
[33] S. Monteleone, "Addressing the Failure of Informed Consent in Online Data Protection: Learning the Lessons from Behaviour-Aware Regulation," Syracuse Journal of International Law and Commerce, vol. 43, no. 1, pp. 69–120, 2015.
[34] S. Y. Soh, "Privacy Nudges:," Eur. Data Prot. Law Rev., vol. 5, no. 1, pp. 65–74, 2019, doi: 10.21552/edpl/2019/1/10.
[35] Belgian DPA v Roularta Media Group Decision 85/2022. 2022. Accessed: Sep. 28, 2022. [Online]. Available: https://www.autoriteprotectiondonnees.be/publications/decision-quant-au-fond-n-85-2022.pdf
[36] F. J. Zuiderveen Borgesius, "Consent to Behavioural Targeting in European Law - What are the Policy Implications of Insights from Behavioural Economics?," SSRN Electron. J., pp. 1-58, 2013, doi: 10.2139/ssrn.2300969.
[37] Article 29 Data Protection Working Party, "Guidelines on transparency under Regulation 2016/679 Rev. 01," 2018.
[38] G. Simmel, "The Metropolis and Mental Life," in The Sociology of Georg Simmel, New York: The Free Press, pp. 409–424, 1950.
[39] A. E. Waldman, "Committee On The Internal Market And Consumer Protection," presented at the Public hearing: Dark patterns and how such practices harm consumers and the Digital Single Market. Accessed: Sep. 28, 2022. [Online]. Available: https://multimedia.europarl.europa.eu/en/webstreaming/committee-on-internal-market-and-consumer-protection_20220316-0945-COMMITTEE-IMCO
[40] T. Jakobi, M. von Grafenstein, P. Smieskol, and G. Stevens, "A Taxonomy of user-perceived privacy risks to foster accountability of data-based services," J. Responsible Technol., vol. 10, p. 100029, Jul. 2022, doi: 10.1016/j.jrt.2022.100029.